D1003569

Preventive Diplomacy at the UN

United Nations Intellectual History Project

Ahead of the Curve? UN Ideas and Global Challenges
Louis Emmerij, Richard Jolly, and Thomas G. Weiss

*Unity and Diversity in Development Ideas: Perspectives from the
UN Regional Commissions*
Edited by Yves Berthelot

Quantifying the World: UN Ideas and Statistics
Michael Ward

UN Contributions to Development Thinking and Practice
Richard Jolly, Louis Emmerij, Dharam Ghai, and Frédéric Lapeyre

The UN and Global Political Economy: Trade, Finance, and Development
John Toye and Richard Toye

UN Voices: The Struggle for Development and Social Justice
Thomas G. Weiss, Tatiana Carayannis, Louis Emmerij, and Richard Jolly

*Women, Development, and the UN: A Sixty-Year Quest for Equality
and Justice*
Devaki Jain

Human Security and the UN: A Critical History
S. Neil MacFarlane and Yuen Foong Khong

Human Rights at the UN: The Political History of Universal Justice
Roger Normand and Sarah Zaidi

Preventive Diplomacy at the UN

Bertrand G. Ramcharan

Foreword by Leon Gordenker

Indiana University Press
Bloomington and Indianapolis

This book is a publication of

Indiana University Press
601 North Morton Street
Bloomington, IN 47404-3797 USA

http://iupress.indiana.edu

Telephone orders   800-842-6796
Fax orders   812-855-7931
Orders by e-mail   iuporder@indiana.edu

The paper used in this publication meets the minimum requirements of American National
Standard for Information Sciences—Permanence of Paper for Printed Library Materials,
ANSI Z39.48-1984.

Manufactured in the United States of America

Library of Congress Cataloging-in-Publication Data

Ramcharan, B. G.
  Preventive diplomacy at the UN / Bertrand G. Ramcharan ; foreword by Leon Gordenker.
    p. cm. — (United Nations intellectual history project series ; 10)
  Includes bibliographical references and index.
  ISBN 978-0-253-35147-0 (cloth : alk. paper) — ISBN 978-0-253-21983-1 (pbk. : alk. paper)
1. United Nations—History. 2. Diplomatic negotiations in international disputes. 3. Pacific
settlement of international disputes. 4. Conflict management. 5. United Nations. Secretary-
General. I. Title. II. Title: Preventive diplomacy at the United Nations.
  JZ4971.R36 2008
  341.5'2—dc22
                              2007049752

1 2 3 4 5 13 12 11 10 09 08

Dedication

To Lily and Robin Ramcharan, I need say no more.
They know.

Preventive Diplomacy is not an option—it is a necessity. As we know too well, dealing with the aftermath of violent conflicts is costly. Lives are needlessly lost. Economics are destroyed. Hopes for development are dashed. Resolving conflicts, before violence occurs, is one of the smartest investments we can make.

Ban Ki-moon, UN press release SG/SM/11318,
10 December 2007

I am reasonably convinced that man can build diplomatic institutions, norms and procedures that will at least reduce the incidence of war. I do not share those pessimistic views that see war as a necessary concomitant of man's genetic make-up, a perpetual "struggle for power" among nations, or an inevitable consequence of international anarchy.

Kalevi J. Holsti, *Peace and War: Armed Conflicts and International Order 1648–1989*

Contents

Series Editors' Foreword

Surprisingly no comprehensive history exists of the United Nations family of organizations. True, in the last few years, histories of the United Nations Development Programme[1] and the World Food Programme[2] have been completed—to add to the two histories of UNICEF produced in the 1980s and 1990s.[3] And the United Nations Educational, Scientific and Cultural Organization, the World Health Organization, and the United Nations Conference on Trade and Development have been preparing internal volumes bringing together different perspectives about the evolution of these organizations. But these are still patchy and incomplete, all the more so sixty years after the founding of the current generation of international organization. More serious and complete accounts of UN activities and contributions should be expected of all intergovernmental organizations, along with enhanced efforts to organize their archives so that independent researchers can also document and analyze dispassionately their efforts, achievements, and shortcomings. These are essential parts of compiling the record of global governance during the last half of the twentieth century and the beginning of the current millennium.

Faced with this major omission, which has substantial implications for the academic and policy literatures, we decided to undertake the task of writing an *intellectual* history—that is, a history of the ideas launched or nurtured by the United Nations. Observers should not be put off by what may strike them as a puffed-up billing. The working assumption behind our undertaking is straightforward: Ideas and concepts are a main driving force in human progress, and they arguably have been one of the most important contributions of the world organization. And as the various volumes of our project have been completed, the more our early assumptions about the importance of ideas among the UN's various contributions, and for its wider influence, have been confirmed by the actual record.

The United Nations Intellectual History Project (UNIHP) was launched in 1999 as an independent research effort based at the Ralph Bunche Institute for International Studies at The Graduate Center of The City University of New York. We are extremely grateful for the enthusiastic backing from the seventh Secretary-General, Kofi Annan, and other staff, as well as from scholars and analysts and governments. We are also extremely appreciative for the generosity of the governments of the Netherlands, the United Kingdom, Sweden, Canada, Norway, Switzerland, Finland, and the Republic and Canton of Geneva; of the Ford, Rockefeller, and MacArthur Foundations; the Carnegie Corporation of New York; the UN Foundations; and an individual contribution of Ms. Alice Lobel of Paris. This support ensures total intellectual and financial independence. Details of this and other aspects of the project can be found on our Web site: www.UNhistory.org.

The work of the UN can be divided into two broad categories: economic and social development, on the one hand, and peace and security, on the other. The UNIHP is committed to produce fifteen volumes on major themes, mainly in the first arena, but we are also penetrating the second. These volumes are being published in a series by Indiana University Press. Oxford University Press is publishing a related volume, *The Oxford Handbook on the United Nations.*[4]

In addition, the UNIHP has completed an oral history collection of some seventy-nine lengthy interviews of persons who have played major roles in launching and nurturing UN ideas—and sometimes in hindering them! Extracts from these interviews were published in 2005 as *UN Voices: The Struggle for Development and Social Justice,* and authors of the project's various volumes, including this one, have drawn on these interviews to highlight substantive points made in their texts. Full transcripts of the oral histories are now available on CD-ROM to facilitate work by researchers and other interested persons worldwide.

There is no single way to organize research, and certainly not for such an ambitious project as this one. We have structured this historical effort by topics—ranging from trade and finance to human rights, from transnational corporations to development assistance, from regional perspectives to sustainability. We have commissioned world-class experts for each topic, and the argument in all of the volumes is the responsibility of the authors whose names appear on the covers. All have been given freedom and responsibility to organize their own digging, analyses, and presentations. Guidance from us as the project directors as well as from peer review groups has helped to ensure accuracy and fairness in depicting where the ideas came from, how they were developed and disseminated within the UN system, and what happened with them. We are hoping that future analyses will build upon our series, and indeed go well beyond. Our intellectual history project is the first, not last, installment in depicting the history of the UN's contributions to ideas.

Preventive Diplomacy at the UN is the tenth volume in the series, and in many respects represents a departure. We asked Bertrand G. Ramcharan to explore the unusual creation of preventive diplomacy. Whereas all of our other books, even the ones on human security and global governance, bring in the economic and social dimensions of the UN's work, the main justifications for this project, preventive diplomacy clearly is in the domain of international peace and security.

We were keen to have at least one volume in the series about peace and security and more importantly on the Secretary-General's role. As we noted in our overview of the first several books from the project as part of our analytical contributions for the UN's sixtieth anniversary, the Charter incorporates four pillars, breathtaking in their boldness and universality: peace, development, human rights, and independence.[5]

We are delighted that our colleague "Bertie" Ramcharan has been willing to take on this volume. He has just assumed a teaching position as Professor of International Human Rights Law at the Geneva Graduate Institute of International Studies and is Chancellor of the University of Guyana. He completed a 32-year distinguished career in the UN Secretariat, which gave him substantial personal exposure to and experience with the kind of UN diplomacy about which he writes: early warning, conflict prevention, preventive diplomacy, peacemaking, peacekeeping, peacebuilding, and human rights. He served in the Office for Research and the Collection of Information, which Secretary-General Pérez de Cuéllar established to strengthen the capacity of the Secretariat for preventive diplomacy. He contributed substantial parts of the first internal draft of *An Agenda for Peace* and was a director in the Department of Political Affairs dealing with African issues. He was director of the International Conference on the Former Yugoslavia, in which capacity he worked with Cyrus Vance, Lord David Owen, Thorvald Stoltenberg, and Carl Bildt in their efforts to negotiate peace in the Balkans. He also was director of the Office of the Special Representative for the Former Yugoslavia responsible for the UN Protection Force in the Former Yugoslavia and was involved in the establishment of the first preventive deployment force for Macedonia. He served in the positions of deputy and then UN high commissioner for human rights ad interim, cumulatively over six years. In addition to this myriad of responsibilities, he somehow found the time and energy in that period to author or edit some twenty-five books on international law, human rights, and the United Nations.

The UNIHP is about forward-looking history. Based on the works already published in the series, we seek to identify the UN's intellectual challenges today. These include measures of human security, for which integrated approaches toward comprehensive collective security should be explored beyond the traditional compass of either the military or national security forces. They also include issues of global economic inequalities, once front and center on the United Nations agenda, which should return to that agenda, along with international measures to moderate and diminish those inequalities and their consequences.[6]

The books in this series have been inspired by recognition of the interdependence among peace, development, and human rights, which themselves are the indispensable prerequisites for meaningful independence. The books on development and economic and social affairs have repeatedly stressed that peace requires economic and social progress based on equality within and among nations and on respect for basic human rights.

The latest book in the series on human rights brought out the difficulties of advancing a human rights agenda in a world of political, economic, and social disequilibria.[7] The challenges are formidable in implementing the human rights principles of the Charter and of the Universal Declaration of Human Rights. In our contemporary world, human rights problems stem from poverty, conflicts, terrorism, inequality, bad governance, and gross violations of human rights inflicted by governments and others on their own people. Once again, the problems and challenges are interlinked.

The world organization has sought to take forward its peace agenda to the extent that political and economic circumstances make this possible. Hence, the backdrop consists of severe economic and social problems, widespread human rights violations, disequilibria in political and economic power, the Cold War, post–Cold War instability, global terrorism, and numerous armed conflicts.

At the most basic level, one could argue that through all of its activities the UN has routinely sought to contribute to conflict prevention and to peacemaking. At the end of the day, the primary responsibility lies with what we have labeled the "first UN" of member states and the "second UN" of international civil servants can be most helpful when governments so wish and cooperate. From the organization's very inception, however, successive Secretaries-General have used preventive diplomacy and peacemaking even when governments resisted, which suggests more room for initiative by the second UN than is commonly thought possible. The establishment of UN observer and peacekeeping forces was one of the great inventions of the world body, and the idea of peacekeeping, foreshadowed by

Secretary-General Trygve Lie and implemented by Secretary-General Dag Hammarskjöld, Lester Pearson, and a succession of other senior UN officials, must rank among the great accomplishments of the world body.

Indeed, Hammarskjöld is the "hero" of the story in this book. He situated peacekeeping within the intellectual stream of preventive diplomacy, a concept that he first articulated. He foresaw preventive diplomacy in the political as well as economic spheres. In the long term, he considered economic prevention to be even more important than crisis management. Subsequently, all of his successors on the 38th floor have been practitioners of preventive diplomacy and sought to highlight the economic and social dimensions as well. Indeed, Secretary-General Boutros Boutros-Ghali, alongside his widely acclaimed *An Agenda for Peace,* a primer of preventive diplomacy, also published toward the end of his term *An Agenda for Development* and *An Agenda for Democratization.*[8] Preventive diplomacy, development, and democracy (and one might add human rights) thus went hand in hand in his conception. This had been well brought out in *Perspectives for the 1990s*[9] of his predecessor, Javier Pérez de Cuéllar. It made the case for a comprehensive global watch in all of these as well as related areas. Kofi Annan took forward the ideas of his predecessors and sought to develop interagency collaboration in the implementation of preventive strategies and the development of a "culture of prevention."[10] We await next steps by the eighth head of the world organization, Ban Ki-moon, who assumed office just before this book went to press.

Alongside the concepts of early warning, a comprehensive global watch, preventive diplomacy, peacekeeping, development, democracy, and human rights, the establishment of the Peacebuilding Commission by the 2005 World Summit emphasized a concept articulated in *An Agenda for Peace.* As such, peacebuilding is recognized to have explicit preventive dimensions.

This book, which is devoted to the intellectual journey of preventive diplomacy at the United Nations, weaves these strands together in a historical examination of one of the powerful ideas promulgated by the world organization, namely that quiet diplomacy may head off some armed conflicts. There are no exaggerated claims. Like many UN tools, preventive diplomacy is a specific and useful tool that helps in some instances. Ramcharan is clear that it promises not salvation but a modestly improved international society.

While running with the intellectual threads of the concept in the political, economic, social, human rights and humanitarian spheres, this book also documents the available practice, showing significant contributions in situations such as the Cuban missile crisis of 1962, tracing the role of the Security Council, representatives of the Secretary-General, and regional conflict prevention centers and examining the application of the concept in new areas, such as the prevention of genocide and terrorism. In its conclusion, the book makes a series of recommendations that include the designation of internal regional rapporteurs in the Security Council for a more systematic approach to conflict prevention, and for the pursuit of forward-looking diplomacy when it comes to the promotion of democracy. It recalls an idea first put forward by President George H. W. Bush in 1990 to establish a position of special coordinator for electoral assistance backed up by a commission on electoral assistance comprised of distinguished experts from around the world, and it advocates the resuscitation of these ideas. It also advances a policy agenda for preventive diplomacy by Ban Ki-moon.

We are convinced that the UN story in general deserves to be better documented if it is to be better understood and appreciated. *Preventive Diplomacy at the UN* makes a significant contribution. As Secretary-General Kofi Annan wrote in the "Foreword" to the first publication in this book series, *Ahead of the Curve? UN Ideas and Global Challenges,* "With the publication of this first volume in the United Nations Intellectual History Project, a significant lacuna in twentieth-century scholarship and international relations begins to be filled."[11] The present volume is another important step in closing the gap in the historical record.

We hope that readers will feel engaged, confronted, and perhaps provoked by this account, at once a journey through time and ideas and a challenge for all who are committed to mitigating the incidence of war. As always, we welcome comments from our readers.

Louis Emmerij
Richard Jolly
Thomas G. Weiss
New York
May 2007

Foreword

Two words—*preventive diplomacy*—that have given form to the practice of the United Nations and international relations provide the foundation of this penetrating and informative study by Bertrand Ramcharan. That pair of words was introduced by Secretary-General Dag Hammarskjöld during some of the tensest days of the Cold War. They immediately became a guide to senior officials in the UN Secretariat and an invitation to representatives of UN member governments to shift to the international organization some of the focus of difficult diplomacy to maintain peace.

While the methods of preventive diplomacy, as Ramcharan points out, had a substantial base in earlier practice, the tension of the Cold War did little to ensure that the novel formulation would have the far-reaching use that this volume traces. Yet the history that Ramcharan follows shows that in succeeding years, the concept of collective diplomacy applied first to active conflict situations and then to related issues that over the long term condition international relations. These include the promotion of human rights, economic improvement, humanitarian relief, and the prevention of terrorism. Moreover, adaptations of the idea of preventive diplomacy have spread through the UN system and its relationships with regional and sub-regional organizations.

Ramcharan's use of the concept of preventive diplomacy yields a close-up account of the UN system; its practices; its ambitious, far-flung, and quite specific programs; and its omnipresence in international politics. He deals not only with the process by which the concept arose and was elaborated but also with its practical application and consequences. His work focuses especially clearly on the policies that UN member states have approved in the form of specific resolutions to which they pledge to give effect. He cites chapter and verse in official documentation supplemented by references to a wide range of authoritative studies. But the book neither pretends that governments always do what they undertake in the United Nations nor that all of the rhetoric leads to the hoped-for—or, for that mat-

ter, any—results. In that sense, Ramcharan deals with the reality of organized international cooperation as well as the underlying concept.

While Ramcharan persuasively shows how the idea of preventive diplomacy has informed UN practice generally, he necessarily points repeatedly
to what the Secretaries-General have done as the "lead actors." This account
adds substantially to knowledge of the actions by the first seven Secretaries-
General and even includes an initial glance how the eighth, Ban Ki-moon,
has voiced aspirations that fit with and presumably advance preventive
diplomacy.

Meticulous attention to the specific details of UN practice reflects Ramcharan's training in and use of international law. His three-decades-long career as an international civil servant with special concentration on human
rights required the precision and clarity displayed in this historical study.
Part of that career brought him to service as a speechwriter in the office of
the Secretary-General. This gives his comments on and observation of the
UN executive process an unusually insightful quality. It also provides new
information on the UN diplomatic process, especially during the repeated
crises of the last six decades.

As may be expected from a close observer who has worked in a long career with policy propositions and the normative aims of international law,
Ramcharan makes, mildly and almost in passing, a series of recommendations about improving the use of preventive diplomacy. Treated in a general
sense in his concluding chapter, these add persuasiveness to his judgment
that "preventive diplomacy . . . will remain one of the great ideas at the UN
for as long as the organization lasts."

Leon Gordenker
Princeton University
August 2007

Preface and Acknowledgments

The UN Charter sought to anchor the future of international peace and security of the world in the international rule of law, the peaceful settlement of disputes, collective security, universal respect for human rights, and equitable economic and social development. In all of these areas it has registered some progress but encountered many problems. During the Cold War, post–Cold War, and post–September 11, 2001, periods, the world organization has resorted to idealism and pragmatism to help it take forward its global mission.

Across the 60-plus years of its history, two ideas have proved of enduring value: preventive diplomacy and peacekeeping. Sometimes peacekeeping is seen as an integral part of preventive diplomacy.

The intellectual thread that has led to today's preventive diplomacy can be traced back to modest beginnings in the Concert of Europe, the Hague peace conferences of 1899 and 1907, the League of Nations, and now the United Nations itself. Regional and subregional organizations have also absorbed the idea in their policies and practice.

This book, written for the United Nations Intellectual History Project, seeks to trace the intellectual journey of the idea of preventive diplomacy. The emphasis is on the diplomacy of prevention, not on preventive strategies more broadly. There are many studies on the latter, including the report and extensive background papers of the Carnegie Commission on the Prevention of Deadly Conflict.[1]

Preventive diplomacy has been an enduring idea because people think that whatever might be done to head off conflicts should at least be considered and tried where possible. A central purpose of the book is to document the practice of preventive diplomacy at the UN to see when and where it has worked—and when it has not. In the world organization, ideas are developed and given shape through practice. I seek, therefore, to set out the practice as faithfully as possible to be true to the intellectual history of what actually took place. I have also sought to keep in mind how the concept of preventive diplomacy could be drawn upon in the future.

The idea of a Comprehensive Global Watch, advanced by Secretary-General Pérez de Cuéllar in 1987, is something that the entire UN system should have in its sights. Within this frame, I note that the Secretary-General is the principal actor when it comes to the practice of preventive diplomacy. He or she must use good judgment for each situation or issue. While others argue for higher decibel levels and visibility, the reader will find that I argue for prudence, tact, and discretion by the Secretary-General. The Secretary-General must be a person of trust, confidence, and wisdom. Careful diplomacy, not headlines, are required.

I am grateful to UNIHP's directors (Louis Emmerij, Richard Jolly, and Thomas G. Weiss) for their encouragement, support, friendship, and counsel. Two are economists and one is a political scientist. Their insights (and their suggestions) greatly enriched the process of interactions and learning for this lawyer whose training and subsequent experience with practice through a professional lifetime in the UN was in the areas about which I am writing—peacemaking, peacekeeping, political affairs, speechwriting for the Secretary-General, and human rights. The final frame is mine, but I am grateful for the insights from my colleagues' disciplines and backgrounds. I particularly appreciated the encouragement to explore the economic dimensions of preventive diplomacy, especially since, from the outset, the principal proponent of preventive diplomacy, Dag Hammarskjöld, underlined that development would be the key to prevention.

I am also particularly appreciative of the detailed comments from three colleagues: James S. Sutterlin, Edward C. Luck, and Elizabeth Lindenmayer. Sutterlin has inspired and guided my interest in preventive diplomacy for two decades. I consider him the preeminent expert on preventive diplomacy. He was also a leading practitioner as a director in the Office of the Secretary-General. Luck is a scholar and practitioner whose views I have also valued for two decades now. His insights helped me sharpen the focus of the work. My former colleague and friend Ms. Elizabeth Lindenmayer has been an experienced practitioner of preventive diplomacy in the Office of the Secretary-General, and her comments helped me deepen the work. I had the privilege of working with her on the Algerian case, about which I write in this volume.

I should like, finally, to single out and thank Tom Weiss, the director of the Ralph Bunche Institute for International Studies, and his staff for their support in the development of this project and as a senior fellow of the institute. Tom brought me to the institute and was a faithful discussion partner. I have enjoyed the friendship and cooperation of the administrative director, Nancy Okada, for a long time now, and I should like to say a particular word of appreciation to her. I also acknowledge the inspiration and continuing support on matters of preventive diplomacy from my much-valued UN colleague, Tapio Kaaninen. He has contributed immensely to the development of preventive strategies at the UN and has been a real pioneer and leader in this field.

The Geneva Graduate Institute of International Studies made me the First Swiss Human Rights Chair while I was finishing this book. The intellectual environment and inspirational setting on the picturesque shores of Lake Geneva helped me complete the book.

Bertrand G. Ramcharan
Geneva
May 2007

Abbreviations

ANC	African National Congress
ARF	ASEAN Regional Forum
ASEAN	Association of Southeast Asian Nations
CEMAC	Economic and Monetary Community of Central African States
CEWARN	conflict early warning and response mechanism
CSCAP	Conference on Security and Cooperation in the Asia-Pacific
DRC	Democratic Republic of the Congo
ECE	Economic Commission for Europe
ECOSOC	Economic and Social Council
ECOWAS	Economic Community of West African States
FAO	Food and Agriculture Organization
IAEA	International Atomic Energy Agency
IFP	Inkatha Freedom Party
INTERFET	International Force for East Timor
IRIN	Integrated Regional Information Networks
MDG	Millennium Development Goal
MONUC	United Nations Observer Mission in the Democratic Republic of the Congo
NPA	National Peace Accord
OAS	Organization of American States
OAU	Organization of African Unity
OCHA	Office for the Coordination of Humanitarian Affairs
OHCHR	Office of the UN High Commissioner for Human Rights
OSCE	Organization for Security and Co-operation in Europe
TAC	Treaty of Amity and Cooperation
UNAMET	UN Mission in East Timor
UNCTAD	UN Conference on Trade and Development
UNDOF	UN Disengagement Force

UNDP	UN Development Programme
UNDRO	UN Disaster Relief Organization
UNEF	UN Emergency Force
UNEP	UN Environment Programme
UNESCO	UN Educational, Scientific and Cultural Organization
UNICEF	UN Children's Fund
UNOMSA	UN Observer Mission in South Africa
UNOWA	UN Office for West Africa
UNPA	UN Protected Area
UNPREDEP	UN Preventive Deployment Force
UNPROFOR	UN Protection Force in the Former Yugoslavia
WFP	World Food Programme
WHO	World Health Organization

Secretaries-General on Preventive Diplomacy

[A] comparatively small United Nations Guard Force, as distinct from a striking force . . . could be recruited by the Secretary-General and placed at the disposal of the Security Council. Such a force would have been extremely valuable to us in the past and it would undoubtedly be very valuable in the future.

—Secretary-General Trygve Lie, Commencement Address at
   Harvard University (June 1948)[1]

Experience indicates that the preventive diplomacy, to which the efforts of the United Nations must . . . to a large extent be directed, is of special significance in cases where the original conflict may be said either to be the result of, or to imply risks for, the creation of a power vacuum between the main blocs. Preventive action in such cases must in the first place aim at filling the vacuum so that it will not provoke action from any of the major parties, the initiative for which might be taken for preventive purposes but might in turn lead to counteraction from the other side. The ways in which a vacuum can be filled by the United Nations so as to forestall such initiatives differ from case to case, but they have this in common: Temporarily, and pending the filling of a vacuum by normal means, the United Nations enters the picture on the basis of its non-commitment to any power bloc, so as to provide to the extent possible a guarantee in relation to all parties against initiatives from others.

The special need and the special possibilities for what I here call preventive United Nations diplomacy have been demonstrated in several recent cases, such as Suez and Gaza, Lebanon and Jordan, Laos and the Congo.

The responsibilities and possibilities of the Organization in the exercise of preventive diplomacy apply also to the economic sphere. Far less dramatic in their impact as the economic activities must be, they are of decisive long-term significance for the welfare of the international community. In the end, the United Nations is likely to be judged not so much by the criterion of how successfully it has overcome this or that crisis as by the significance of its total contribution towards building the kind of world community in which such crises will no longer be inevitable.

—Dag Hammarskjöld, Annual Report (1960)[2]

I believed at that time, and I still believe in retrospect, that preventive diplomacy . . . is far more effective—and incidentally much cheaper—than attempting to resolve a conflict that has been allowed to reach an acute stage. It of course requires total discretion on the part of the Secretary-General, and the cooperation, restraint, and good will of the parties concerned.

—U Thant, *View from the UN* (1978)[3]

I myself advocate what some call "preventive diplomacy," which has to be conducted calmly, without fanfare. One runs the risk, of course, of acquiring a reputation for passivity, since the substance of direct, intensive talks with heads of state and foreign ministers can never be heedlessly disclosed—but the strength of such diplomacy lies in that very feature. If it goes well, the crisis is averted, and no one is the wiser. If it goes badly, it is merely dubbed another UN failure.

The ground rule here is: the Secretary-General should negotiate only at the request of the parties to the dispute. Nothing is worse, and nothing would be less wise, than for him to force himself upon a situation. Successful mediation stands a chance only if it is wanted and worked for by all involved. During such negotiations, I always find it wise to refrain from making too many public statements. These can be easily distorted, sometimes intentionally, and only complicate matters. On the other hand, reticence poses another kind of dilemma, since a sensible public reaction to the initiatives of the United Nations can be elicited only if all aspects of a problem are openly and objectively presented. As you can see, it is a path strewn with booby-traps. If too much is said, the negotiations are in danger of being scuttled; silence, on the other hand, gives rise to all sorts of speculation in the mass media, which can lead to a hardening of the negotiating process. Diplomatic skill consists in steering precisely the right middle course.

—Kurt Waldheim, *Memoirs* (1980)[4]

Nowhere is the saying that an ounce of prevention is worth a pound of cure more true than in the field of international security, especially since the cure for conflict has proven so elusive. The United Nations must therefore give very high priority . . . to monitoring potential causes of conflict and to communicating warning signs to those in a position to alleviate the situation. First responsibility should lie with the Security Council and with the Secretary-General who will need to have the means to mount a global watch. Given the strong economic and social factors in regional violence, economic and social developments will have to be followed and assessed in terms of their relevance to international security.

—Javier Pérez de Cuéllar (1987)[5]

Preventive diplomacy is action to prevent disputes from arising between parties, to prevent existing disputes from escalating into conflicts and to limit the spread of the latter when they occur.

—Boutros Boutros-Ghali, *An Agenda for Peace* (1992)[6]

No task is more fundamental to the United Nations than the prevention and resolution of deadly conflict. Prevention, in particular, must be central to all our efforts.

—Kofi Annan, *In Larger Freedom* (March 2005)[7]

Today, war continues to threaten countless men, women and children across the globe. It is the source of untold suffering and loss. And the majority of the UN's work still focuses on preventing and ending conflict. But, the danger posed by war to all of humanity—and to our planet —is at least matched by the climate crisis and global warming.

Global warming has profound implications for jobs, growth and poverty. It affects agricultural output, the spread of disease and migration problems. It determines the ferocity and frequency of natural disasters. It can prompt water shortages, degrade land and lead to the loss of biodiversity. And, in coming decades, changes in our environment and the resulting upheavals—from droughts to inundated coastal areas to loss of arable lands—are likely to become a major driver of war and conflict.

—Ban Ki-moon (2007)[8]

Preventive Diplomacy at the UN

Introduction

The idea of preventive diplomacy has captivated the United Nations ever since it was first articulated by Secretary-General Dag Hammarskjöld nearly half a century ago. Successive generations of diplomats, state actors, and believers in the UN have put great faith in the idea in the hope that diplomatic efforts might be able to head off conflicts or human-made catastrophes. Every Secretary-General since Hammarskjöld has professed belief in the idea of preventive diplomacy, and even his predecessor, Trygve Lie, acted on similar ideas, although he did not refer to them as preventive diplomacy.

There have been dramatic successes, such as in the Cuban missile crisis of 1962, when preventive diplomacy by Secretary-General U Thant helped head off a nuclear confrontation between the Soviet Union and the United States. There have also been dramatic failures, such as the inability to head off the invasion of Iraq in 2003 and the subsequent disastrous consequences. Failures have probably numbered more than successes, but still, the idea of preventive diplomacy is potent and will continue to be so because of a simple belief by people that, whenever feasible, everything possible should be done to head off a conflict or disaster.

Article 99 of the UN Charter presaged the idea of preventive diplomacy. For the first time in the history of international organizations, that article gave the Secretary-General the competence to bring matters that might threaten international peace and security to the Security Council for its consideration. From the outset of the institution, Secretary-General Trygve Lie used this competence to gather information about situations, establish contacts with those concerned, send emissaries to examine situations more closely, and do whatever he could to help head off or contain crises of international concern. Lie had been a lawyer, trade unionist, government minister, and UN delegate before he was elected Secretary-General, and he sought to give content to the Secretary-General's responsibilities. He did not have many successes in heading off conflicts, but he pioneered the Secretary-General's use of this competence under Article 99.

Secretary-General Dag Hammarskjöld was an economist and lawyer with a philosopher's bent. He had held important positions in Swedish government service and as a delegate to the UN before he was elected Secretary-General. He was a conceptual and political thinker, and he sought to develop the role of the institution and the Secretary-General by introducing concepts and practices that would enable the UN to make tangible contributions to the quest for peace and prosperity. He had distinct ideas about diplomacy at the UN and on preventive diplomacy in particular. He considered the presence in New York of the permanent missions of the member states an asset for the conduct of diplomacy on issues of concern to the United Nations, and he had thoughts on the use of UN diplomatic representatives in different parts of the world. He knew that the UN could do little in the area of preventive diplomacy where there was a direct clash of interests between the superpowers in the Cold War. But he hoped that he might be able to head off disputes between lesser powers from being drawn into the gravitational pull of the superpower contest.

Hammarskjöld put down markers on the practice of preventive diplomacy that are still in use today. For example, he always used his judgment in decisions about whether his efforts might be useful; his involvement was not automatic. He sent representatives on special missions or outposted them in particular situations. He envisaged the eventual deployment of a ring of representatives in trouble spots where the UN might be able to play a role. His concept of preventive diplomacy focused on turmoil-ridden areas and kept root causes in mind. He understood that it would be important to tackle the economic and social causes of conflict. To use some of the terms that are currently fashionable, he had an operational and structural approach to preventive diplomacy.

Hammarskjöld's ideas fired the imagination of diplomats, scholars, state actors, and believers in the UN. In 1965, the first textbook on preventive diplomacy was published, *From Collective Security to Preventive Diplomacy*.[1] Another scholarly text—*Dag Hammarskjöld and Crisis Diplomacy*—was written in 1961.[2] Brian Urquhart's biography of Hammarskjöld devoted several chapters to his practice of preventive diplomacy.[3] A new idea had taken hold at the United Nations.

Secretary-General U Thant took this vision forward, practiced preventive diplomacy, and made a distinctive contribution in calling for the UN to deal with natural disasters and head off human-made disasters. U Thant, a devout Buddhist, was a schoolteacher-turned-diplomat who represented Burma at the UN before being elected Secretary-General. His role in helping head off a nuclear confrontation during the Cuban missile crisis is one

of the best examples of preventive diplomacy. His visionary establishment
of the office of UN disaster relief coordinator had elements of response as
well as prevention. U Thant also pleaded for attention to how the UN might
be able to deal with human-made disasters such as humanitarian emergencies and gross violations of human rights. He exercised the Secretariat's
good offices in many such situations.

Secretary-General Kurt Waldheim continued the practice of preventive
diplomacy. A soldier during World War II (whose service would be a cause
of controversy after he left office), Waldheim was a lawyer who served most
of his career as an Austrian diplomat, representing his country at the UN
and later as its foreign minister. In his own words, he was a believer in careful diplomacy, not grand designs. He did not establish any new policies or
doctrinal markers in the development of the concept. But he had his successes in particular situations, such as the border disputes between Iran and
Iraq in the 1960s. He resorted to appeals in dangerous situations such as the
Arab-Israeli War of 1973. He acted speedily to dispatch UN peacekeepers
to contain and control that situation. He showed inventiveness in dealing
with delicate situations such as the Soviet Union's refusal to accept a Secretary-General's special representative on Afghanistan, which the General Assembly had called for. He appointed a personal representative instead,
which the Soviet Union accepted.

Secretary-General Javier Pérez de Cuéllar was of the same diplomatic
school as U Thant and Waldheim. A lawyer by training, he had served in his
country's diplomatic service, representing it at the UN, and had also served
as an under-secretary-general. He was a careful diplomatic practitioner, and
this skill served him well when the opportunity came to help end the dev-
astating war between Iran and Iraq. He sought to head off the war between
Argentina and the United Kingdom over the Falkland/Malvinas Islands
(and nearly succeeded). He sent a discreet fact-finding mission to Bulgaria
and Turkey in 1989 to help head off the deterioration of a dispute between
those two countries. He added to the concept and practice of preventive
diplomacy in two significant respects: He called for the maintenance of a
comprehensive global watch over threats to human security and welfare,
and he established a unit within the offices of the Secretary-General dedicated to the collection and analysis of information intended to help the head
of the UN provide alerts to the Security Council about situations that could
threaten or breach international peace and security.

Secretary-General Boutros Boutros-Ghali, a lawyer and political scientist, was a professor of international law and international relations for many
years before serving as his country's minister of state for foreign affairs. He

was on the team of President Anwar Sadat when he launched his peace initiative with Israel and participated in the Camp David talks. He had a stellar academic record and significant scholarly publications, and his assumption of the office of Secretary-General in 1992 came shortly after the end of the Cold War during a time of hope for a new world order. At the first summit meeting of the Security Council, in January 1992, he was requested to write a report on the UN's future role in conflict prevention, peacemaking, and peacekeeping, which led him to submit the widely acclaimed *An Agenda for Peace*.[4] This was one of the most influential documents in the intellectual journey of preventive diplomacy. Unfortunately, two and a half years after its publication, Boutros-Ghali felt that it was necessary to issue a supplement to *An Agenda for Peace* that signaled practical difficulties in implementing the ideas in the forward-looking document.

Boutros-Ghali reorganized the Secretariat and made information-gathering and analysis for early warning a core part of the responsibilities of a strengthened Department of Political Affairs. He practiced preventive diplomacy in cases such as the war between Eritrea and Yemen, and his proposal led to the establishment of the first preventive deployment of UN peacekeepers in the Former Yugoslav Republic of Macedonia.

Secretary-General Kofi Annan took this work forward and gave pronounced emphasis to preventive strategies. A lifelong international civil servant before he was elected Secretary-General, he did graduate work in management during his career in the world organization. He served mainly in the personnel, administrative, management, and budgetary parts of the UN before becoming assistant-secretary-general and then under-secretary-general in the Department of Peacekeeping Operations prior to being elected Secretary-General. He maintained the arrangements in the Department of Political Affairs, although he reduced the number of regional divisions from six to four. He submitted three reports on preventive diplomacy, the last of which categorized preventive actions into structural, operational, and systemic measures.[5] He exercised preventive diplomacy successfully in cases such as the border conflict over the Bakassi Peninsula between Cameroon and Nigeria.

As of the time of writing, the eighth Secretary-General—Ban Ki-moon— had just entered into office. A lawyer by training and a lifelong career diplomat, he served as his country's foreign minister at the time of his election to the post of Secretary-General. He has announced his intention to emphasize diplomacy, tact, and discretion during his term as Secretary-General. He will undoubtedly take the practice of preventive diplomacy at the

UN forward. He has already drawn attention to the dangers of conflict that could ensue from global warming.

In tracing the journey of the idea of preventive diplomacy, I have emphasized the roles of the Secretaries-General because they have been the lead practitioners of the art. While the Security Council and the General Assembly have contributed to preventive diplomacy, they were both constrained by political differences during the Cold War. The Secretaries-General were likewise constrained during that period but had a little more room for maneuver on a case-by-case basis and could therefore establish a stronger practice. Through its establishment of the interim committee in its early years, the General Assembly came close to a preventive role, but the committee did not operate long in practice. In the "Uniting for Peace" resolution, the General Assembly sought to establish a mechanism of urgent response, which has been used on occasions.[6]

As a deliberative body of the entire membership, however, the General Assembly is slower off the mark, and speed counts when one is trying to head off conflicts. The General Assembly has encouraged the Secretary-General's discharge of his responsibilities under Article 99 of the Charter. However, in the post–Cold War period, especially after Boutros-Ghali's *An Agenda for Peace* was published, many developing countries displayed caution about agendas of early warning and urgent response out of concern regarding unwarranted interferences in their internal affairs. The General Assembly has thus been guardedly encouraging when it comes to pursuing preventive strategies.

For its part, the Security Council has always been and remains a careful organ in dealing with political situations. This probably explains why it has generally preferred to leave preventive diplomacy to the Secretary-General when possible, retaining its own room for maneuver. In the aftermath of *An Agenda for Peace,* the Security Council has pledged itself to contribute to preventive diplomacy where appropriate and has encouraged the Secretary-General's efforts. On occasion, the Security Council president has taken an initiative. In some instances, the council has sent fact-finding or visiting missions and has designated a committee on conflict prevention in Africa.

From all of this, it can be concluded that Secretaries-General have promoted broad preventive approaches, exercised preventive diplomacy in cases where they thought their efforts might be helpful, and sought to build up the Secretariat's capacity to gather and analyze information for early warning and preventive diplomacy. The General Assembly and the Security

Council have been cautiously supportive in recent practice, but the Security Council retains its freedom to act as it deems appropriate.

The Secretary-General, the Security Council, and the General Assembly are not the only actors at the UN. Senior officials under the authority of the Secretary-General may also engage in preventive efforts. Some regional and subregional organizations operate their own systems of early warning and preventive actions and are often in contact with their counterparts in the UN. Cooperation between the UN and regional or subregional organizations is thus developing in the practice of preventive diplomacy. Documenting this cooperation is relevant to the story of preventive diplomacy at the UN.

Tracing the intellectual history of preventive diplomacy at the UN requires recognition that in the post–Cold War, post–September 11 periods, the organization has been called on to deal not only with the risks of interstate or intrastate conflicts but also with new threats and challenges such as international terrorism and the possibility that terrorists might use weapons of mass destruction, fears about genocide, and problems of governance and gross violations of human rights that result in widespread humanitarian emergencies and conflicts. To the extent that it might be possible and appropriate, preventive diplomacy might have a role to play in some of these issues, and indeed, efforts have already been launched, such as the designation of a special adviser to the Secretary-General on the prevention of genocide.

This book follows the intellectual journey of the idea of preventive diplomacy at the UN with an eye toward the future: What role should the concept play in the UN's grand strategy of the future, particularly for the Secretary-General? It is clear that while the concept of preventive diplomacy has been invoked often, its essence has not been quite understood, leading to unrealistic expectations. Preventive diplomacy is an idea with limitations as well as promise. There are uses to which it might be put and situations or issues that are not susceptible to its treatment.

In July 2006, following Hezbollah's incursions into Israel, the killing of some Israeli soldiers, and the kidnapping of two others, Israeli forces moved against Hezbollah positions in Lebanon and, with the support of the United States, remained on the offensive for several weeks. Appeals from Secretary-General Annan and others for a cease-fire were rebuffed because Israel, supported by the United States, had determined that Hezbollah should be put out of action to prevent future Hezbollah offensives against it. In this case, Israel, supported by the United States, chose war as a means of preventing future attacks. The world, including the Security Council, stood by helplessly.

One should distinguish between preventive diplomacy and broader preventive strategies or actions. The two are closely related but not identical. The UN Charter offers many preventive strategies and diverse activities for peace, development, and human rights that are potentially preventive. Preventive diplomacy, especially by the Secretary-General, entails marshaling diplomacy on selected issues, threats, or situations where the Secretary-General considers that her or his efforts, discreetly pursued, might be of assistance.

The elements of discretion and judgment are crucial. Preventive diplomacy should be distinguished from public advocacy.[7] There may be occasions when careful advocacy about an issue or threat might help lay the groundwork for preventive diplomacy. But for the most part, preventive diplomacy must be carried out prudently and discreetly, with tact and discernment. Trust and confidence are key ingredients of preventive diplomacy. Preventive diplomacy must be exercised in a world of uneven power distribution.[8] Moving forward even in the face of a complex political environment is a challenge to the diplomatic skills of the practitioner.

When Hammarskjöld first coined the term "preventive diplomacy,"[9] he wanted to develop an independent role for the UN in dealing with Cold War crises that were not in the direct line of confrontation between the East and West and to prevent nations from falling within the gravity of that contest. That was his objective, not the prevention of conflicts around the world.[10] Hammarskjöld's use of the expression "preventive diplomacy" was understandable, however, inasmuch as the insulation of some situations from the East-West confrontation did have a preventive rationale.

Subsequently, the term "preventive diplomacy" was given what has become its current signification: diplomacy to head off conflicts, mitigate their effects, and prevent their recurrence. Notwithstanding an understandable preference in recent UN practice to use the wider term "conflict prevention," "preventive diplomacy" remains the key concept, closely linked to the Secretary-General's exercise of it under Article 99 of the Charter.

Preventive diplomacy involves the exercise of the good offices of the Secretary-General, but the two concepts are not identical. Preventive diplomacy, especially in contemporary practice, might go beyond the provision of good offices. On some issues, preventive diplomacy might have world-order dimensions and may call for the Secretary-General to resort to action that is quite novel, depending on the issue at hand.[11] Promoting democracy, reducing extreme poverty, and responding to climate change are examples.

The practice of preventive diplomacy in heading off, alleviating, or resolving conflicts will continue to be part art and part science, and future Secretaries-General will continue to use their judgment about whether and how good offices, mediation, or other forms of preventive action might be used. Documenting the practice of preventive diplomacy can help future Secretaries-General in their efforts.

There are those who argue that preventive diplomacy has a long historical tradition. "Traditional preventive diplomacy," as Mohammed Bedjaoui termed it, was diplomacy exercised by a state to protect its interests or reduce threats of attacks by its neighbors or adversaries.[12] This practice continues.

However, Bedjaoui argues, contemporary preventive diplomacy is new. It is diplomacy that must be brought to bear on issues of peace, development, and human rights. In his view, development, education, and human rights are the keys. Dynamic peace, he submits, is a ceaseless activity toward the banishment of all social ills that generate tension, violence, and war. Preventive diplomacy would thus do well to focus on the struggle against underdevelopment in poor regions of the world. To ensure the observance of human rights, preventive diplomacy must engage in a vast preventive campaign against underdevelopment. According to Bedjaoui, human dignity is the crucial guiding value.

There is much in Bedjaoui's presentation that is morally attractive—even if he may be speaking more of preventive policies or advocacy. Generically, one can make the case that diplomacy should be deployed for the ends he sets out. But it is a broad agenda and is indistinguishable from the UN's overall efforts for peace, development, and human rights. Preventive diplomacy, especially by the Secretary-General, is best focused on threats, situations, or issues where the Secretary-General or another UN actor has a reasonable chance of making headway. The prevention, containment, and resolution of conflicts will always be the central focus.

Preventive diplomacy must be strategic. It takes place alongside leadership and advocacy, but it must be subtle, nimble, and deft. Leadership and advocacy may pursue the big-picture issues and grand designs. Preventive diplomacy pursues specific objectives. The Secretary-General is a moral leader, a moderator, a harmonizer, a custodian of the Charter's principles, and a promoter of a global watch over human security and welfare. Preventive diplomacy situates itself within the framework of harmonization, and its ends must be carefully thought through.

This study, while taking account of the regional and subregional experiences, is mainly concerned with UN practice. It also examines the Concert of Europe, the Hague Peace Conferences, and the League of Nations to determine whether the germ of the idea of preventive diplomacy may be detected in earlier periods. Key provisions of the UN Charter, particularly Article 99, are also considered

Chapters 2, 3, and 4 examine UN policies and doctrines of preventive diplomacy, paying attention to the Secretaries-General, the Security Council, and the General Assembly. The practice of preventive diplomacy by the Security Council and the Secretary-General are also examined. Chapter 5 focuses on the Cuban missile crisis of 1962, when Secretary-General U Thant performed perhaps the most important exercise of preventive diplomacy in the institution's history. Chapter 6 considers the practice of preventive diplomacy by representatives of the Secretary-General and UN subregional offices, while chapter 7 examines the preventive role of UN observers and peacekeepers. The following chapters—8 and 9—take a look at preventive diplomacy from different perspectives, first its practice in the fields of economic, social, human rights and humanitarianism and then in the age of genocide, terrorism, and nontraditional threats to security. Finally, chapter 10 explores cooperative preventive diplomacy with regional and subregional organizations.

The book's conclusion offers some thoughts for preventive diplomacy in the years to come, suggesting that the future calls for the pursuit of careful preventive diplomacy while building up a comprehensive global watch. The conclusion finishes with a seven-point agenda for the Secretary-General to that end.

1

Preventive Diplomacy in the Concert of Europe, the Hague Peace Conferences, the League of Nations, and the UN Charter

- The Development of Preventive Diplomacy in the Pre-UN Period
- Preventive Diplomacy within the UN System
- Implicit or Explicit Invocations of Article 99
- Conclusion

During each historical epoch, the UN has had to respond to changing circumstances and contexts. The practical expression of the idea of preventive diplomacy has necessarily reflected these changing demands and circumstances. Methods of action respond to the needs and circumstances of the situation or issue. That will continue to be the case in the future.

Hence, even as the evolution of the idea of preventive diplomacy is recorded, it is necessary to be aware of its contemporary and future relevance. The idea may be useful with regard to situational as well as thematic, traditional, and nontraditional threats. Secretary-General Ban Ki-moon brought this out well when he sounded the alert that the danger posed by war was matched by the dangers posed by climate crisis and global warming. He cautioned that in the coming decades, changes in the environment and the resulting upheavals were likely to become major drivers of war and conflict.[1] This book argues that attention must also be paid to grave threats from the dangers of genocide, nontraditional threats to security, and terrorists using nuclear, chemical, or biological weapons.

In *Peace and War: Armed Conflicts and International Order 1648–1989*, Kalevi Holsti particularly emphasized the need to be attentive to the problems of the past and the threats of the future.[2] After a detailed examination of peace agreements since Westphalia, Holsti found that all the great peace settlements had failed in one important respect: The architects of peace had looked backward and had focused on resolving the issues that had been the source of the previous war. They had attempted to construct international orders that would prevent a recurrence of previous crises, but most were not far-sighted enough to note important new issues appearing on the diplomatic horizon. His comments on the post–World War II settlement were particularly instructive. Holsti argued that in 1945, insufficient attention was given to future problems such as colonialism, state creation, and population growth.

It was in this inhospitable environment that the concept of preventive diplomacy made its way at the UN. What, if anything, did it have to build on? In *Power and the Pursuit of Peace,* historian F. H. Hinsley traced peace plans going back to Dante's *Monarchia* and concluded:

> It was in the last years of the nineteenth century that for the first time in the history of the present . . . world civilization—if not in all history—peace proposals were propagated for fear of the danger of war rather than in consequence of its outbreak. Warfare has become even more extensive and destructive since then, and at an even more rapid rate. It is unlikely that the problem will ever again recede from the forefront of people's minds even if further large-scale war is avoided.[3]

This led to the search for preventive approaches.

The principal strands in ideas of prevention that were advanced up to the nineteenth century included ideas such as the balance of power, cooperation among states for maintaining peace, development of the international rule of law (an idea closely associated with Grotius), the establishment of international organizations dedicated to maintaining peace, collective security, establishment of an international (European) army, the development of international arbitral and judicial procedures, and the systematization and development of international law, an idea first implemented with the Hague peace conferences of 1899 and 1907 but one that had been much emphasized by Immanuel Kant, who had argued for a "union of nations which maintains itself, prevents wars, and steadily expands."[4] He "was as convinced that the development of the rule of law between states would eventually produce international peace as he was convinced that it was the only means of producing it and that it would take a long time to develop."[5]

The Development of Preventive Diplomacy in the Pre-UN Period

Some of the early ideas in the Concert of Europe, the Hague peace conferences, and the League of Nations pertain to the development of preventive diplomacy in the pre-UN period.

The Concert of Europe

The Concert of Europe was born in a circular letter written by Count Kaunitz dated 17 July 1791. In the letter, Kaunitz, in the name of Emperor Leopold, impressed on the imperial ambassadors the duty of all powers to make common cause to preserve "public peace, the tranquillity of states, the inviolability of possessions, and the faith of treaties."[6] The Concert of Europe provided direct antecedents for the idea of preventive diplomacy that became prominent in the twentieth century.

Diplomacy was intended as the principal method of action within the concert, and preventive diplomacy was precisely the hope. At its core was the idea that by combining their efforts through diplomatic action, the principal powers of the time—Austria, France, Great Britain, Prussia, and Russia, subsequently joined by Turkey—could help avoid another European conflagration in the aftermath of the Napoleonic Wars. In some situations, the Concert succeeded, such as during the Belgian revolt of 1830 and with regard to the Eastern Question. In others, such as the Crimean War, it failed.

The Concert of Europe broke down after 1870, when it could not stem wars between Prussia and Denmark, Prussia and Austria, and then Prussia and France. This breakdown left the major European powers without a framework of cooperation that could help prevent the slide to war in the first half of the twentieth century. Notwithstanding its eventual failure, the Concert passed on a set of ideas and methods closely related to the practice of preventive diplomacy in current times.[7]

The Congress of Vienna of 1815 led to the birth of the congress system, which some historians consider an integral part of the concert system. At the Vienna Congress, the great powers were moved by a desire to reestablish the law of nations against a conqueror's ambitions. Their aim was to reestablish a world where order prevailed, not war and revolution. They sought to promote peace, security, and order within states as well as between them.

Article VI of the Treaty of Defensive Alliance of 1815—the Quadruple Alliance—provided for periodic meetings of the allies to consider measures to maintain peace in Europe. The article reads as follows:

> To facilitate and to secure the execution of the present Treaty, and to consolidate the connections which at the present moment so closely unite the Four Sovereigns for the happiness of the world . . . the High Contracting Parties have agreed to renew their meeting at fixed periods . . . for the purpose of consulting

upon their common interests, and for the consideration of the measures which at each of these periods shall be considered the most salutary for the repose and prosperity of Nations, and for the maintenance of the peace of Europe.[8]

Like the congress system, the Concert of Europe continued to emphasize the role of the great powers and was based on the concept of the balance of power among them. The principles of the concert were the responsibility of the great powers for dealing with European problems and maintaining the territorial status quo, an agreement among these powers not to make unilateral changes to arrangements and understandings among them, and consensus in decision-making among the great powers.[9]

In 1856, the Concert of Europe introduced an historic innovation that laid the foundations for what would be called preventive diplomacy a century later. Protocol 23 of the Declaration of Paris of 1856 contained the following provision:

> The Plenipotentiaries do not hesitate to express in the name of their governments the desire that States . . . should, before appealing to arms, have recourse, so far as circumstances allow, to the good offices of a friendly Power. The Plenipotentiaries hope that governments not represented at the Congress will unite in the sentiment which has inspired the desire recorded in the Protocol.[10]

British prime minister William Gladstone welcomed this declaration as "the first time that . . . the principal nations of Europe have given an emphatic utterance to sentiments which contain at least a qualified disapproval of the results of war." The London *Times* hoped that it would make "all Europe one court of appeal."[11] Hinsley noted that "it was certainly the first clause of its kind to be included in a multilateral treaty."[12] Not until forty-three years later was the thread of prevention picked up at the first Hague peace conference of 1899 and continued at the second conference in 1907.

The Hague Peace Conferences

The idea of the prevention of war through resort to good offices or mediation, expressed for the first time in Protocol 23, would be picked up explicitly at the Hague peace conferences of 1899 and 1907. As their fundamental aim, the two conferences intended to avoid war through the use of international law, the promotion of peaceful methods for settling disputes, the advancement of international arbitration, and the lessening of human suffering in war by codifying and developing the rules for protecting non-combatants during warfare.[13] The Permanent Court of Arbitration and the Hague provisions on the laws of war came out of the Hague peace conferences.

In Article 2 of the Hague Convention on the Pacific Settlement of International Disputes (18 October 1907), the contracting powers agreed to have recourse to the good offices or mediation of one or more friendly powers before resorting to arms. Article 3 gave the right to nations not involved in the dispute to offer good offices, even during hostilities. The exercise of this right was not to be considered an unfriendly act.

The ideas for the peaceful settlement of disputes and, thereby, the prevention of war, that were elaborated at the Hague peace conferences were picked up after the devastation wrought by World War I and inserted into the Covenant of the League of Nations.

The League of Nations

The prevention of war was the central idea of the Covenant of the League of Nations. In Article 8, League members recognized that maintaining peace required reducing national armaments to the lowest point consistent with national safety and enforcing international obligations by common action. In Article 10, members agreed to respect and preserve the territorial integrity and existing political independence of all members against external aggression.

Article 11 declared that any war or threat of war, whether it immediately affected any of the members of the League or not, was a matter of concern to the entire League. The article also declared it the friendly right of each member to bring to the attention of the assembly or of the council any circumstance that threatened to disturb international peace or the good relations between nations. Under Article 11 of the Covenant, the council or the assembly could intervene or mediate in any circumstances affecting the peaceful relations of members. Article 12 provided for resort to arbitration or judicial settlement or to inquiry by the council, and members agreed that they would not resort to war until three months after the award by the arbitrators or the judicial decision or the report by the council. In Article 13, the members agreed that if a dispute arose that they recognized as suitable for submission to arbitration or judicial settlement that could not be settled by diplomacy, they would submit the subject to arbitration or judicial settlement. Taking forward the ideas developed at the Hague peace conferences, Article 14 established a Permanent Court of International Justice.

Under Article 15, if a member did not choose to go to arbitration or judicial settlement, the dispute was to be submitted to the Council of the League of Nations. Any party to the dispute could make such a submission by giving notice of the dispute to the secretary-general, who would arrange for a full investigation and consideration of the matter. The council would then endeavor to reach a settlement. The council could refer a dispute to the assembly.

If any member of the League resorted to war in disregard of Articles 12, 13, or 15, it would be deemed to have committed an act of war against all members of the League, who were then authorized to institute sanctions against the aggressor. In such a case, the council could recommend to the governments concerned what military, naval, or air force resources League members should contribute to the armed forces to be used to uphold the Covenant provisions.

The council of the League developed procedures for dealing with potential hostilities, which included immediate intervention by its president, who could issue a warning to the disputants and call for a cease-fire; immediate convening of the council, to which representatives of the disputants were summoned for the purpose of ending hostilities; the appointment of a commission of officers to supervise the cessation of hostilities, secure the maintenance of the status quo, or execute some other provisional arrangement, pending a settlement of the dispute; and the establishment of a commission to examine the facts and make a report with recommendations for a solution to the dispute.

When Sweden and Finland could not decide in 1921 who owned the Aaland Islands, which were an equal distance from both countries, the council, on the initiative of Great Britain, took up the matter before hostilities could begin.[14] Eric Drummond, secretary-general of the League, led efforts to avoid the dispute from escalating into war. Drummond suggested that the council establish a commission of inquiry to settle the matter by mediation and secure agreement between the parties. This course of action was adopted and proved successful.

Arthur W. Rovine has observed that the "pattern for the Drummond model was determined from the start—he would work quietly and his diplomatic activity would take the form of recommendation and suggestion, even on consequential procedural or political matters."[15] In February 1921, Drummond brought a border dispute between Panama and Costa Rica that had resulted in fighting to the attention of the council. Drummond did so without a request from either party or a member of the League as required by the Covenant.[16]

When skirmishes developed on the common border of Greece and Bulgaria in 1925, Drummond and the president of the council took action just hours after hostilities had begun.[17] Rovine's assessment of Drummond's efforts in this case was as follows:

> Drummond, as always working quietly, attempted to exert some authority in matters of vital concern to the League and world politics, and in so doing, he maintained the reality of a political function for the Secretary-General as mediator and aide in shaping the terms of settlement, and as a leading channel for communications between the parties to the conflict and the international community.[18]

Unfortunately, the League, too, eventually suffered the fate of the Concert of Europe and the Hague peace conferences and was unable to avoid the recurrence of another global conflagration. It was the turn of the United Nations to take the torch of conflict prevention forward.

Preventive Diplomacy within the UN System

According to the opening article of its Charter, the first purpose of the UN is to maintain international peace and security and take effective collective measures to prevent and remove threats to peace. In addition, according to the Charter, the UN will bring about, by peaceful means and in accordance with the principles of justice and international law, adjustment or settlement of international disputes or situations that may lead to a breach of the peace.

The Security Council is mandated to determine the existence of any threat to the peace, any breach of the peace, or any act of aggression and to make recommendations or decide what measures should be taken to maintain or restore international peace and security. The Security Council may call on the parties concerned to comply with such provisional measures as it deems necessary or desirable. The Security Council may also decide which measures should be employed to give effect to its decisions; these measures cannot involve the use of armed force.

The Charter thus places primary responsibility for prompt and effective action on the Security Council. Next, according to Article 99, the Secretary-General may bring any matter that threatens the maintenance of international peace and security to the Security Council's attention.

The General Assembly may also discuss any question relating to maintaining international peace and security brought before it by any member state, the Security Council, or a state that is not a member of the UN. Under paragraph 3 of Article 11, the General Assembly may call situations that can endanger international peace and security to the Security Council's attention. The Security Council may also indicate provisional measures. Finally, the International Court of Justice may also indicate interim measures in cases where it is vested with jurisdiction.

Article 99 of the Charter

Article 99 of the Charter and the Secretary-General's status as a principal organ of the UN are the principal legal bases and inspiration for the development of the concept of preventive diplomacy at the UN. This is the case even if diplomatic actions have also been pursued at the request of the Security Council and the General Assembly.

When Article 99 was discussed at the 1945 San Francisco conference that established the UN, different views existed regarding whether the exercise of the competence should be obligatory or optional. The majority agreed that the right should be exercised at the Secretary-General's discretion and should not be made a duty.[19] The preparatory commission felt that the responsibility conferred on the Secretary-General by Article 99 required the exercise of the highest qualities of political judgment, tact, and integrity.[20]

In one of the early studies on the Office of the Secretary-General, Stephen Schwebel, who later served as a judge and president of the International Court of Justice, identified "seven interlocking powers" flowing from Article 99, including, among others, the Secretary-General's right to make such inquiries and investigations necessary to determine whether or not to invoke the powers under Article 99 and the Secretary-General's right to choose the most appropriate means of implementing the article. He also noted that Article 99 supplied the Secretary-General with a springboard at the Security Council for a dramatic appeal to world public opinion comparable to that provided for the General Assembly in Article 98.[21]

In order to be able to act pursuant to Article 99, the Secretary-General must be provided with up-to-date information, analysis, and risk assessment. Historically, all three of these have been in short supply, although the regional divisions of the Department of Political Affairs attempt to gather and analyze such information and submit risk assessments to the Secretary-General.

Risk Assessment in the Secretariat

When Secretary-General Boutros-Ghali established the Department of Political Affairs in 1992, he set out five tasks it should carry out in support of preventive and peacemaking efforts: first, collecting information about potential or actual conflicts; second, analyzing this information to identify situations where the UN, with the agreement of the parties concerned, could play a useful preventive or peacemaking role; third, preparing recommendations for the Secretary-General about the specific forms of that role; fourth, assisting the Secretary-General in obtaining such authority as may be required from the relevant intergovernmental body; and fifth, executing the approved policy.[22]

The Department of Political Affairs currently has four regional divisions with desk officers who cover every country of the world. On average, a desk officer covers five to six countries. Typically, a desk officer follows political developments within a country to provide background and briefing papers for the Secretary-General or other senior officials. They are also expected to provide talking points for the Secretary-General during his meetings. The preparation of background and briefing papers and talking points takes up a great deal of the time of the desk officers.

However, a key mandate of the department is to help the Secretary-General discharge his responsibilities under Article 99 by monitoring each country and alerting him or her to situations of concern. To do so, each desk officer should have an up-to-date risk analysis of the country that monitors issues that could trigger unrest, crisis, or conflict. At times, desk officers have been given training in risk analysis. One such initiative was an extensive training program carried out beginning in 1996 under the auspices of the United Nations Staff College.[23] Over the years, hundreds of UN officials from several departments have attended training sessions in risk analysis, early warning, and preventive diplomacy. It is difficult to determine whether this program contributed meaningfully to a risk-sensitivity approach in the Department of Political Affairs. Broadening the courses systemwide throughout the UN made the training available to many more people, but the Department of Political Affairs, where it was needed most, was no longer the principal focus of the training courses. Risk assessment by Department of Political Affairs desk officers should be a key part of the Secretariat's approach to the discharge of the responsibilities of the Secretary-General under Article 99 of the Charter.

Before the Secretary-General formally invokes Article 99, he or she and senior political officers may decide that the appropriate step is to brief Security Council members informally. This has become a regular occurrence in the Security Council.

Briefings and Informal Consultations in the Security Council[24]

Security Council briefings may relate to situations already on its agenda; these are meant to address issues of containment or settlement. Briefings may also be held on new situations or issues at the council's request. The aim here may be prevention or containment. Thirdly, briefings may be about new situations of concern to the Secretary-General. The aims here are, once again, prevention or containment.

In a typical briefing, the Secretariat aims to provide a succinct factual account of the situation. It may also provide an analysis of the situation, identifying issues for consideration, presenting options, or offering recommendations. Often, recommendations are advanced only if they have been cleared with senior officials or the Secretary-General and then provided in response to specific questions or comments; discipline among members of the Secretariat adds to the trust accorded by council members. Because council members wish to make their own political assessments, they need as good factual information as can be provided. If they so wish, they may ask for the comments, analysis, or advice of the Secretariat.

In the normal run of things, the under-secretary-general for political affairs, one of the assistant-secretaries-general for political affairs, or a director in the Department of Political Affairs does the briefing. Where the Secretary-General considers the matter sufficiently grave, he or she may personally conduct the briefing. During a briefing in informal consultation, members pose questions, ask for supplementary information, offer thoughts or recommendations, and suggest lines of approach or response for the council. The Secretary-General can also raise situations that seem significant at his or her monthly luncheons with Security Council members.

Frequently, after a briefing, if Security Council members agree, the council president may make comments to the press along the lines discussed and agreed on in the council. The president of the Security Council may make a presidential statement, the text of which has been agreed on by council members.

Where the president and council members think helpful, the president may meet the permanent representative(s) of the country or countries concerned for a briefing or to suggest viewpoints that had been distilled by consensus during the informal consultations. This is an example of the council acting in preventive or containment mode.

A debate sometimes arises about whether the Secretary-General should consider formally invoking Article 99 even as the council is considering a situation under informal procedures. Article 99 has been formally invoked only a few times. But the case of Darfur leads one to ask whether Secretary-General Annan should have exercised the option because of the gravity of that situation. That could have dramatically raised the stakes for council members, forcing them to consider the option of a no-fly zone over Darfur, possibly combined with aerial monitoring and enforcement. According to press reports, this idea was under active consideration in London and Washington in the closing weeks of 2006, nearly three years after the situation in Darfur was brought to the attention of the Security Council.[25] However, it had been canvassed as an option on 1 February 2006 in an article in the *International Herald Tribune.*[26]

Implicit or Explicit Invocations of Article 99

Although Article 99 has been implicitly or explicitly invoked on only a few occasions, the practice quite richly illustrates the options of the Secretary-General.

In 1946, during the Security Council's consideration of the situation in Greece, the United States proposed establishing a commission to investigate the facts relating to incidents along Greece's northern frontier. Secretary-General Lie advised the council that if the proposal was not carried, he would reserve his right to engage in fact-finding:

> I hope that the Council will understand that the Secretary-General must reserve his right to make such inquiries or investigations as he may think necessary in order to determine whether or not he should consider bringing any aspect of this matter to the attention of the Council under the provisions of the Charter.[27]

Subsequent Secretaries-General have continued to act on this basis. The designation of a special representative to keep the Secretary-General informed of developments in a situation of international concern has been a long-standing practice.[28]

On 25 June 1950, the Security Council met to deal with the situation in Korea. The formal request for the meeting had come from the United States, but Secretary-General Lie had also received a cable from the United Nations Commission on Korea suggesting that he exercise his right under Article 99. The letter was circulated to the Security Council members.[29]

Secretary-General Lie informed the council that "the present situation is a serious one and is a threat to international peace. The Security Council is, in my opinion, the competent organ to deal with it. I consider it the clear duty of the Security Council to take steps necessary to re-establish peace in that area."[30]

In the Suez crisis of 1956, the Security Council was called into session by the United States. Secretary-General Dag Hammarskjöld told the Security Council that he would have used his right to call for an immediate meeting of the Security Council if the U.S. government had not done so the previous night.[31]

Secretaries-General have claimed and exercised the right to visit a country or countries to brief themselves at first hand. On 8 November 1959, during the Security Council's consideration of the situation in Laos, Secretary-General Hammarskjöld announced that he had accepted an invitation to visit the country to gather independent and full knowledge that would enable him to discharge his responsibilities. Similarly, in July 1961, while the Security Council was examining the situation in Tunisia, Secretary-General Hammarskjöld accepted an invitation from Tunisia to visit the country for an exchange of views.[32]

Hammarskjöld explained his action:

> Quite apart from the fact that it is naturally the duty of the Secretary-General to put himself at the disposal of the Government of a Member State, if that Government considers a personal contact necessary, my acceptance of the invitation falls within the framework of the rights and obligations of the Secretary-General, as Article 99 of the Charter authorizes him to draw to the attention of the Security Council what, in his view, may represent a threat to international peace and security, and as it is obvious that the duties following from the article cannot be fulfilled unless the Secretary-General, in case of need, is in a position to form a personal opinion about the relevant facts of the situation which may represent such a threat.[33]

In relation to the situation in Laos in 1959, Secretary-General Hammarskjöld requested that he be allowed to make a statement on a matter within the council's responsibility "as he considers called for under the terms of his own responsibilities" without formal invocation of Article 99.[34]

In a letter dated 13 July 1960 to the council president, Hammarskjöld wrote:

> I want to inform you that I have to bring to the attention of the Security Council a matter which, in my opinion, may threaten the maintenance of interna-

tional peace and security. Thus, I request that you call an urgent meeting of the Security Council to hear a report of the Secretary-General on a demand for United Nations action in relation to the Republic of the Congo.[35]

In July 1961, Secretary-General Dag Hammarskjöld, citing his right under Article 99, considered it his duty to make an urgent appeal to the Security Council to take immediate action regarding calls for a cessation of hostilities in Tunisia. The Secretary-General was mindful of the risks of irreparable damage to international peace and security.[36] Secretary-General U Thant used this competence to great effect during the Cuban missile crisis of 1962.

In December 1954, the General Assembly asked Hammarskjöld to seek the release of U.S. airmen being held in China, a nation that did not recognize the validity of the General Assembly resolution. Secretary-General Hammarskjöld invoked his general authority under the Charter in carrying out his mission.[37] Some of his successors also used this strategy, as when the General Assembly requested Secretary-General Waldheim to push for the withdrawal of Soviet forces from Afghanistan. The Secretary-General chose to act on the basis of his inherent powers under the Charter. In 1979, Waldheim invoked Article 99 regarding the situation between Iran and the United States following the seizure of the U.S. Embassy in Tehran.[38]

Conclusion

As illustrated in this rapid survey, the intellectual thread of preventive diplomacy runs from the Congress of Vienna of 1815 to the European Congress system and the Concert of Europe to the Hague peace conferences and the League of Nations directly to the United Nations. In the history of humanity's quest to prevent war, they provided valuable intellectual building blocks that the UN built upon. The UN experiment is still under way, and it has had modest successes and many failures. But what is of importance is how that institution has sought to take the idea of preventive diplomacy forward and give it practical meaning in the six decades of its history.

Article 99 and the Secretary-General's status as a principal organ remain the primary foundation for the Secretary-General's exercise of preventive diplomacy, although they may also be exercised at the request of a UN organ. The Secretariat's practice of keeping abreast of risk analysis holds great potential for preventive diplomacy, and in the future, consideration should be given to how the Security Council might benefit more from this work. Briefings to and informal consultations within the Security Council are meant to operate a substantive partnership between the Secretary-General or the Secretariat and the council in the quest for conflict prevention. Briefings and informal consultations make it less necessary to invoke Article 99. In the case of a major crisis such as Darfur, it is difficult to understand why Secretary-General Annan did not elect to use this option.

2

UN Policies and Doctrines of Preventive Diplomacy

- The General Assembly
- The Security Council
- The Secretaries-General
- Conclusion

The General Assembly

The General Assembly has not been a lead player in the development and practice of preventive diplomacy.[1] On occasion, the president of the General Assembly has sought to head off or stem particular conflicts; for example, in 1948, the president tried, together with the Secretary-General, to defuse the Berlin crisis. There have also been times when major crises erupted while the General Assembly was in session and members sought to restrain parties from going to the brink. This happened in 1962 with the Cuban missile crisis.

At a meeting of presidents of the General Assembly organized by the UN Institute for Training and Research in June 1985, Paul Lusaka of Zambia, president of the assembly at that time, suggested establishing a new committee on science and technology, issues considered to be the major factor of change at the time. Lusaka felt that the General Assembly often reacted on an ad hoc basis when a new world crisis required attention and suggested that all assembly committees consider classifying their agendas into three categories: immediate current problems, medium-term problems, and long-term problems.[2] Unfortunately, the General Assembly did not take up these suggestions.

The General Assembly has sought to promote the rule of law in international affairs and the peaceful settlement of disputes. Its Declaration on the Principles of International Law Concerning Friendly Relations and Cooperation among States (1970) codified the Charter's legal principles and the duties of member states to settle their disputes peacefully on the basis of respect for the Charter and international law. The Manila Declaration of 1988 on the prevention of disputes highlighted the role of the Secretary-General in heading off conflicts and gave prominence to the Secretary-General's exercise of preventive diplomacy.

More recently, the General Assembly has promoted the peaceful settlement of disputes and encouraged the development of capacity for preventive action. Following the publication of Secretary-General Boutros-Ghali's *An Agenda for Peace* in 1992, the assembly held extensive consultations with member states to encourage the pursuit of preventive strategies. However, developing countries feared that prevention might be used as a pretext to interfere in their internal affairs. They particularly objected to suggestions for preventive action in the field of human rights.

From the point of view of the intellectual history of preventive diplomacy, some early experiences of the General Assembly are worth recalling. The assembly's early efforts to establish an urgent action procedure were significant. In 1945, the Netherlands suggested the creation of a standing committee on peace and security to the Preparatory Commission for the United Nations. This proposal was not taken forward, but on 13 November 1947, the General Assembly established an interim committee that was assigned the task of considering whether any matter under discussion in the committee might require summoning a special session of the General Assembly and the prerogative to conduct investigations and appoint commissions of inquiry.[3] The interim committee never really functioned substantively, and in 1950 it was overtaken by the "Uniting for Peace" resolution (General Assembly resolution 377). Theoretically, the interim committee is still in existence, as resolution 295 (IV) made it an indefinite committee that would meet when the General Assembly was not in regular session.

According to the "Uniting for Peace" resolution, if lack of unanimity among the permanent members causes the Security Council to fail to exercise its primary responsibility to maintain international peace and security in a case of a threat to the peace, breach of the peace, or act of aggression, the General Assembly can consider the matter immediately. If the General Assembly is not in session, it can meet in emergency special session within twenty-four hours if so requested by any seven (now nine) members of the Security Council or by a majority of the UN member states. The General Assembly has met in several special sessions.

More recently, the General Assembly has taken important policy positions on preventive strategies, including preventive diplomacy. On 5 December 1988, the General Assembly adopted the "Declaration on the Prevention and Removal of Disputes and Situations Which May Threaten

International Peace and Security and on the Role of the United Nations in this Field" (resolution 43/51, known as the Manila Declaration). In that resolution, the assembly declared that states should act to prevent the emergence or aggravation of disputes or situations in their international relations. It encouraged the Secretary-General to approach the states involved in a dispute to prevent the dispute from becoming a threat to international peace and security, to respond swiftly by offering his good offices if he were approached by a state directly concerned with a dispute, to make full use of fact-finding capabilities, and to use—at an early stage—the right accorded to him or her under Article 99 to bring to the Security Council's attention any matter that might threaten international peace and security.

In resolution 57/26 of 19 November 2002, the General Assembly urged the "strengthening of cooperative mechanisms for information-sharing, planning and the development of preventive measures . . . [and] the development of a comprehensive plan for a revived early-warning and prevention system for the United Nations."[4]

The Security Council

A separate chapter below discusses the practice of preventive diplomacy by the Security Council.[5] Even though it is vested with primary responsibility to maintain international peace and security, the council has not been the lead actor in the exercise of preventive diplomacy. Previously, this may have been due to the Cold War environment, but, even in the post–Cold War and the post–post–Cold War eras, the Security Council has not led the charge in spearheading preventive diplomacy, most likely due to political calculations of its individual members. This role has been left with the Secretary-General.

Nevertheless, the Security Council has laid down important policies of preventive action in a number of resolutions and statements. Resolution 1366 (2001), which outlines the policies of the Security Council in this area, is one of the most significant. The Security Council starts from the premise that conflict prevention is within the responsibilities of member states. In other words, member states should act in accordance with the norms of international law and should settle their disputes peacefully.

The resolution acknowledges the essential role of the Secretary-General in preventing armed conflict and the importance of efforts to enhance that role in accordance with Article 99. It expresses the Security Council's "willingness to give prompt consideration to early warning or prevention cases brought to its attention by the Secretary-General" and encourages the Secretary-General to convey to it his or her assessment of potential threats to international peace and security with due regard to relevant regional and subregional dimensions.

The council has stressed the need to enhance the Secretary-General's role in conflict prevention including by increased use of UN interdisciplinary fact-finding and confidence-building missions to regions of tension, developing regional prevention strategies with regional partners and UN organs and agencies, and improving the capacity and resource base for preventive action in the Secretariat. In a significant statement, the council recognized the role of other relevant organs, offices, funds and programs, and the specialized agencies of the UN and other international organizations including the World Trade Organization and the Bretton Woods institutions, as well as the role of nongovernmental organizations, civil society actors, and the private sector in preventing armed conflict.

The council has stressed the need to address the root causes and regional dimensions of conflicts. It has expressed serious concern over the threat to peace and security caused by the illicit trade in—and the excessive and destabilizing accumulation of—small arms and light weapons in areas of conflict and their potential to exacerbate and prolong armed conflicts. The council called on all member states to ensure timely and faithful implementation of the UN Programme of Action to Prevent, Combat and Eradicate the Illicit Trade in Small Arms and Light Weapons in All its Aspects (July 2001)[6] and to take all necessary measures to prevent and combat the illicit flow of small and light weapons in conflict areas.

The resolution stresses the need to create conditions for durable peace and sustainable development by addressing the root causes of armed conflict. To that end, it calls on member states and relevant UN bodies to contribute to the effective implementation of the United Nations Declaration and Programme of Action for a Culture of Peace.[7] The resolution reiterates that early warning, preventive diplomacy, preventive deployment, practical disarmament measures, and post-conflict peacebuilding are interdependent and complementary components of a comprehensive conflict prevention strategy. It calls on member states as well as regional and subregional organizations and arrangements to support the development of a comprehensive conflict prevention strategy as proposed by the Secretary-General.

The resolution invites the Secretary-General to refer to the Security Council information and analyses from within the UN system on cases of serious violations of international law, including international humanitarian law and human rights law, and on potential conflict situations arising from ethnic, religious, and territorial disputes, poverty, or lack of development. The council also expresses its determination to give serious consideration to such information and analyses regarding situations that it deems to represent a threat to international peace and security.

In the operative part of its resolution, the council expresses its determination to pursue conflict prevention as an integral part of its primary responsibility to maintain international peace and security. It stresses that the essential responsibility for conflict prevention rests with national governments and that the UN and the international community could play an important role supporting these national efforts and could assist in building national capacity in this field. In this regard, it recognizes the important role of civil society. The council expresses its commitment to take early and effective action to prevent armed conflict and, to that end, to employ all appropriate means at its disposal, including its missions to areas of potential conflict, with the consent of receiving states.

The council says that it will keep situations of potential conflict under close review as part of a conflict prevention strategy and expresses its intention to consider cases of potential conflict brought to its attention by any member state, a state that is not a member of the UN, the General Assembly, or on the basis of information furnished by the Economic and Social Council (ECOSOC).

The council expressed its willingness to consider preventive deployment on the Secretary-General's recommendation and with the consent of the member states concerned. Since the preventive deployment in the Former Yugoslav Republic of Macedonia in 1993, the Security Council has not authorized any preventive deployments. One wonders whether the lack of proposals by Secretary-General Annan for preventive deployments in particular situations might have contributed to this.

As with the General Assembly, the policy framework of the Security Council is impressive on paper. But how does it translate into practical action? Experience indicates that the Security Council still depends heavily on the Secretary-General to take the initiative in bringing to its attention situations that are considered a threat to international peace and security.

The Secretaries-General[8]

The concept of preventive diplomacy was first articulated by Secretary-General Hammarskjöld in his annual report for 1959 and elaborated in his annual report for the next year. Even before that, Secretary-General Trygve Lie sought to use his good offices for preventive purposes and, in his proposal to establish a corps of UN guards, launched an idea considered by some to be the precursor of Hammarskjöld's ideas of preventive diplomacy and a UN presence. Yet the League of Nations had already resorted to the use of peacekeeping and observer forces.

Secretary-General U Thant continued the practice of good offices for preventive purposes and took the lead in calling for arrangements to deal with natural and human-made disasters. His initiative led to the establishment of the United Nations Disaster Relief Office (UNDRO). Secretaries-General U Thant, Waldheim, Pérez de Cuéllar, Boutros-Ghali, and Annan all provided statements of their understanding of the concept of preventive diplomacy and sought to contribute to the pursuit of preventive strategies globally. As of the time of writing, Secretary-General Ban Ki-moon had begun to set out his views. The following sections provide snapshots of the core policies and doctrines of preventive diplomacy put forward by the Secretaries-General.

Trygve Lie

It was the historic responsibility and achievement of Trygve Lie, the first Secretary-General, to establish the Secretariat and give shape to the political role of the Secretary-General under Article 99 of the Charter. He is credited with charting the UN course to the exercise of the good offices of the Secretary-General, claiming the powers of investigation with a view to exercising them under the Secretary-General's mandate of Article 99, asserting the Secretary-General's right to submit written or oral views to the Security Council, and communicating his views to the Security Council about whether a situation amounted to a threat to or breach of international peace and security. He was also forthright in defending the Charter's principles, speaking out publicly on occasion.

Initially, he made a case for discreet diplomacy, and in the Berlin crisis of 1948, for example, he attempted to play a role in defusing the crisis. The Security Council's role in this case was far more significant than that of the Secretary-General. According to Arthur W. Rovine, former legal adviser of the U.S. State Department and one of the foremost authorities on the Office of the Secretary-General, although Lie's efforts were unsuccessful, he may have helped create space for the major powers to negotiate an outcome to the crisis. In the Korean crisis, however, Lie publicly condemned North Korea's crossing of the 38th parallel, and Rovine has questioned whether Lie compromised his ability to work behind the scenes by taking such a high profile and voicing his criticism so publicly.[9] It has been pointed out, how-

ever, that Lie had to bear in mind the failure of the League of Nations in de-
nouncing aggression and the subsequent fatal consequences for that organization.[10]

In view of the importance and contemporary relevance of the question,
it would be helpful to look at the issues Rovine raised. He wrote:

> Until Korea, the Secretary-General had made strenuous efforts to present at
> least the appearance of neutrality in East-West conflict. . . . Lie's switch in the
> Korean War was highly significant for the future of the Office. . . . Whether Lie's
> abandonment of neutrality was justified in terms of the political and legal pos-
> ture deemed appropriate for a Secretary-General is a difficult question. . . . Yet
> it might appear that the true difficulties involved here were not so much matters
> of conflicting substantive obligations as a matter of style and procedure. . . . Per-
> haps it is simply a matter of the right words or avoiding particular formulations
> that must necessarily result in alienation.

I agree with Rovine that Lie could have been more careful in his presentation. There is ample evidence from Lie's writings and from other sources
about the extensive behind-the-scenes diplomacy in which he engaged. In
Rovine's final assessment, Lie's advocacy of the establishment of a UN guard
composed of neutral contingents acting to keep antagonists apart was a
"conception that approached rather closely the notion of 'preventive diplomacy' as articulated in later years by Secretary-General Hammarskjöld."[11]

In the introduction to his third annual report, Lie advocated a force of
1,000 to 5,000 personnel that could be used for guard duty with UN missions to conduct plebiscites under the UN's supervision and administer
truce terms. The force could also be used as a constabulary under the Security Council or the Trusteeship Council during the establishment of international regimes. It could also be called on to perform provisional measures to prevent the aggravation of a situation threatening the peace.[12]

In explaining, developing, and eventually modifying his idea to establish
UN guards, Lie envisaged them performing five sets of functions relevant
to preventing conflicts and preventive diplomacy. First, the Security Council could have called on it under Article 40 of the Charter, which allows for
provisional measures to prevent the aggravation of a situation threatening
the peace.[13] Second, they might have been observers.[14] Third, they might
have protected weak parties in a conflict.[15] Fourth, they might have supported commissions of inquiry, conciliation, or mediation.[16] Fifth, and this
is a concept Secretary-General Lie added when he modified his idea to that
of a technical field service, they could have served as a panel of field ob-

servers, a list of names of qualified persons that would be available on call to the Security Council or the General Assembly.[17]

Lie's idea of a corps of UN guards did not come to fruition in his time, but he saw the deployment of observers in sensitive situations, a concept that Dag Hammarskjöld built upon.

Dag Hammarskjöld

Although Dag Hammarskjöld built on some of Lie's ideas, such as the Secretary-General's right to undertake fact-finding or provide good offices pursuant to Article 99, he developed the conceptual architecture of the office of Secretary-General in a dramatic manner. He also sought to develop the notion of an independent role for the UN—and the Secretary-General—in the circumstances prevailing in the Cold War. He developed the concept of peacekeeping forces, observer missions, and UN "presences."[18] He had in view both "corrective and preventive peace-keeping operations."[19] He sought to develop the ground rules for political fact-finding or good offices missions.[20] He introduced the practice of designating special representatives in trouble spots and envisaged a ring of such representatives in different parts of the world.[21]

Brian Urquhart writes that Hammarskjöld felt that the UN must rely on negotiation, persuasion, and consent to accomplish its purposes "and above all, on the exercise of enlightened and moral leadership by those in positions of responsibility."[22] He saw as the organization's primary political function the day-to-day effort to control and moderate conflicts through a system of mediation and conciliation developed on the basis of the sovereign equality of states. This primary function went hand in hand with a long-term effort to attain wider social justice and equality. Progress in this direction needed to be based on a growing respect for international law in Hammarskjöld's view of the UN.[23]

Hammarskjöld believed in quiet diplomacy to complement the conference diplomacy of the UN. To him, quiet diplomacy meant that one would nuance what was said with all the richness possible in a private talk, where one could retreat without any risk of losing face and where one could test out ideas rather than put forward proposals.[24] He used good offices in a variety of ways, normally undertaking good offices missions only at a government's request, and he refused to take initiatives if he believed that his right to do so or his chances of success were seriously in doubt. He was also circumspect in situations where he felt he had no chance of being useful.[25]

Hammarskjöld came to believe that the Charter, particularly Article 99, gave the Secretary-General wide political and diplomatic possibilities of action.[26] As Urquhart put it, "Hammarskjöld was increasingly convinced that in the political field the UN could concentrate on preventive action rather than corrective action." In the introduction to his annual report for 1960, he wrote that the efforts to prevent conflict "must aim at keeping newly arising conflicts outside the sphere of bloc differences."[27]

Hammarskjöld articulated the concept of preventive diplomacy for the first time in the organization's history:

> What I should like to call active preventive diplomacy . . . may be conducted by the United Nations through the Secretary-General or in other forms, in many situations where no government or group of governments and no regional organization would be able to act in the same way. That such interventions are possible for the United Nations is explained by the fact that . . . the organization has begun to gain a certain independent position, and that this tendency has led to the acceptance of an independent political and diplomatic activity on the part of the Secretary-General as the "neutral" representative of the Organization.[28]

In the introduction to his 1960 annual report, Hammarskjöld developed the idea further:

> Experience indicates that the preventive diplomacy, to which the efforts of the United Nations must thus to a large extent be directed, is of special significance in cases where the original conflict may be said either to be the result of, or to imply risks for, the creation of a power vacuum between the main blocs. Preventive action in such cases must in the first place aim at filling the vacuum so that it will not provoke action from any of the major parties, the initiative for which might be taken for preventive purposes but might in turn lead to counteraction from the other side. The ways in which a vacuum can be filled by the United Nations so as to forestall such initiatives differ from case to case, but they have this in common: Temporarily, and pending the filling of a vacuum by normal means, the United Nations enters the picture on the basis of its noncommitment to any power bloc, so as to provide to the extent possible a guarantee in relation to all parties against initiatives from others.
>
> The special need and the special possibilities for what I here call preventive United Nations diplomacy have been demonstrated in several recent cases, such as Suez and Gaza, Lebanon and Jordan, Laos and the Congo.[29]

The instrumentalities of preventive diplomacy Hammarskjöld used have influenced the development of the concept ever since and have continuing relevance to the present and the future.

U Thant

U Thant took Hammarskjöld's commitment to preventive diplomacy forward. He felt that the Secretary-General's role was to build bridges between peoples, governments, and states.[30] Recalling that President Roosevelt had initially suggested that the chief officer of the UN should be called "moderator," he thought this the best word to describe his conception of the office of Secretary-General. He thought it the most important political duty of the Secretary-General to concentrate on the harmonizing function of the UN.[31]

He did five things that were significant for the journey of the idea of preventive diplomacy at the UN. In the first place, he practiced preventive diplomacy. Second, he offered his thoughts on the role of the Secretary-General. Third, he articulated the notion of the good offices of the United Nations and practiced them. Fourth, he made a strong case for a UN role in dealing with natural and human-made disasters. (U Thant established UNDRO, which is now an integral part of the Office for the Coordination of Humanitarian Affairs. Historically, UNDRO was meant not only to respond to human-made disasters but also to engage in preventive efforts.) Fifth, U Thant played a crucial role in defusing the most dangerous moment in the UN's history—the Cuban missile crisis of 1962.

In his memoirs, U Thant wrote that he had exercised his good offices "in a large number of disputes or difficulties." He believed that preventive diplomacy of this kind was far more effective and cheaper than attempting to resolve a conflict that had reached an acute stage. He thought that in his exercise of good offices, the less publicity that surrounded his efforts, the more successful they were likely to be. Two considerations were paramount for him. First, the Secretary-General must always be prepared to take an initiative, no matter what the consequences to his office or to him personally, if he sincerely believed that it might mean the difference between peace and war. Second, the Secretary-General must always maintain an independent position.[32]

Kurt Waldheim

While in office, Secretary-General Waldheim offered a clear statement of his position on preventive diplomacy:

> I myself advocate what some call "preventive diplomacy," which has to be conducted calmly, without fanfare. One runs the risk, of course, of acquiring a reputation for passivity, since the substance of direct, intensive talks with heads of

state and foreign ministers can never be heedlessly disclosed—but the strength of such diplomacy lies in that very feature. If it goes well, the crisis is averted, and no one is the wiser. If it goes badly, it is merely dubbed another UN failure.

The ground rule here is: the Secretary-General should negotiate only at the request of the parties to the dispute. Nothing is worse, and nothing would be less wise, than for him to force himself upon a situation. Successful mediation stands a chance only if it is wanted and worked for by all involved. During such negotiations, I always find it wise to refrain from making too many public statements. These can be easily distorted, sometimes intentionally, and only complicate matters. On the other hand, reticence poses another kind of dilemma, since a sensible public reaction to the initiatives of the United Nations can be elicited only if all aspects of a problem are openly and objectively presented. As you can see, it is a path strewn with booby-traps. If too much is said, the negotiations are in danger of being scuttled; silence, on the other hand, gives rise to all sorts of speculation in the mass media, which can lead to a hardening of the negotiating process. Diplomatic skill consists in steering precisely the right middle course.[33]

Waldheim provided glimpses into his practice of preventive diplomacy. There were occasions, he wrote, when discreet personal intervention helped ease the tensions between states and checked the outbreak of hostilities. Whether by open appeal or quiet diplomacy—or whatever other procedure he judged would best achieve practical results—those opportunities to intercede in the cause of peace and justice entailed a challenge that he perceived to be both duty and reward.[34] Many times he was able to save a human life, even free entire groups of people from persecution, through personal intervention.[35]

He used his judgment when deciding whether or not to intercede. In the 1979 conflict between Ethiopia and Somalia, for example, the problem was seen as internal to Africa and thus as falling within the purview of the Organization of African Unity (OAU). He contacted the OAU chair, who had made it clear that that organization preferred to resolve the problem within its own framework. He therefore did not consider it appropriate to exercise his Charter prerogative of calling on the Security Council to concern itself with the situation.[36]

He saw a number of opportunities to act preventively: exercising his competence under Article 99, drawing attention to a situation in his annual report, or inscribing an item on the General Assembly's agenda. In 1972, he proposed that the General Assembly look into international terrorism.[37] In 1973, he described the situation in the Middle East as explosive. In 1976, he drew the Security Council's attention to the seriousness of the situation in Lebanon.[38]

He attached great importance to trust and confidence. He considered that his success depended mainly on the degree to which he could retain the support and confidence of the UN member states: "Long experience has taught me that an abrupt gesture, an ill-chosen word, or an unthinking remark can prove disastrous. As the leader of the international community, the secretary-general must never forget his every word is scrutinized by every member state and heard by every people."[39]

In his assessment, the UN had been able to forestall full-scale military conflict repeatedly. He felt that in 1974, for example, he and his colleagues had played a significant role in defusing the tensions that had poisoned relations between Iran and Iraq for decades. The frequent border clashes between the two countries were likely to escalate into a major confrontation. His special representative, Luis Weckmann-Muñoz, negotiated an agreement whereby the two sides observed a cease-fire and withdrew troops along the entire frontier. They also resumed conversations aimed at a comprehensive settlement of all bilateral issues ahead of schedule.[40]

He sought to help contain crises in other situations, such as the Vietnam conflict in 1972[41] and the Arab-Israeli War of 1973.[42] He tried to help defuse the crisis between Iran and the United States over the seizure of the American embassy in Tehran in 1979. In his memoirs, he recounted his contacts with both sides and his harrowing mission to Tehran.[43] He also related his efforts to be of service after the Soviet invasion of Afghanistan in 1979. The General Assembly asked him to play a role and to appoint a special representative, which the Soviet Union opposed. He successfully proposed that he designate a personal representative, which the Soviet Union accepted. (He appointed Under-Secretary-General Pérez de Cuéllar as his personal representative.)[44] He commented: "This deliberate ambiguity would allow one side to assume that I was proceeding as directed by the Assembly while the other side could assume that I was not. This indeed resolved the problem."[45] He eventually obtained Soviet acquiescence to negotiations between Afghanistan and Pakistan with the participation of the Secretary-General's personal representative.

Javier Pérez de Cuéllar

During the UN's fortieth anniversary in 1985 and in later years, Javier Pérez de Cuéllar made a determined push to develop the UN's capacity for early warning and preventive diplomacy. In a series of speeches, he repeatedly pressed this theme. He strongly advocated the development of a comprehensive global watch over threats to human welfare.

He was a careful Secretary-General. While calling for a capacity for information-gathering and analysis, he was prudent in the way he approached his political responsibilities. In his Cyril Foster Lecture at Oxford in 1986, he spoke on the political role of the Secretary-General. The Secretary-General, he observed, sometimes remained the only channel of communication between parties in conflict and therefore must be able to improvise in the context of good offices missions. A disciple of quiet diplomacy, Pérez de Cuéllar believed that the Secretary-General must not only be impartial but must be perceived to be so. He observed that a Secretary-General needed enormous patience. He did not have the option of being frustrated or discouraged. At the same time, the Secretary-General is called upon to exercise wise judgment. He explained this in his discussion of Article 99:

> Before invoking the Article, the Secretary-General has to consider carefully how his initiative will fare, given the agreement or lack thereof among the permanent members and also the positions of the non-permanent members. A situation may in certain cases be aggravated and not eased if the Secretary-General draws attention, under Article 99, and the Security Council then does nothing. Situations that threaten the peace are usually highly complicated and require a flexible and finely tuned response from the Secretary-General. Hence, the discretion allowed him by Article 99.
>
> Two situations of equally dangerous potential may have to be dealt with in two different ways, depending on how far they can be insulated from great-power rivalries, how far the parties are susceptible to moral suasion and, in some cases, whether one or both of them is reluctant to face exposure in the Security Council. It is worth adding that the possibility that invocation of Article 99 might displease a member state, whether or not a party to the dispute, most certainly ought not to be a consideration inhibiting the Secretary-General.[46]

In March 1987, in a push to develop the Secretariat's capacity for early warning and preventive diplomacy, he established the Office for Research and the Collection of Information (ORCI) with the following aims:

- Consolidating information-gathering and analytical activities in the political area of the Secretariat into one specialized office
- Bringing together research, analysis, information-gathering, the drafting of the Secretary-General's speeches, and political advisory services for the Secretary-General in a single organizational unit
- Establishing links to the outside academic community to keep the Secretary-General informed of the latest research advances and findings

- Integrating data management in the design and development of the office, with the specific aim of creating a modern data bank for the political sector of the Secretariat
- Assigning responsibility to the office for early warning of refugee flows and comparable developments
- Monitoring global trends for purposes of early warning and preventive diplomacy[47]

Pérez de Cuéllar must be credited with having made the most serious structural efforts in the Secretariat to advance early warning and preventive diplomacy. His successors built on his work in other ways, but the architecture he created for pursuing preventive diplomacy has not kept pace.

In his discussion of the powers of the Secretary-General under Article 99 of the Charter, Stephen Schwebel pointed out that the Secretary-General's authority extends to the reporting of any developments that could have serious political implications. Such developments could be in the economic and social field. This gives the Secretary-General a vital link between the Security Council and the other organs of the organization.[48]

Secretary-General Pérez de Cuéllar followed up on this important idea in *Perspectives for the 1990s*, which he presented to the General Assembly in 1987 as the introduction to the medium-term plan, a document setting out the UN's goals for the coming five to ten years. This document, drafted by James S. Sutterlin, is one of the most important ever presented in the quest for comprehensive prevention strategies. In the plan's vision, international security, including disarmament and international law, development and international economic cooperation, social advancement, basic rights and fundamental freedoms, and human well-being would be the broad areas on which the future programs of the United Nations should concentrate.[49]

The document presented the problems facing the world: "Conflict and resort to force, the inordinate utilization of resources for arms, continuing social and economic inequities, hunger, terrorism, the abuse of human rights—these and other negative elements in the world condition cast their shadow forward on the future."[50]

Making the case for the further development of early warning and prevention activities, the document stressed that nowhere was the expression that "an ounce of prevention was worth a pound of cure" more valid than in the field of international security, especially since the cure for conflict had proven so elusive. The UN therefore, needed to give very high priority to monitoring potential causes of conflict and to communicating warning signs to those in a position to alleviate the situation. First, responsibility should lie with the Security Council and the Secretary-General, who would need the means to mount a global watch. Given the strong economic and social factors in regional violence, economic and social developments would have to be followed and assessed in terms of their relevance to international security.[51]

The document pointed out that much could be foreseen in the economic and social fields that required advance planning. A crowded world of strained resources could not be managed on an ad hoc basis. The UN also needed to be able to meet emergencies that called for collective effort, whether to contain violent political conflicts or to meet natural or human-made disasters. Both in looking ahead and in meeting new crises, information was an indispensable tool. In the previous decades, many of the greatest shocks to the international community had been unanticipated, partly because warning signals had not been communicated. A communication gap had kept environmental, population, and development assistance groups apart for far too long. Conflicts could best be peacefully resolved before shots were fired. For such preventive action, information and communication were highly important.[52]

Offering thoughts "towards peace and security in a new century," the document cautioned that a world of limited resources and growing needs could not support the enormous cost of regional conflicts. A world of reason could not accept the risk of global desolation that conflicts bring. A world of human compassion could not ignore the death, homelessness, and despair that such armed conflict inevitably entails. Bringing an end to regional wars that still persist and preventing others from erupting needed to be two principal focal points for UN efforts in the future on behalf of international security. In addition, the number of arms needed to be reduced and nuclear weapons—the element that could transform armed conflict from human tragedy to human annihilation—needed to ultimately be eliminated. The acquisition of arms by both developed and developing countries is a destructive extravagance that would, if uncurbed, have fatal consequences.

Offering ideas for the prevention of conflicts, *Perspectives for the 1990s* argued for better understanding of the following issues:

- The disparate nature of the origins of regional disputes
- The structural anomalies left by colonialism, which were sometimes at the root of conflict
- Societal pressures resulting from inadequate economic and social development, which were the primary causes of instability in some areas

- Ethnic identity factors centered on race or belief, which were increasingly the cause of tensions that brought countries and peoples to violence
- Terrorism, which also shared some of the foregoing roots[53]

Mindful of the above, the report argued that the UN needed to give very high priority to monitoring potential causes of conflict and to communicating warning signs to those in a position to act. It stated that the UN's role in disarmament could be broadened because of the significance of this objective as well as the organization's potential to contribute further to its achievement. The Secretary-General said:

> I foresee in particular, possible new tasks for the United Nations in helping to monitor compliance with disarmament agreements, a function for which the United Nations has special advantages. The United Nations could also monitor developments that might inadvertently lead to a nuclear exchange. Both functions could involve the use of high technology.[54]

The Secretary-General also believed that the UN could usefully formulate disarmament concepts for specific circumstances that could be helpful in disarmament negotiations.

Staking out a position on the future role of the United Nations, the Secretary-General pleaded:

> I believe it will be even more evident than now, as we approach a new century of unprecedented demands on our habitat, that multilateral cooperation and the rational utilization of multilateral institutions provide the key to common well being. This should be a persuasive factor in bringing Governments to formulate national policies in such a way as to ensure that their commitments under the Charter are fully honored.[55]

The document argued for coherent and integrated policies and preventive strategies in the economic and social areas at the national, regional, and international levels. Regional cooperation would need to be strengthened. The state of the human condition necessitated such policies and strategies. The trends were stark:

- By the beginning of the 21st century, the world population will increase to about six billion. Virtually all of this growth will take place in developing countries, further straining their efforts to provide an adequate standard of living for their citizens. The proportion of the elderly will also increase, increasing demands for social services with a proportionately smaller base to bear the costs. The reduction of unemployment will also require hundreds of millions of new jobs. Problems associated with urban migration will intensify as part of the search for rural/urban equilibrium in the context of balanced development.

- The satisfaction of basic human needs will impose a further toll on the world's natural resources, including energy. Desertification, deforestation, and problems of transboundary pollution will become acute.

- Technological advances will have a major impact in enhancing productive capacities and in changing traditional patterns of comparative advantage. Transnational ownership, global financial transactions, and rapid communications will change significantly the nature of the global market and financial regimes.[56]

The document predicted the future accurately, and the trends identified are accelerating. The Secretary-General stated: "I think particularly of disease, of drug abuse, of terrorism and all other such threats that respect no national boundaries and, increasingly, claim universality in their victims." These predictions made the case for a comprehensive global watch all the more urgent.

The report offered some ideas to preventively address these economic and social problems.

- There must be a broad educational base among populations. Social progress will always be closely related to progress in education. While the provision of education is a national responsibility, multilateral efforts to assist national authorities to meet this responsibility will be needed and will be of fundamental importance not only in dealing with social threats but also in assuring better protection of vulnerable groups in the global society and in combating destructive social forces that breed from ignorance.

- Cooperation among countries is needed to promote a more hospitable global environment for growth and development. Such cooperation is a basic tenet of the Charter and must continue to be a major focus in the UN's work.

- The continued existence of widespread poverty must be avoided. If poverty is allowed to increase with population growth, there will be negative consequences for social harmony, ecological integrity, and international security. The UN must accord high priority to poverty reduction—not only as a critical element in development but also as a human responsibility and a requirement of international security.

- The UN has a two-fold role—as a multilateral framework for support to national development efforts, especially through technical cooperation, and as a universal forum for dealing with the issues of world cooperation for development.

- Development-related programs need to take account of the larger base of what are increasingly perceived as interrelated factors. A productive, healthy, global environment must be preserved and, where damaged, restored.

- In addition to causing unacceptable suffering, hunger debilitates the base for development and brings ecological degradation and thus must be eliminated.

- The human population, the earth's greatest resource, must live within the earth's supportive capacity.

- The protection of vulnerable groups must be enhanced.

- Health for all must be progressively achieved through preventive action and through the fight against diseases.

- The wasteful use of resources for arms, both conventional and nuclear, must be drastically curbed.

- The growth of population in the poorer countries could result in massive migratory pressure on relatively more developed countries. The result could be grave internal tensions, severe hardship for the people involved, and hostility between countries that could ultimately pose a threat to international security. National and multilateral attention is necessary to the modes and timing of development to reduce the catalysts for such mass movement of people. The possibilities of migrant resettlement in the best-suited countries or regions will need attention, too, as one of the means of accommodating a doubling of the population in poor countries.

- Enhancement of safety in nuclear energy production, including the disposal of nuclear waste, warrants sustained multilateral attention, given its importance for present and future generations that extended beyond any national border.[57]

The document cautioned:

Each of these aspects of development can be seen as distinct but, if not taken into account as integral parts of a complex equation, development programmes will be less than fully effective and, as experience has shown, the results can be flawed. The United Nations, drawing on the capacities of the system as a whole, will need . . . to be the fulcrum for a globally integrated approach to development. The technical cooperation activities of the United Nations will have to be so adapted.[58]

The document emphasized the role of human rights protection as a preventive strategy. It argued that respect for basic human rights and for the dignity and worth of the human person as called for in the Charter was a fundamental element in the vibrant and productive global society toward which UN efforts needed to continue to be directed. In the future, the main focus of United Nations human rights activities should be on bringing about universal respect for the norms that had been agreed on in practice. The challenge of promoting respect for human rights is global, and the goal of UN bodies needed to be to translate the wide commitment to human rights into an increasingly persuasive means to eliminate abuses wherever they occurred.

This was a powerful presentation of the role of the UN in the operation of a comprehensive global watch. It was based on a view of the role of the United Nations in which its activities would be necessary if the objective required multilateral action. There would be need for a UN capability to identify compelling global and regional needs susceptible to multilateral alleviation and to concentrate available resources where they could most effectively be used to meet the identifiable need.

This was, without a doubt, a seminal report, put forward on the Secretary-General's own initiative during the Cold War. It was a penetrating and visionary document that provided a blueprint for the future that envisioned the world organization working on problems that could be solved by multilateral action and coordinating a comprehensive global watch over issues of peace and security, environmental protection, economic and social welfare, and the protection of human rights. The concept of a global watch would require renewed attention, and the role of the UN as a "reliable source of timely information across the range of human activities" could help give intellectual and policy thrust to the United Nations in the future.

Boutros Boutros-Ghali

Boutros-Ghali's landmark contributions to the intellectual history of preventive diplomacy are to be found in three reports he put forward during his tenure, *An Agenda for Peace* (1992), *An Agenda for Development* (1995), and *An Agenda for Democratization* (1996).

He also put forth his views on the challenges of preventive diplomacy in a chapter in a 1996 collection of essays, where he set out five generic conditions that should be fulfilled if the Secretary-General is to be able to apply preventive treatments effectively.[59] First, the Secretary-General should have the necessary capacity to collect and analyze information. He or she should also have the clinical capacity to prescribe the "correct treatment" for the condition diagnosed. Third, the parties to the potential conflict should accept the action the Secretary-General proposed. Fourth, the Secretary-General needed to persuade the other member states, and especially Security Council members, to give him or her steady political support. Finally, the Secretary-General needed to persuade member states to provide the necessary resources to finance the preventive action.

In 1992, Secretary-General Boutros-Ghali integrated the functions of ORCI into the Department of Political Affairs. Some functions related to news-gathering and distribution were given to the Department of Public Information. The abolition of ORCI was unfortunate. The regional divisions of the Department of Political Affairs have a broad range of briefing and political functions, but ORCI was meant to project the notion that the Secretariat supported a global watch and was a focal point for early warning and preventive diplomacy. The policy, analytical, early warning, and speech-writing functions had been deliberately brought together when ORCI was established. The dispersal of these functions meant the loss of an institutional blueprint that has not been matched since.

Interestingly enough, in August 2000, the Brahimi Panel examined, once again, the consolidation of various departmental units related to policy and information analysis. It proposed—for a second time—to bring information and news-gathering (which is done by the Department of Public Information) and political analysis and strategic planning (which is done by the Department of Political Affairs, the Department of Peacekeeping Operations, and the Office for the Coordination of Humanitarian Affairs) under one entity—the Information and Strategic Analysis Secretariat for the Executive Committee for Peace and Security.[60] This idea is still on the drawing board.

An Agenda for Peace

In the intellectual journey of the idea of preventive diplomacy at the UN, Secretary-General Boutros-Ghali's 1992 report *An Agenda for Peace: Preventive Diplomacy, Peacemaking and Peacekeeping* is highly ranked as an inspirational work that has influenced developments for the past decade and a half and that will continue to influence preventive activities and diplomacy for a long time to come. It is true that barely two and a half years later, he issued his *Supplement to Agenda for Peace,* which identified difficulties in implementing the ideas in *An Agenda for Peace.* But he considered that the set of general principles of the 1992 *An Agenda for Peace* remained valid. Their reinterpretation in the light of experience was necessary. He stated: "Most of the ideas in an *Agenda for Peace* have proved themselves. A few have not been taken up. The purpose of the present position paper, however, is not to revise *An Agenda for Peace* nor to call into question structures and procedures that have been tested by time. Even less is it intended to be a comprehensive treatise on the matters it discusses. Its purpose is, rather, to highlight selectively certain areas where unforeseen, or only partly foreseen, difficulties have arisen and where there is a need for the Member States to take the 'hard decisions' I referred to two and a half years ago."[61]

In contrast, although it is a highly original and pathbreaking document, Pérez de Cuéllar's *Perspectives for the 1990s* has not enjoyed the same status. The reasons for this are probably because it was written in 1987, during the Cold War, and was not launched in such solemn circumstances as *An Agenda for Peace,* which was written at the request of the Security Council's first summit meeting and at the advent of what some deemed a new world order.

When Boutros-Ghali assumed office at the beginning of 1992, the quest for preventive strategies was very much in the air. On 31 January of that year, the Security Council met at the level of heads of state and government and adopted a decision that called on the Secretary-General to present a report containing an "analysis and recommendations on ways of strengthening and making more efficient within the framework and provisions of the Charter the capacity of the United Nations for preventive diplomacy, for peacemaking and for peace-keeping."[62]

The Secretariat gave the preparation of this report the highest priority. A group of senior officials convened to discuss the report and offer their thoughts and suggestions. After they had met for some weeks, they asked the chief of the Secretary-General's speechwriting service to go through the numerous papers they had assembled and put together a first draft. The flagship idea of this draft was that the Secretary-General should brief the Security Council in informal sessions once a fortnight about situations where preventive diplomacy might be exercised.

After members of the senior group had reacted to the draft report, it was sent to Boutros-Ghali who, in turn, made detailed comments and suggestions. The document was then revised and sent back to him for further reflection. Thereafter, successive efforts were made within the Secretary-General's office, involving several drafters, including James Sutterlin, to continue the drafting process and to reflect the further thinking of the Secretary-General. The report, when finally released, was widely praised in the media and by well-wishers of the United Nations as a visionary document of historic importance.

An Agenda for Peace defines preventive diplomacy as "action to prevent disputes from arising between parties, to prevent existing disputes from escalating into conflicts and to limit the spread of the latter when they occur." The aims of UN action must be: "To seek to identify at the earliest possible stage situations that could produce conflict and to try through diplomacy to remove the sources of danger before violence results."[63]

Other aims included peacemaking, peacekeeping, peacebuilding, "and in the largest sense, to address the deepest causes of conflict, economic despair, social injustice and political oppression."[64]

An Agenda for Peace contains a range of ideas regarding the use of preventive diplomacy:

- Preventive diplomacy should be used to ease tensions before they result in conflict.
- If conflict breaks out, preventive diplomacy should be used to act swiftly to contain it and resolve its underlying causes.
- Preventive diplomacy may be performed by the Secretary-General or though senior staff or specialized agencies and programs, by the Security Council or the General Assembly, and by regional organizations in cooperation with the UN.
- Preventive diplomacy requires measures to create confidence.
- Preventive diplomacy needs early warning based on information-gathering and informal or formal fact-finding.
- Preventive diplomacy may involve preventive deployment and, in some situations, demilitarized zones.[65]

An Agenda for Peace elaborated on measures to build confidence, fact-finding, early warning, preventive diplomacy, and demilitarized zones. Its key ideas on these issues are summarized below. First, mutual confidence and good faith, the report argued, were essential to reducing the likelihood of conflict between states. Systematic exchanges of military missions, the formation of regional or subregional risk reduction centers, and arrangements for the free flow of information, including the monitoring of regional arms agreements, were examples of confidence-building measures. Boutros-Ghali announced:

I ask all regional organizations to consider what further confidence-building measures might be applied in their areas and to inform the United Nations of the results. I will undertake periodic consultations on confidence-building measures with parties to potential, current or past disputes and with regional organizations, offering such advisory assistance as the Secretariat can provide.[66]

Preventive steps, the Secretary-General argued, needed to be based on timely and accurate knowledge of the facts. Beyond this, an understanding of developments and global trends based on sound analysis was necessary. The information the UN needed had to encompass economic and social trends as well as political developments that might lead to dangerous tensions. Hence:

- An increased resort to fact finding was needed, in accordance with the charter, initiated either by the Security Council, the General Assembly, or the Secretary-General to enable him to meet his responsibilities under the Charter, including Article 99.
- Contacts with the governments of member states could provide the Secretary-General with detailed information on issues of concern. "I will supplement my own contacts by regularly sending senior officials on missions for consultations in capitals or other locations."
- Formal fact-finding could be mandated by the Security Council or by the General Assembly, either of which might elect to send a mission under its immediate authority or invite the Secretary-General to take the necessary steps, including designating a special envoy.
- In exceptional circumstances, the Security Council might meet away from UN headquarters (as the Charter provided) to inform itself directly and also to bring the authority of the organization to bear on a given situation.[67]

The Secretary-General noted that in recent years, the UN system had been developing a valuable network of early warning systems concerning environmental threats, the risk of nuclear accident, natural disasters, mass movements of populations, the threat of famine, and the spread of disease. There was a need, however, to strengthen arrangements so information from those sources could be synthesized with political indicators to assess whether a threat to peace existed and to analyze what action might be taken to alleviate this threat. This process would continue to require the close cooperation of the various UN specialized agencies and functional offices. The Secretary-General pledged that the analyses and recommendations received would be made available, as appropriate, to the Security Council and other UN organs.

The Secretary-General noted that UN operations in crisis areas had generally been established after conflict had occurred. The time had come to plan for circumstances warranting preventive deployment, which could take place in a variety of instances and ways. In each situation, the mandate and composition of the UN presence would need to be carefully devised and be clear to all. In conditions of crisis within a country, when the government requested assistance or all parties consented, preventive deployment could help alleviate suffering and limit or control violence.

The report noted that in the past, demilitarized zones had been established by agreements of the parties at a conflict's conclusion. It stated that in addition to the deployment of UN personnel in such zones as part of peacekeeping operations, consideration should be given to the usefulness of such zones as a form of preventive deployment by separating potential belligerents. The zones should be on both sides of the border and should be established with the agreement of both parties. Such zones could also be established on one side of the border at the request of one party to remove any pretext for attack. Demilitarized zones would serve as symbols of the international community's concern that conflict be prevented.

The report advanced the idea of peace enforcement. When a recalcitrant government openly flouted the will of the international community, the latter should be ready to enforce the peace. If, for example, a peacekeeping force was interposed between two states and one became uncooperative, the international community should insist on its cooperation.

As mentioned earlier, the *Supplement to Agenda for Peace,* published on the UN's fiftieth anniversary, maintained that the set of principles of the 1992 *Agenda for Peace* have proved themselves. The supplement reported that the greatest obstacle to success in preventive diplomacy and peacemaking was not, as was widely supposed, lack of information, analytical capacity, or ideas for UN initiatives. Success was often blocked by the reluctance of the parties to accept the UN's help. That was true of both interstate and internal conflicts. Collectively, member states encouraged the Secretary-General to play an active role in this field, but individually they were often reluctant when they were a party to the conflict. It was difficult to know how to overcome this reluctance. Clearly the UN could not impose its preventive and peacemaking services on member states that did not want them. Legally and politically, their request for, or at least acquiescence in, UN action was a sine qua non. The solution could only be long term. It might lie in creating a climate of opinion or ethos within the international community in which the norm would be for member states to accept an offer of good offices.

The supplement identified two practical problems that had emerged in preventive diplomacy and peacemaking. The first was the difficulty of finding senior persons who had the diplomatic skills and who were willing to serve as a special representative or special envoy of the Secretary-General. As a result of the streamlining of the senior levels of the Secretariat, the extra capacity that had been there in earlier years no longer existed.

The second problem related to establishing and financing small field missions for preventive diplomacy and peacemaking. Although special envoys could achieve much on a visiting basis, their capacity was greatly enhanced if continuity could be assured by the presence on the ground of a small full-time support mission. Two solutions were possible: The first was to include a contingency provision in the regular budget that might be in the range of $25 million per biennium for such activities. The second would be to enlarge the existing provision for unforeseen and extraordinary activities.[68]

The Security Council adopted a series of presidential statements expressing its views on different proposals the Secretary-General advanced in *An Agenda for Peace.* It reiterated its readiness to cooperate fully with the Secretary-General in strengthening the organization's capacity to exercise preventive diplomacy. It encouraged all member states to provide the Secretary-General with detailed information on issues of concern to facilitate effective preventive diplomacy. Because of its awareness of the increased responsibilities of the UN in the area of preventive diplomacy, the Security Council invited the Secretary-General to consider appropriate measures to strengthen the Secretariat's capacity for information-gathering and in-depth analysis.

The council welcomed and supported the Secretary-General's proposals in *An Agenda for Peace* with regard to fact-finding. It stated that an increased use of fact-finding as a tool of preventive diplomacy, in accordance with the Charter and the Declaration on Fact-finding by the United Nations for the Maintenance of International Peace and Security (1991), could result in the best possible understanding of the objective facts of a situation, which would enable the Secretary-General to meet his responsibilities under Article 99 and facilitate Security Council deliberations.

The council noted with concern the incidence of humanitarian crises, including mass displacements of population, becoming or aggravating threats to international peace and security. In this connection, it deemed it important to include humanitarian considerations and indicators under the rubric of early warning information capacities. The council also invited regional arrangements and organizations, within the framework of Chapter VIII of the Charter, to study, on a priority basis, ways to strengthen their functions to maintain international peace and security within their areas of competence.[69]

The General Assembly, for its part, adopted a resolution on 18 December 1992 emphasizing that, together with the Security Council and the Secretary-General, it has an important role in preventive diplomacy.[70] The General Assembly recognized that it needs to work closely with the Security Council and the Secretary-General in accordance with the Charter and consistent with their respective mandates and responsibilities. It decided to explore ways to support the Secretary-General's recommendations in *An Agenda for Peace* to promote the utilization of the General Assembly by member states in order to have greater influence on preempting or containing any situation that is potentially dangerous or might lead to international dispute.

To follow up on the ideas for preventive diplomacy contained in *An Agenda for Peace,* Secretary-General Boutros Boutros-Ghali established six regional divisions within the consolidated Department for Political Affairs whose principal task was to gather and analyze information to assist him in preventing conflicts. He also designated a senior under-secretary-general to be principally responsible for liaising with and informally briefing the Security Council about developments in situations of concern to the council.[71]

At the end of 1992, the year of the publication of *An Agenda for Peace,* Vladimir Petrovsky, under-secretary-general for political affairs, submitted a "Report on Preventive Diplomacy" to Boutros-Ghali.[72] According to the report, between March and December 1992, the Department of Political Affairs had undertaken thirty-one missions to various trouble spots on the initiative either of the Secretary-General or a member state. Of the thirty-one missions, eight concerned the conflict in Nagorno-Karabakh; six, the former Yugoslavia; four, Guatemala; two, Moldova; two, Haiti; two, Georgia; and two, Tajikistan. The under-secretary-general also undertook two missions to Libya at the request of the Secretary-General. In Petrovsky's assessment, "these missions were of great use to the Department as they helped collect reliable information on a given situation. . . . Some of the missions were successful and some were not."[73]

Petrovsky's report was an admirable initiative that has not been maintained. Since the publication of *An Agenda for Peace,* a mindset has developed in the Secretariat and the Security Council that the UN must remain on the alert to do whatever is possible to prevent conflicts and catastrophes.

Subsequent reports by Boutros-Ghali's successor, Kofi Annan, focused on prevention. Officers of the regional divisions of the Department of Political Affairs are expected to conduct risk analyses of the countries and bring situations of concern to their supervisors' attention with the aim of briefing the Secretary-General. A training program aims to develop the skills of political and other officers on early warning and preventive diplomacy. The impact of *An Agenda for Peace* has thus been of lasting significance.

However, in the pool of ideas for preventive diplomacy, *An Agenda for Peace* must, in the future, be linked more with the pathbreaking *Perspectives for the 1990s* and its central concept of a comprehensive global watch.

An Agenda for Development

According to Boutros Boutros-Ghali, the lack of economic, social, and political development is the underlying cause of conflict.[74] He advocated a renewed vision of development to get at the roots of conflict. In his *An Agenda for Development*, he warned that if poverty persists or increases and the human condition is neglected, political and social strains will endanger stability over time. Reducing poverty requires development in which access to the benefits of economic progress is as widely available as possible and is not concentrated excessively in certain localities, sectors, or groups of the population.[75]

To Boutros-Ghali, development is a "fundamental human right and the most secure basis for peace."[76] Peace is the foundation of development. Unfortunately, the absence of peace is a pervasive reality in many parts of the world. Many carry the burden of recent devastation and continuing ethnic strife. None can avoid the realities of ongoing arms proliferation, regional war, and the possibility of a return to potentially antagonistic spheres of influence.[77]

The lack of development, Boutros-Ghali underlined, contributes to international tension and to a perceived need for military power. This, in turn, heightens tensions. Societies caught up in this cycle find it difficult to avoid involvement in confrontation, conflict, or all-out warfare.[78] Even while recognizing that development activities yield their best results in conditions of peace, they should start prior to the end of hostilities, Boutros-Ghali argued. Emergency relief and development should not be regarded as alternatives. Conflict, terrible as it is, can provide opportunities for major reforms.[79]

Conflict situations require a different development strategy than the strategies used in peacetime, and the characteristics of development differ according to the nature of the situation. Development in the context of international war does not involve the same problems as development during guerrilla warfare or development when governmental institutions are under military control.[80]

Boutros-Ghali defined peacebuilding as action to identify and support structures that tend to strengthen and solidify peace to avoid a relapse into conflict. As preventive diplomacy aims to prevent the outbreak of conflict, peacebuilding starts during the conflict to prevent its recurrence. Only sustained cooperative work on underlying economic, social, cultural, and humanitarian problems can place an achieved peace on a durable foundation. Unless there is reconstruction and development in the aftermath of conflict, there can be little expectation that peace will endure.[81]

An Agenda for Development argued that the most immediate task of peacebuilding is to alleviate the effects of war on the population. Food aid, support for health and hygiene systems, the clearing of mines, and logistical support to essential organizations in the field represent the first peacebuilding task. As food aid is provided, food production capacities need to be developed. Mine clearance is a unique post-conflict undertaking. The reintegration of combatants is crucially important to stability in the post-conflict period. Post-conflict efforts need to pay special attention to the mechanisms of governance, and the underlying conditions that led to conflict must be addressed. Reduction of military expenditure is a vital link in the chain between development and peace. Imports of armaments require attention. Transition toward smaller militaries should be promoted. Arms control and disarmament measures reduce the threat of destruction, economic decline, and tensions that lead to war.[82]

An Agenda for Democratization

In *An Agenda for Democratization,*[83] Boutros-Ghali dealt indirectly with the nexus between democratization and conflict prevention. He believed that over time, nondemocratic states tend to generate conditions inimical to development: a politicized military rule, a weak middle class, a population constrained to silence, a prohibition on travel and censorship, restrictions on the practice of religion or imposition of religious obligations, and pervasive and often institutionalized corruption. Without democratic institutions to channel popular pressures for development and reform, popular unrest and instability will result. Democracy is thus a practical necessity and has the capacity to foster good governance, which is perhaps the single most important development variable within the control of the individual state.[84]

Peace, development, and democracy, Boutros-Ghali continued, are inextricably linked. Peace is essential because without some degree of peace, neither development nor democracy is possible. Yet both development and democracy are essential for peace to endure. Over the long term, democracy is an essential ingredient of sustainable development.[85]

There are potential dangers in democratization, and a cautious approach is necessary. Democratization requires a comprehensive approach that addresses not only free and fair elections but also the construction of a political culture of democracy and the development and maintenance of institutions to support the ongoing practice of democratic politics. Democratization must seek to achieve a balance between state institutions and the institutions of civil society. In order to succeed over time, democratization within states must also be supported by a process of democratization among states and throughout the international system. Democratization might require the reduction of the North-South gap, so that all states are empowered to participate in the international political system to which they all belonge.[86]

The special power of democratization, he concluded, was in its logic, which flowed from the individual human person, the one irreducible entity in world affairs, the logical source of all human rights. Just as democratization relies on individual commitment to flourish, it fosters the conditions necessary for the individual to flourish.[87]

Kofi Annan

In June 2001, Secretary-General Kofi Annan presented a report to the General Assembly on the *Prevention of Armed Conflict* and measures taken to promote a "culture of prevention."[88] Using terms that had been advanced by the Carnegie Commission on the Prevention of Deadly Conflict, he made a distinction between operational and structural prevention. He defined operational prevention as short-term actions taken when facing an immediate crisis and structural prevention as long-term and comprehensive undertakings aimed at ensuring that crises did not happen in the first place.[89] On 31 August 2001, the Security Council passed resolution 1366, which called on member states and regional and subregional organizations to support the development of comprehensive regional conflict prevention strategies.

Secretary-General Annan's overall approach sought to give impetus to a move from early warning to early action. In his opinion, the availability of information was not the biggest problem; rather, using information efficiently for early action was the biggest challenge. He sought to orient an interdepartmental framework for coordination, or the framework team, toward conflict prevention.[90]

After 2002, the framework team concentrated on helping the different parts of the UN system to propose and implement pre-conflict initiatives aimed at structural prevention, understood in terms of building sustainable in-country capacity to prevent violent conflicts. A secretariat, supported by voluntary contributions, was also established for the framework team in 2003, in light of the fact that the team had grown from an original membership of three to up to seventeen UN departments and agencies.

At the same time, the UN Staff College pressed ahead with courses to train UN staff to sharpen their skills in carrying out assessments and analyses (including with relevant national actors) of existing tensions and their potential for generating violent conflict. In some instances, these analyses were used to modify development activities to better integrate the prevention perspective into ongoing programs.

In 2003, the United Nations Development Programme (UNDP) and the Department of Political Affairs joined hands to develop and launch the Joint Programme on Building National Capacities for Conflict Prevention to help selected UNDP country offices in pre-conflict situations develop and implement initiatives aimed at building the capacity of relevant national actors to settle disputes. The joint program drew on a number of precedents for successful collaboration between the development and political arms of the UN. For instance, in 2003 and 2004, UNDP and the Department of Political Affairs collaborated in supporting key national actors in Niger in developing a common vision of national priorities through the National Forum on Conflict Prevention and then implementing the recommendations from the forum. This program of support was executed through the UNDP country office.

The joint program also drew on several new types of development programs aimed explicitly at building national capacity for dispute resolution. For instance, with the support of the UN Department of Economic and Social Affairs the UNDP country office in Zimbabwe has supported the Programme on Building Skills for Constructive Negotiation and Conflict Transformation since 2002. This program aimed to build the capacity of key national actors such as the government, parliamentarians, public officials, educators, and civil society members to peacefully settle internal tensions and disputes. The program did not seek a UN role in facilitating dialogue or negotiations but instead sought to provide the relevant actors with the skills, relevant forums, policy expertise, and other tools to initiate their own efforts to build consensus on these issues.

Similarly, through the 1990s and the early 2000s, UNDP has supported "democratic dialogues" in a number of countries in the Latin American and Caribbean region. In addition, since 2001 the Department of Economic and Social Affairs has implemented—in collaboration with UNDP—a program to help selected member states in Africa build capacity for public administration and government institutions that can peacefully settle disputes.

Drawing on these precedents, the joint program has established a concrete framework where UNDP and the Department of Political Affairs can assist UNDP country offices (and UN country teams as appropriate) in meeting some of the challenges of pre-conflict prevention. Rather than presenting conflict prevention to the concerned national actors as a set of interventions aimed at helping them resolve specific disputes, the joint program engages them on the basis of partnerships aimed at building specific capacities—skills, institutions, and processes—to peacefully settle disputes and meet critical internal challenges.

The joint program is not intended to substitute capacity-building initiatives for diplomatic interventions aimed at resolving specific disputes. Where the UN is invited to play that role, it is under the leadership of its political arm. Where such interventions are not feasible or invited, other forms of support for national actors can still lead to a de-escalation of the most pressing tensions. Conversely, where diplomatic interventions have yielded a peaceful settlement of a specific dispute, capacity-building initiatives are still necessary to ensure that in the future such disputes will be resolved peacefully and that the concerned parties will have the relevant skills to continue implementing the initial agreement achieved with international assistance.

In Guyana and Ghana, the support of the Joint Programme for UNDP country offices in 2004–2005 was provided under the auspices of the framework team. These were instances of sustained, on-the-ground implementation of the overall approaches developed under the auspices of the framework team and augur well for systematic partnership within the UN in service of the new prevention agenda. In addition, in both instances, funds from the UN Trust Fund for Preventive Action have been provided in addition to funds specifically raised for the joint program.

Annan's Final Prevention Report

In his final comprehensive report on the prevention of armed conflict,[91] prepared at the request of the General Assembly, Annan built on his earlier report, again using a frame of analysis put forward earlier by the Carnegie Commission on the Prevention of Deadly Conflict, namely the concepts of structural and operational preventive actions. However, he advanced a third category of preventive measures, namely systemic prevention, referring to measures to address global risks of conflict that transcend particular states.

According to Annan, in view of the complex nature of effective preventive action, no state or organization can act alone. Sovereign governments, while fully accountable for maintaining peace within their borders, must be able to rely on the support of external actors to help prevent conflict. However, the fact that prevention is a shared responsibility does not diminish the primary obligation of member states to exercise their sovereign duties to their citizens and neighbors. In the case of both intrastate and interstate armed conflict, the key is to equip states and societies to manage their own problems in ways most appropriate to them. He argued for internally driven initiatives to develop local and national capacities for prevention, fostering home-grown, self-sustaining infrastructures for peace. The aim, he explained, should be to develop a society's capacity to resolve disputes in internally acceptable ways, reaching a wide constellation of actors in government and civil society. External support for such efforts must be informed by an understanding of the countries and the societal dynamics concerned.

Elaborating on the concept of systemic prevention, Annan submitted that some of the main sources of societal tension could be and were being addressed at the systemic global level. These include, for instance, international efforts to regulate trade in resources that fueled conflicts, such as diamonds; attempts to stem illicit flows of small arms and light weapons and the spread of nuclear, chemical, and biological weapons; efforts to combat narcotics cultivation, trafficking, and addiction; action against HIV/AIDS; and steps to reduce environmental degradation and its associated economic and political fallout. Many of these endeavors include international regulatory frameworks and the building of national capacities. Measures in these areas should all be underpinned by a more energetic and committed approach to development and poverty reduction.

Dealing with the challenges of structural prevention, Annan advanced the concept of national responsibility for conflict prevention. Much armed conflict, he pointed out, is caused by failures in governance and public administration systems, institutions, and practices. That is the case particularly when public policies fail—deliberately or inadvertently—to achieve even-handed responses to social, economic, and political needs. Horizontal inequalities that are or are perceived to be the result of poor governance frequently lead to conflict that can turn violent. That is particularly the case when existing ethnic, regional, or religious cleavages are overlaid by the inequitable allocation of public goods.

If, despite systemic and structural measures, conflict is staring in the face of a country, operational measures such as good offices of external actors can help prevent the outbreak of armed conflict in the first place.[92] Good offices, in his understanding, include any diplomatic initiative undertaken by a third party acting as an honest broker and a channel of communication between parties to a dispute, with functions ranging from passing messages from one party to another to brokering a limited agreement to negotiating a comprehensive accord. This encompasses many of the activities listed in Article 33, paragraph 1 of the Charter, including negotiation, inquiry, mediation, conciliation, and the use of regional agencies or arrangements or other peaceful means of the parties' choice.

The Secretary-General commented:

> My predecessors and I have provided our good offices in a wide range of situations and on countless occasions, offering an avenue for the resolution of inter-State wars, intra-State wars, border disputes, maritime disputes, constitutional disputes, electoral disputes, questions of autonomy and independence, hostage crises and a vast range of other disagreements and problems. My good offices are always at the disposal of Member States, especially in cases where I or my envoys could help to avoid the outbreak of conflict.[93]

He considered that meeting humanitarian needs in a timely way could contribute to preventing the outbreak or recurrence of armed conflict. Tackling food insecurity and related problems of agricultural underproduction and resource scarcity can do much to stabilize a fragile situation. The information produced by famine and other humanitarian early warning systems can forecast possible political deterioration. Bringing communities together to tackle humanitarian concerns such as food insecurity, water supplies, health, and the needs of children can also serve a conflict prevention purpose by opening avenues for dialogue and mutual cooperation.

He stressed the importance of democracy as a universal value. He felt that countries prone to armed conflict merit special assistance with respect to democratization. Democratic governance depends both on a legal framework that protects basic human rights and provides a system of checks and balances and on functioning rule-of-law institutions. It is the absence of these characteristics that often leads people to feel that they must resort to violence to be heard. Individual governments must find their own path to democracy, but the UN and its partners offer a variety of important services at the request of member states. These include electoral assistance, constitutional assistance, human rights capacity-building, support for good governance, anti-corruption initiatives, and reforms in key sectors, including the security and judicial sectors.

Annan welcomed emerging regional initiatives to take a stand against the violent overthrow of representatives of legitimately elected governments. He noted that member states had formed two important groups to advance principles of democracy—the new or restored democracies and the community of democracies. He encouraged them to explore how the two movements could complement each other to optimum effect. Regional organizations also contribute significantly to advancing democratic institutions and principles. Regional conflict-prevention mechanisms were making a valuable contribution in different parts of the world. He noted the growing role of visiting missions of the Security Council.

Annan considered it important to advance an international culture of peace and understanding. He defined a culture of peace as a set of values, attitudes, modes of behavior, and ways of life that rejected violence and prevented conflicts by tackling their root causes to solve problems through dialogue and negotiation among individuals, groups, and nations. He thought that a global movement of civil society organizations was emerging to advance the concept of a culture of peace. He discussed the role of parliamentarians, the private sector, the media, and women as vital resources for conflict prevention. He stressed that meaningful diplomatic intervention could not be achieved without intimate knowledge of political, cultural, and geographical reality combined with the patient groundwork of building critical local relationships, trust, and capacity over a long period.

He saw a reciprocal relationship between human rights and conflict prevention. Violations of human rights were a root cause of conflict as well as a common consequence of it. It was, therefore, imperative that resilient national human rights institutions and protection systems be established to safeguard those rights.

In his recommendations, he made a series of exhortations to member states, international and regional organizations, and civil society. He invited the international community to embrace more explicitly the responsibility to prevent conflict and invited member states to consider creating elements of a national infrastructure for peace. He called for a more robust and strategic approach to assistance in democracy-building, elections, and constitutional capacity. He asked the newly established Human Rights Council "to include in the implementation of its important new mandate recommendations on specific conflict-prevention measures to member states, the

United Nations system and other actors."[94] In the same vein, he called on the newly established Peacebuilding Commission to provide recommendations to prevent the recurrence of conflicts. He invited member states and relevant parts of the UN system to launch a dialogue on conflict prevention.

Ban Ki-moon

At the time of the completion of this book at the beginning of March 2007, Secretary-General Ban Ki-moon had been in office for just over two months. His policies and doctrines of preventive diplomacy were thus in the process of development. However, he had already established his imprint in three important respects: First, in his acceptance statement and in other declarations, he emphasized the importance of quiet diplomacy, marking a difference from his predecessor. Second, he proposed that the Security Council establish peacekeeping operations on the border between Sudan and the Central African Republic and between Sudan and Chad in an effort to prevent the Darfur conflict from spilling over. Third, he made a stirring case for preventive strategies in respect of climate change and global warming, which he considered likely to engender conflicts.[95]

Conclusion

Following the journey of preventive diplomacy at the UN yields an examination of efforts by the General Assembly and the Security Council to provide encouragement and support for preventive diplomacy and preventive actions. However, neither of these are lead actors in the practice of preventive diplomacy, a role that has been left mostly to the Secretary-General.

The Secretary-General's exercise of preventive diplomacy is a delicate business. Lie was facilitatory, inventive, and bold. Through his outspokenness on the Korean situation, he lost out politically in the end. But he built up important precedents, such as the right of the Secretary-General to engage in fact-finding. Hammarskjöld, the articulator and shaper of the concept of preventive diplomacy, exhibited a creative brilliance. His models of action are the ones largely still in use today.

U Thant walked the path of Hammarskjöld and took a major initiative when he called for the establishment of UNDRO. His preventive diplomacy during the Cuban missile crisis was a class act. Secretary-General Waldheim walked the careful path. He was a diplomatic practitioner rather than an innovator, but his practice of preventive diplomacy yielded results in different situations.

Secretary-General Pérez de Cuéllar was also a careful diplomatic practitioner. He walked the path of his predecessors in the practice of preventive diplomacy and had some successes. In his establishment of ORCI and in his advocacy of a comprehensive global watch, he set down ideas whose structural and strategic importance were significant and have not since been matched by his successors. The abolition of ORCI so shortly after its establishment was unfortunate. Although the notion of comprehensive preventive strategies has subsequently been canvassed, the notion of a comprehensive global watch has been lost along the way, and one can only hope that it will be resurrected in the future.

Secretary-General Boutros-Ghali's *An Agenda for Peace* was a historic document whose path was traced in Pérez de Cuéllar's advocacy of a comprehensive global watch. Boutros-Ghali's three agendas—for peace, development, and democratization—continue to provide inspiration and ideas for the development of preventive diplomacy at the UN.

Secretary-General Annan advocated "comprehensive preventive strategies," and structural and operational (and, later, systemic) prevention. He also sought to foster institutional coordination in favor of preventive action and diplomacy. During his tenure, there was significant cooperation on preventive measures between the political, economic, and development parts of the UN. His concept of systemic prevention covered a broad range of UN programs. Secretary-General Hammarskjöld had already pointed out that

> the responsibilities and possibilities of the Organization in the exercise of preventive diplomacy apply also to the economic sphere. Far less dramatic in their impact as the economic activities must be, they are of decisive long-term significance for the welfare of the international community. In the end, the United Nations is likely to be judged not so much by the criterion of how successfully it has overcome this or that crisis as by the significance of its total contribution towards building the kind of world community in which such crises will no longer be inevitable.[96]

Annan's discussion of the role of national systems for conflict prevention was important because the best form of prevention is within each country. This idea had already been put forward in Pérez de Cuéllar's *Perspectives for the 1990s* and Boutros-Ghali's *An Agenda for Peace.* His discussion of the relevance of economic and social equity and of human rights and humanitarian considerations, to the extent that they brought these perspectives more to the fore, was useful.

Secretary-General Ban Ki-moon has put down crucial building blocks of future preventive diplomacy strategies, particularly his proposal for preventive deployments and his warning of the threats posed by climate change and global warming.

From the point of view of future development of preventive diplomacy at the UN, one should retain the concept of a comprehensive global watch advanced by Pérez de Cuéllar as a policy framework. In addition, one would need to keep in mind the issues discussed in the reports of the Secretaries-General from the point of view of whether, when, and how there might be room for targeted diplomacy by the Secretary-General and continue to emphasize, from the perspectives of the Secretary-General, the exercise of preventive diplomacy that in his discretion and judgment might be most effective in particular circumstances.

3

The Practice of Preventive Diplomacy by the Security Council

- The World of the Council
- The Regional Working Group on Prevention of Conflicts in Africa
- The Role of the President
- Fact-Finding and Visiting Missions
- Strengthening the Role of the Security Council in Preventive Diplomacy: Designating Internal Regional Rapporteurs
- The Peacebuilding Commission
- Conclusion

The World of the Council

In the UN Charter, the Security Council is given the primary responsibility for maintaining international peace and security. The prevention of conflicts is thus at the core of its mandate. During the Cold War, the practical possibilities for action within the council were limited by considerations of power and politics. Yet the deliberations of the Security Council during the Cuban missile crisis made a contribution to containing and managing the situation.

In the post–Cold War period, the council has been considerably more active in efforts to stem, resolve, and settle conflicts and to encourage preventive strategies within the UN as well as within the regional and subregional organizations. The council nevertheless continues to be influenced by considerations of power and politics, and this will probably always be the case. The council is a political body, and whether or how it can act in a particular situation or marshal efforts toward preventive diplomacy depends on the interests and power alignments at play. In the light of these considerations, the interaction between the Security Council and the Secretary-General becomes particularly relevant in practicing preventive diplomacy.

In February 2001 the International Peace Academy organized a Security Council workshop on the theme of strengthening UN capacities for the prevention of violent conflict that provided some useful insights on the role of the Security Council in conflict prevention. At the workshop, concerns were expressed about the council's composition and the perceived selectivity of its actions. Participants recognized that council attention might, in some cases, be counterproductive, drawing unhelpful political attention to sensitive situations and legitimizing rogue actors. Participants observed that the council had traditionally become involved after a conflict was underway. Potential preventive roles suggested for the council included more regular discussion about early warning alerts, establishing ad hoc mechanisms to follow early warning cases, and more frequent discussion between council members and experts within and outside the UN system about early warning and prevention when appropriate.

There was a strong sense among some workshop participants that the lead role regarding prevention needed to rest with the Secretary-General, given the council's already heavy work load, "its leaky operations, and its lack of universally accepted mandate in this area."[1]

Some commentators have been quite harsh in their criticism of the Security Council's failure to prevent or end conflicts in situations such as Bosnia, the Great Lakes region of Africa, and Iraq.[2] One can understand these judgments without necessarily sharing them. In Bosnia, the parties were determined to fight and had the means to fight. The same can be said of the Great Lakes region of Africa, where conflict is fueled by the sale of diamonds and other natural resources. In the recent invasion of Iraq by the coalition powers, the Security Council was torn asunder in the diplomatic battle between the defenders of the Charter and the determination of the United States, in particular, to force Saddam Hussein to comply with Security Council decisions.

In the Israeli offensive against Hezbollah in Lebanon in July 2006, Israel, supported by the United States, chose military action in self-defense and would not entertain thoughts of a cease-fire until it had achieved its military objectives. What, realistically, could the Security Council do in such circumstances? The idea that the Security Council can prevent or quickly resolve every conflict is simply unrealistic, a fact that must be recognized.

Nevertheless, the Security Council's central mandate is to attempt to prevent the outbreak of wars, and the council must be faithful to this mandate. In its own way, the body is striving for prevention. The council has worked for prevention through its deliberations and decisions on cooperation with regional organizations. It has done so through its consideration and response to reports of the Secretary-General on preventive strategies. It has done, and continues to do so, through its consideration of Secretariat briefings on situations of concern and through its informal consultations and its open meetings. It has done so by developing new links between human security and international peace and security. Council deliberations and actions on issues such as HIV/AIDS, terrorism, children and armed conflict, and women and international peace and security are cases in point.[3]

The Security Council thus strives to prevent conflict in general and in particular situations where possible. The preventive role of the Security Council lies simply in its existence and in its overall efforts to maintain international peace and security. It is this story of striving that is presented in this chapter, paying particular attention to the council's practice of preventive diplomacy. A recapitulation of the policies and practice of the council is the departure point for this examination.

Policies and Practice

Chapter 2 noted that the Security Council's policies regarding preventive strategies and preventive diplomacy have expressed its "willingness to give prompt consideration to early-warning or prevention cases brought to its attention by the Secretary-General."[4] The Security Council has attempted to keep situations of potential conflict under close review as part of a conflict prevention strategy and expressed its intention to consider cases of potential conflict brought to its attention by any member state, a state that is not a member of the United Nations, or by the General Assembly or on the basis of information furnished by ECOSOC. The Security Council has also expressed its willingness to consider preventive deployment on the Secretary-General's recommendation and with the consent of the member states concerned. It has called for enhancing the regional organizations' capacity for conflict prevention.

The Security Council's policy pronouncements amount to a major and comprehensive strategy of conflict prevention and are impressive on paper. But how are they faring in practice? In a 2004 essay, Elizabeth Cousens of the International Peace Academy stated that the council's record was "only modestly promising": "The generally held view about the Council, in particular, is that it needs to be cajoled, resourced, and pressured to take more action rather than less."[5]

She notes that in cases where powerful member states were directly involved—especially the permanent five members—the council was unlikely to be able to act except minimally as an arena for the coordination of bilateral positions. In cases where there were no major powers directly implicated, council unity might be more likely. Even then:

One need only survey the long list of crises and conflicts that have been unaddressed in any significant measure—Algeria, Burundi, Chechnya, Colombia, Nepal, Sudan, and, curiously, even the Israeli-Palestinian conflict, which despite being an object of Council consideration has not seen the Council contribute productively to its resolution—to be reminded that the UN and its member states have far to go in matching outcome to normative aspiration.[6]

One can understand such comments. The Security Council has experienced many problems in discharging its primary role of maintaining international peace and security, and numerous academic and other commentaries have pointed this out. The council has been unable to prevent conflicts on many occasions, and there have been many occasions when it has not even been able to bring about settlements. The Security Council is a political organ of power and interests, and, except where one or more major power is determined to do so and obtains Security Council authorization, it is rarely able to impose its writ. But the council's overall contribution is somewhat more positive. It is a story of striving, even in the midst of difficulties. The council's deliberations are a good place to begin.

The Preventive Role of Meetings and Consultations of the Security Council

Fair-minded analysis requires us to ask: What is the significance, if any, of the Security Council's overall work and its deliberations in the face of the threatened outbreak of conflict? Do Secretariat briefings of the Security Council president or formal and informal meetings to discuss situations of concern have some preventive effect on the parties? Might these efforts allow more time to head off conflicts? Might the views of international public opinion that are marshaled at the Security Council have some restraining influence on the parties?

Security Council deliberations are among the possibly restraining and possibly deterrent instrumentalities of the United Nations. In October 1962, when the world faced the possibility of an imminent nuclear exchange during the Cuban missile crisis, and in October 1973, during the Arab-Israeli War, when the United States placed its forces on high alert, including nuclear readiness, the Security Council deliberations helped wiser counsel prevail at two particularly difficult moments.

The council's annual report for 1 August 2004–31 July 2005 noted that the previous twelve months had reaffirmed the trend observed in recent years toward a continuous increase in the volume and scope of its activities.

Africa had featured, once again, at the forefront of its agenda. The council had held an extraordinary session in Nairobi, its fourth outside of UN headquarters since the council began meeting in New York, to try to end Africa's most protracted conflict—that in the Sudan.[7]

All of the council's activities represented significant action to promote international peace and security and must be acknowledged as preventive diplomacy.

- On 2 December 2004, at the request of the government of the Democratic Republic of the Congo (DRC), the council held an urgent meeting and was briefed by the under-secretary-general for peacekeeping operations on alleged military operations by the Rwandan army in the DRC's eastern province of North Kivu. On 7 December, the council adopted a presidential statement concerning the situation in the border area between Rwanda and the DRC, calling on all governments in the region to make use of the mechanisms they had agreed to establish and to devote their resources to the promotion of peace and security.
- On 30 March 2005, the presidency organized a public debate on the African dimension of the council's work. Delegations underlined the root causes of conflict in Africa and the need to combine peace and security efforts with long-term development strategies to move from resolution to prevention.
- The council considered cross-border issues in West Africa at an open meeting on 25 February 2005 that was based on a report of the Secretary-General on this topic. It adopted a presidential statement reiterating the need for a wider strategy of conflict prevention, crisis management, and peace-building in the region. It called on member states and key international partners to explore practical ways of assisting the Economic Community of West African States (ECOWAS) to enhance its capacities in conflict prevention, peacekeeping, and peacemaking.
- A council meeting in Nairobi on the institutional relationship with the African Union, held on 19 November 2004, led to the adoption of a presidential statement inviting the Secretary-General to explore new means of cooperation between the UN and the African Union. On 25 February 2005, the council adopted a presidential statement reiterating the need for a wider strategy of conflict prevention, crisis management, and peacebuilding in the region and to explore practical ways of helping ECOWAS enhance its capacities in conflict prevention, peacekeeping, and peacemaking.

- The council continued to closely monitor the situation in the Middle East through its monthly open briefings. It continued consideration of the situation in Haiti and sent a council mission to the country in April 2005.
- On general issues, counter-terrorism continued to be a matter of top priority for the council, which held regular meetings on developments in the various peacekeeping operations with troop-contributing countries.
- It also held an open meeting on peacekeeping issues. The council discussed the work of the international tribunals for the former Yugoslavia and Rwanda and the International Court of Justice.
- On thematic issues, the council met at the ministerial level on 22 September 2004 to consider civilian aspects of conflict management and peacekeeping and adopted a presidential statement on this issue.
- On 6 October 2004, it held an open meeting on justice and the rule of law and adopted a presidential statement.
- On 28 October 2004, it held an open debate on women and peace and security and adopted a presidential statement.
- On 14 December 2004, it held an open debate on the protection of civilians in armed conflict and adopted a presidential statement.
- On 17 February 2005, the council held an open debate on the Secretary-General's report on small arms, adopting a presidential statement calling on all member states to enforce resolutions on sanctions, including those imposing arms embargoes.
- On 23 February 2005, the council held an open debate on children and armed conflict and adopted a presidential statement reiterating the need for a systematic and comprehensive monitoring and reporting mechanism on this issue.
- On 26 May 2005, the council held an open debate on post-conflict peacebuilding and adopted a presidential statement underlining priorities in the post-conflict environment, the need for significant international assistance for the economic and social rehabilitation and reconstruction of countries emerging from conflicts, and the importance of cooperation between UN peacekeeping operations and UN funds and programs and the specialized agencies.
- On 12 July 2005, the council held an open debate on maintaining international peace and security and its role in humanitarian crises. It adopted a presidential statement reiterating the importance of the urgent restoration of justice and the rule of law in post-conflict societies and the increasing importance of civilian aspects of conflict manage-

ment in addressing complex crisis situations and preventing the recurrence of conflict.
- On 28 July 2005, the council held informal consultations at which the
High Commissioner for Human Rights briefed it on the human rights
dimensions of issues on the council's agenda.

The council president is sometimes called on to take particular initiatives
in preventive diplomacy. The council stepped in when faced with a possible
Rwandan army incursion into the DRC. This is a pattern of activity that is
often seen in the council, particularly regarding African situations. In 2001–
2002, the council maintained "constant and even-handed pressure" on all
parties to the Lusaka Agreement to fulfill their responsibilities under the
peace process in the DRC.[8] This approach had had some success in keeping
up the momentum for peace. Progress on the core issues—foreign troop
withdrawal, internal dialogue and disarmament, demobilization, repatriation, resettlement, and reintegration—was slow, however, and there were
reports of cease-fire violations and human rights violations in the east of the
country. The lack of trust among the parties could be addressed only by
more progress in addressing the root causes of the conflict. The various initiatives by the council and others to promote direct contacts among the
leaders of the Lusaka parties have had limited success so far.

During a mission to the region in May 2002, led by Ambassador Jean-
David Levitte of France, the council pressed for progress in implementing
the Lusaka Agreement and identified the need for agreement on a comprehensive and inclusive transitional government for the DRC as a key element, together with the final withdrawal of foreign troops. The mission also
demonstrated the Security Council's continuing commitment to UN engagement in the Great Lakes region.[9]

During 2003–2004, the council expressed its concern about continued
violence and instability in the country by means of press statements, presidential statements, and resolutions. The council continued to put pressure
on all Congolese parties to remain fully committed to the peace process. On
numerous occasions, it called on all the states in the region to play a constructive role. It solemnly warned states neighboring the DRC of the consequences of providing support to armed rebel groups.

On 14 May 2004, in a presidential statement, the council expressed its
serious concern regarding reports of an incursion into the DRC by elements of the Rwandan army and demanded that the Rwandan government
take measures to prevent the presence of any of its troops in the DRC. The
council also called on the governments of the DRC and Rwanda to jointly

investigate the substance of reports of armed incursions across their mutual border with the assistance of the United Nations Observer Mission in the Democratic Republic of the Congo (MONUC).

In a presidential statement on 7 June 2004, the council condemned the seizure of Bukavu five days earlier by dissident forces and stressed that such actions constituted a serious threat to the peace process and to the transition. On 22 June 2004, the council reiterated its grave concern about the continued violence and instability in the DRC and condemned in the strongest terms any involvement in the DRC by outside forces. The council warned all parties against any attempt to engage in belligerent actions or violations of the embargo imposed by resolution 1493 (2003) and invited the Secretary-General to look into the need for a rapid reaction capability for MONUC.[10] The skeptic might comment that the situation in the DRC has continued precariously since then, but we do not know what might have happened without the preventive and deterrent effect of these council actions.

The same might be said of the urgent Security Council response to the situation in the Central African Republic. During 2002–2003, the council continued to monitor the country's political situation, which had remained tense, and supported the deployment of troops of the Economic and Monetary Community of Central African States (CEMAC) there in October 2002. The council later condemned the coup d'état of 15 March 2003. In July 2003, the council noted with satisfaction that the Central African authorities had opted for consensual management of the transition period by involving all the political factions and other actors of civil society. The council invited the Central African authorities to fulfill their commitment to holding presidential elections before the end of 2004. It recognized the importance of donor support to the Central African authorities to bring about the return of constitutional order and lasting peace.[11]

The council's report the next year stated that it continued to monitor the situation in the Central African Republic. In July 2004, the council encouraged the Central African authorities to maintain their efforts to organize free, transparent, and democratic presidential and legislative elections in the beginning of 2005. The council recognized CEMAC's considerable efforts and called, once again, on the international community to provide assistance to the country as soon as possible.[12]

The council's actions regarding the DRC and the Central African Republic were intended to contain the situations and prevent them from deteriorating and help head off further conflict. The council was thus doing its utmost in prevention as well as settlement.

The Regional Working Group on Prevention of Conflicts in Africa

In January 2002, the council established the Ad Hoc Working Group on Conflict Prevention and Resolution in Africa. The group began work on a range of issues, including improving relations with the Organization of African Unity/African Union and subregional organizations, using "groups of friends" to handle country-specific issues, and following up on thematic debates on Africa.[13] The group has also done preparatory work on African issues before it comes to the council, notably the workshop session on the Mano River Union in July 2002. The council had an exchange with member states that were not council members during an interactive session on the group's work in an open debate on 22 May 2002. On 11 July, following a report by the chair of the working group on its activities for the last six months, the council endorsed two sets of recommendations on cooperation with the Organization of African Unity/African Union and the establishment of groups of friends.[14]

In April 2003, the group held meetings on the DRC and held joint meetings on Guinea-Bissau with the Advisory Group of ECOSOC and the group of friends of Guinea-Bissau. The chair of the working group was actively involved in preparing the Security Council mission to Central Africa and the Guinea-Bissau leg of the Security Council mission to West Africa.[15] The ad hoc working group had been requested to take a closer look at Guinea-Bissau, and the group's chair, Ambassador Jagdish Koonjul of Mauritius, participated in a visit of ECOSOC's Ad Hoc Advisory Group on Guinea-Bissau in November 2002. The Security Council was concerned about the serious economic situation in the country and called on the government to take the necessary steps to facilitate dialogue with the international community and endorse the partnership approach the ECOSOC advisory group defined after its visit.[16]

A Security Council mission to West Africa visited Guinea-Bissau on 27–28 June 2003 with a mission of the ECOSOC group. The mission urged that the electoral registers be completely revised and that measures be taken to ensure that all parties could campaign freely.[17]

In March 2004, the Ad Hoc Working Group on Conflict Prevention and Resolution in Africa held joint meetings with the ECOSOC Ad Hoc Advisory Group on Burundi and with nongovernmental experts on regional and international norms regarding unconstitutional regime change in Africa and with the mission of the Security Council to West Africa.[18]

On 30 March 2005, the presidency organized a public debate on the African dimension of the council's work at a wrap-up session of the twenty-five meetings on African issues the council had held during March. Delegations underlined the root causes of conflict in Africa and the need to combine peace and security efforts with long-term development strategies.[19] Delegations agreed that the council's efforts would focus on the continent (African issues amounted to 60 percent of its agenda) and that the UN had learned valuable lessons from past developments in peacekeeping and could benefit from them.

The skeptic might remark that all of these activities have not produced tangible results and that the council and its working group were treading water. However, undramatic though it may be, the above account illustrates the council acting as it is able to do in the circumstances. The council strives in its own way, even if the results might not be spectacular.

The Role of the President

The Security Council president acts under the council's authority. That said, the president has some room to shape the council's policy responses and actions to head off or contain disputes or conflicts. A good example of this was the situation between Eritrea and Yemen in August 1996, when the two countries were on the verge of falling back into a conflict that had subsided the previous December. The president of the council that month, Ambassador Tono Eitel of Germany, played a leading role with Secretary-General Boutros Boutros-Ghali and council members to avert the resurgence of conflict.[20] As described below, the council president in September 1999, Ambassador Peter van Walsum, also played a leading role in developing the council's response to the violence in East Timor.

The council's annual report for 2001–2002 has a rather interesting addendum that contains the monthly assessments of former presidents of the council's work during their presidencies.[21] This addendum, which does not appear in subsequent annual reports, provides insightful information on the role of the president during each month. It shows, for example, that during the Jamaican presidency in July 2000, the president made eleven statements to the press on behalf of council members and briefed countries—not council members—on specific issues considered during consultations. During that month, the president met with the president of the General Assembly, the Secretary-General, chairs of regional groups, representatives of various member states, UN agencies and missions, heads of Secretariat departments, and representatives and special envoys of the Secretary-General, representatives of the International Committee of the Red Cross, and representatives of nongovernmental organizations. The president briefed council members on the discussions.[22]

The report of the Bangladeshi presidency during June 2005 is also revealing. It concluded with a wrap-up discussion on the work of the Security Council during that month, the first time that such a discussion had been held in public. The president recorded salient issues for future attention that included the points that the council should be proactive; that council missions to conflict areas were useful and a proactive instrument; that the council should have increased resources for sending missions to conflict areas; and that the findings and recommendations of such council missions should be followed up effectively.[23]

The Security Council Mission to East Timor (1999) was a case that involved active leadership of the council president, Dutch ambassador Peter van Walsum.[24] On 11 June 1999, the Security Council established the United Nations Mission in East Timor (UNAMET) to conduct a public consultation on the territory's future. After mid-August, there was an upsurge of violence, and in the week before the ballot, UN representatives, diplomats on the Security Council, and regional leaders made many attempts to impress on Jakarta the international consequences of continuing violence.

The Security Council received detailed briefings from Under-Secretary-General for Political Affairs Kieran Prendergast, who, on 24 August, suggested that the council send a mission prior to the announcement of the ballot result to demonstrate the seriousness of its concern. This suggestion was not taken up immediately.

On 3 September, at 9 PM, Secretary-General Annan announced the results of the ballot to the Security Council: 21.5 percent had voted for autonomy and 78.5 against. In other words, the East Timorese had overwhelmingly opted for independence. In East Timor, which was twelve hours ahead of New York time, violence had erupted. The violence was not only aimed at pro-independence East Timorese but also at foreign witnesses—journalists and UNAMET itself. The permanent representative of Portugal formally requested the president to reconvene the Security Council without delay.

On 5 September, the president called consultations with a view to dispatching a Security Council mission. The council swiftly decided that the mission would consist of five members and left further details, such as the mission's composition, to its president. The president asked the permanent representative of Namibia, his immediate predecessor as council president, to chair the mission. As the remaining four members, he chose the permanent representatives of the United Kingdom, Malaysia, and Slovenia and his own deputy.

The mission left New York the following day. On the third day, just as the Indonesian defense minister, General Wiranto, was assuring the mission that everything was quiet in East Timor, the news broke that there had been a militia attack on the UNAMET compound. This enabled the mission to insist that it visit East Timor. Both the mission and Minister Wiranto flew to Dili the following day.

Meanwhile, in New York, a Portuguese request for a formal public Security Council meeting had been seconded by Brazil, which, unlike Portugal, was a member of the council. The president consulted the council and had found that, apart from Brazil, all delegations believed that it would be illogical for the Security Council to dispatch a mission consisting of one-third of its members and not wait for them to return and report. However, in the light of developments, on 10 September, the president informed the council that he was calling a formal meeting on East Timor for the following day. During that meeting, which lasted nearly six hours, fifty delegations took the floor, almost all critical of Indonesia's role in East Timor.

The following day, on 12 September, Indonesian president B. J. Habibie telephoned Secretary-General Annan to request UN assistance to restore security in East Timor. The mission returned to New York on 13 September, the United Kingdom offered a draft resolution authorizing the establishment of a multinational force on 14 September, and fifteen hours later, at about 2 AM on 15 September, that resolution was adopted unanimously. The International Force for East Timor (INTERFET) came into being less than twelve days after the outbreak of the disturbances triggered by the outcome of the referendum. The first INTERFET troops landed in East Timor five days later.

These snapshots show that council presidents can and do play a role in the body's overall political diplomacy and in its preventive diplomacy as well. How can the council president play a more leading role in activating the conflict prevention role of the Security Council? An idea might be for the president, based on materials provided by the Secretariat and in a very discreet setting, to organize a working luncheon or dinner at the start of the presidency, where Security Council members would be invited to consider preventive measures in particular situations of concern.

Fact-Finding and Visiting Missions

Marrack Goulding, former under-secretary-general for peacekeeping and for political affairs, highlights the importance of fact-finding as a way of responding to crises, containing them, and heading them off.[25] Goulding notes that facts and effective methods of collecting them are indispensable in-struments to the peacemaker. After the Secretariat's analysis of the situa-tion, the first task in investigating whether a conflict is brewing is to verify the diagnosis. One of the most frequently used responses to early warning of an impending conflict is the dispatch of a goodwill or fact-finding or good offices mission to the area where the threat exists.

Where such a mission is dispatched, its first function is to verify that the Secretariat's analysis has correctly diagnosed a threat of conflict. Its second function is to discuss with the parties whether they would like or would ac-cept UN help in trying to resolve their dispute. A third function is to make a judgment about whether the dispute is susceptible to treatment by the UN, assuming the parties will cooperate. A fourth function is to make rec-ommendations about immediate therapy. A mission's fifth function is to make recommendations about longer-term treatment.[26]

Goulding points out that the importance of fact-finding for preventive purposes was registered by the General Assembly when it adopted the De-claration on Fact-Finding by the United Nations in the Field of the Mainte-nance of International Peace and Security in 1991.[27] That declaration de-fined fact-finding as any activity designed to obtain detailed knowledge of the relevant facts of any dispute or threatening conflict in which the com-petent UN organs need to effectively exercise their functions pertaining to the maintenance of international peace and security. Fact-finding must be comprehensive, objective, impartial, and timely. Every state that receives a fact-finding mission should cooperate with it.

Probably because of the sensitivities involved, visiting missions of the Se-curity Council are more frequent than fact-finding missions. The Security Council has, on occasion, asked the Secretary-General or, through him, the United Nations High Commissioner for Human Rights to investigate par-ticular incidents or situations and report to it.

Visiting missions are becoming more frequent. To give some examples, from 26 June to 5 July 2003, a mission of the Security Council visited West Africa and submitted a report to the Security Council with observations and recommendations on Guinea-Bissau, Côte d'Ivoire, Liberia, Sierra Leone, and the West African subregion.[28] From 13 to 16 April 2005, Brazilian rep-resentative Ronaldo Mota Sardenberg led a Security Council mission to Haiti in conjunction with the Ad Hoc Advisory Group on Haiti of ECOSOC. On 20 April 2005, Sardenberg briefed the council on the mission's findings, including its assessments on the situation in Haiti. On 13 May, Sardenberg presented the report of the mission at an open meeting.[29]

From 21–25 November 2004, the representative of France, Ambassador Jean-Marc de La Sablière, led a Security Council mission to the DRC, Burundi, Rwanda, and Uganda. On 30 November, Ambassador de La Sablière briefed the council on the mission's findings, including its assessments of the peace process in the DRC and Burundi and the prospects for peace and stability in the region. On 8 December, the ambassador presented the mission report at an open council meeting.[30]

In November 2005, a Security Council mission to Central Africa recommended a series of actions in and around the DRC to put in place measures for sustained peace and make the projected elections free and fair. The mission recommended that the council encourage the DRC's transitional government to strengthen its military forces and pay them regularly and urge the Rwandan rebels in the eastern DRC to disarm and repatriate to Rwanda.

The mission further recommended that the council encourage the UN's peacekeeping mission in the DRC to continue to support the actions taken by the armed forces of DRC "to step up the pressure on foreign armed groups operating in the eastern part of the Democratic Republic of the Congo." Further, the mission stated that the council should call on Uganda "to respect fully the sovereignty of neighboring States and in particular to refrain from any use of force outside its borders" and "to take further measures to ensure the remnant militias operating in the Ituri district receive no support from Ugandan territory."[31]

The mission recommended that both Uganda and Rwanda be encouraged to cooperate with UN efforts toward resolving the continued threat to regional security posed by the presence of foreign armed groups on Congolese territory. It felt that the council should also urge each of the two governments to ensure that the arms embargo imposed by the Security Council on the DRC was respected and enforced in its territory, in particular by establishing stricter controls at its borders with the DRC to curtail the illegal cross-border trafficking of natural resources and arms and the movement of combatants.[32] This was practical preventive diplomacy in action in the Security Council.

Strengthening the Role of the Security Council in Preventive Diplomacy: Designating Internal Regional Rapporteurs

This chapter has attempted to outline the considerable efforts the Security Council has been making to marshal preventive diplomacy regarding threats or breaches of international peace and security. At the same time, it has not ignored criticisms that the council should make stronger efforts. The Security Council has been dynamic and innovative in its own way, given all the circumstances and difficulties. There is no doubt that the Security Council has been carrying a heavy work load in its efforts for peace and security.

The Security Council contains all the power disequilibriums, competing interests, and divisions in the world at large. There will always be occasions when the Security Council can do no more than what is politically possible in the given circumstances. Recognizing this does not lead in the direction of a futile quest for perfection but rather a consideration of ideas for enlarging the positive contribution that the council might be able to make in preventing, managing, and resolving conflicts.

Creating regional rapporteurs inside the council might be one way to accomplish this. From the point of view of maintaining a global watch over threats to international peace and security, the current arrangements inside the Security Council still have one fundamental deficiency that can be easily corrected: the council is too dependent on the Secretariat or a member state to bring potential threats to international peace and security to its attention. The council has not organized itself to take a systematic periodic look at the global scene and benefit from briefings or advice that could be available to it. The council owes it to the international community to systematize its efforts in this respect.

One can readily anticipate the counter-argument that council members, especially the permanent members, already have the information-gathering capacity to know of situations of concern and that what is at issue is the question of political advisability or political will. Considerations of judgment and discretion must obviously come into play in deciding whether a matter should be taken up in the council.

It is precisely for this reason that a case can be made for a system of regional rapporteurs inside the council. A regional rapporteur, one for each of the five political regions of the United Nations, coming from a national or a nonpermanent member on the council, could be briefed by the Secretariat and the relevant regional organizations, could gather information from reliable sources, and could share his or her thoughts with council members, say quarterly, at closed council sessions.

At least one result could be achieved by such a system: the council could be satisfied that it has a system in place that would draw its attention to situations of concern. Whether the council chooses to act or not is a different matter. Issues of judgment and political sensitivity are, of course, involved. Organized reflection in the council, in the most discreet manner, would surely strengthen its efforts and could lead to the initiation of more discreet fact-finding or good offices missions to head off situations of concern.

The Peacebuilding Commission

Peacebuilding, at its core, is a preventive idea. It is meant to head off the resurgence of conflict and, in the long term, remove the root causes that led to conflict.[33] Recent economic studies indicate that around half of all civil wars are due to post-conflict relapses. In the words of Paul Collier, this provides:

> [a]n opportunity for the international system radically to reduce conflict by highly targeted intervention. It is likely that the combined efforts of the international community can make a major difference. The risks of conflict relapse are very high during the first post-conflict decade—typically around 50%. This is partly because the countries that have had a conflict have underlying persistent characteristics such as low income and natural resource dependence that makes them prone to conflict, and also because of the legacy of the conflict itself. The high level of risk is due approximately equally to the pre-conflict characteristics and the legacy of the conflict. The three instruments that can be deployed to reduce post-conflict risks are: political design, economic recovery, and military provision.[34]

In short, what is required is sustained peacebuilding, which was defined in *An Agenda for Peace* of 1992. The 1995 *Supplement to An Agenda for Peace* elaborated on this definition. It includes

> comprehensive efforts to identify and support structures which will tend to consolidate peace and advance a sense of confidence and well-being among people. Through agreements ending civil strife, these may include disarming the previously warring parties and the restoration of order, the custody and possible destruction of weapons, repatriating refugees, advisory and training support for security personnel, monitoring elections, advancing efforts to protect human rights, reforming or strengthening governmental institutions and promoting formal and informal processes of political participation.

The High-level Panel on Threats, Challenges and Change saw peacebuilding as an inherent part of the UN's efforts to prevent, contain, and resolve conflicts. It recommended establishing a peacebuilding commission, which, after a further recommendation of the Secretary-General in his *In Larger Freedom*, was formally established in 2005 as a subsidiary body of the Security Council.[35] It is intended to marshal resources at the disposal of the international community and propose integrated strategies for post-conflict recovery and focus attention on reconstruction, institution-building, and sustainable development in countries emerging from conflict.

The commission is expected to bring together the UN's capacities and experience in conflict prevention, mediation, peacekeeping, respect for human rights, the rule of law, humanitarian assistance, reconstruction, and long-term development. Specifically, the commission will:

- Propose integrated strategies for post-conflict peacebuilding and re-covery
- Help ensure predictable financing for early recovery activities and sustainable investment over the medium to longer term
- Extend the period of attention by the international community to post-conflict situations
- Develop best practices on issues that require extensive collaboration among military, humanitarian, and development actors[36]

The Peacebuilding Commission held its first session in June 2006.[37] On 21 June 2006, the Security Council requested its advice on the situation in Burundi and Sierra Leone.[38] In his second comprehensive report on conflict prevention, Secretary-General Annan called on the Peacebuilding Commission to provide recommendations on preventing the recurrence of conflicts.[39]

That there is a strong preventive component to peacebuilding came out repeatedly and forcefully in the Security Council's discussion on peace consolidation in West Africa on 9 August 2006. A Ghanaian concept paper that was circulated as a background document for the discussion invited the contribution of the Peacebuilding Commission to issues such as the following: "How do we manage conflicts to prevent further escalation and achieve expedited solution? What measures should be taken to prevent the outbreak of new conflicts? Given that several peace agreements have collapsed within five years, how do we prevent the relapse into conflict of countries emerging from conflict?"[40]

Repeatedly in the debate, speakers emphasized the preventive aspect of peacebuilding. The Ghanaian foreign minister, who was the council president, stated:

> From our perspective . . . the strategy for peace consolidation should focus on the following broad priorities: first resolving ongoing conflicts as quickly as possible or at least preventing them from escalating; secondly, preventing a relapse into conflict in countries that have just emerged from war; thirdly, preventing a fresh outbreak of conflict; fourthly, developing the institutional framework and relevant capacities for peace initiatives; fifthly, mobilizing the required resources at the national, regional and international levels for peace initiatives; and sixthly, addressing the underlying causes of conflict in a comprehensive manner.[41]

The secretary-general of ECOWAS, Mohamed Ibn Chambas, told the Security Council: "A proactive initiative composed of peace consolidation and post-conflict reconstruction is an urgent step to prevent conflict back-lash in post-conflict countries. It is also an effective conflict prevention measure."[42]

Time will tell whether the Peacebuilding Commission will rise to these challenges.

Conclusion

The council already does much to head off threats or manage or settle conflicts. It has developed a range of methods for exercising preventive diplomacy. At the same time, the council is preeminently a political body, and its methods of action must be calibrated to allow it to contribute tangibly to preventive efforts without inflaming situations. This is where the emphasis on preventive diplomacy is important. More imaginative preventive diplomacy can indeed allow the Security Council to contribute more effectively to maintaining international peace and security. It would be in order to look to a strengthened role of the president in enhancing its capacity for the exercise of preventive diplomacy. The president can help spearhead preventive diplomacy in the council. Designing a system of internal regional rapporteurs could do a great deal to strengthen the council's preventive diplomacy. It could help identify situations in which discreet fact-finding or good offices missions might be deployed to advantage.

The Peacebuilding Commission could develop into an important organ of preventive diplomacy. For the time being, however, it is still at the initial stages of planning and organizing its work, and it remains to be seen how it will develop.

4

The Practice of Preventive Diplomacy
by the Secretaries-General

- Good Offices
- Initiatives for the Prevention or Containment of Particular Conflicts
- Public Controversy and Quiet Diplomacy

Good Offices

A long-standing tradition of the exercise of the good offices by the Secretaries-General stands at the heart of the practice of preventive diplomacy. A 1972 United Nations Institute for Training and Research study on the "quiet approach," or the good offices of the Secretary-General,[1] advanced the proposition that any dispute or situation could be regarded as suitable for handling through the Secretary-General's good offices if the continuance of that situation might be prejudicial to the purposes and principles of the UN, as set forth in the Charter.

According to the study, to maintain constitutional balance within the UN, the Secretary-General should refrain from action while the Security Council is exercising or is likely to exercise the functions assigned to it by the Charter. He should also seek the council's prior authorization if the action relates to a situation that may require council action in accordance with Chapter VII of the Charter. The Secretary-General should also keep the council informed and consult its members about any involvement in disputes that could endanger the maintenance of international peace and security so the council can take appropriate steps in accordance with Articles 33(2), 34, 36, and 38. Finally, the Secretary-General should report to the council on the outcome of his involvement in the settlement of disputes under Chapter VI of the Charter, with or without a recommendation on appropriate action.

The study identified four types of troubleshooting :

- Rudimentary forms of diplomatic assistance, such as informal contacts and consultations with a view to exposing each side to the other's attitudes and claims and facilitating communications between the parties involved
- Diplomatic action designed to express international concern, to coax the parties into talks before a favorable atmosphere fades away or before they reach a point of no return, and to help them find a suitable framework for settlement
- Mediation, conciliation, and coordination, including taking action aimed at helping parties alleviate human suffering or easing other burdens such as refugee problems
- Inquiries, fact-finding, the supervision of plebiscites or other acts of choice, and the determination of legal rights and duties on a specific issue[2]

This early study, written by an international lawyer, Vratislav Pechota, and inspired by another international lawyer, Oscar Schachter, sought to document the practice of Secretaries-General up to 1972 and offer some prescriptions based on practice. However, there is an obvious need for Secretaries-General to improvise when they seek to do whatever they can in the face of Security Council inaction. As a matter of principle, the Secretary-General should defer to the Security Council and should keep it informed to the extent possible. But Secretaries-General have to give themselves some room for maneuver discreetly behind the scenes, keeping the Security Council informed when considered appropriate.

A 1983 study of the good offices of the Secretary-General in the fields of human rights and humanitarianism documented the practice of Secretaries-General in addressing gross violations through the use of good offices. Secretaries-General used their personal judgment about whether an intercession would be appropriate or helpful. They were guided mainly by the welfare of the persons concerned and acted on humanitarian grounds. Most often, they acted confidentially and discreetly, but when necessary they spoke out publicly. Sometimes they sent a representative to consult with the government concerned, and sometimes they also visited countries to take up particular cases or situations.[3]

Preventive diplomacy has been exercised quite a bit since these two studies were written. The following sections take a look at the contours of the practice of preventive diplomacy by the first seven Secretaries-General.

Initiatives for the Prevention or Containment of Particular Conflicts

Berlin, 1948: Secretary-General Trygve Lie worked to help resolve the crisis caused by the Soviet Union's blockade of West Berlin in 1948. It is noteworthy that in this crisis the nonpermanent members of the Security Council, led by Juan A. Bramuglia, the foreign minister of Argentina, as well as the president of the General Assembly, Herbert Evatt of Australia, also sought to play a role in ameliorating the situation.

Working behind the scenes, Secretary-General Lie sought to use two of his senior officers, an American and a Soviet national, to work on a currency scheme, an issue at the heart of the crisis, and to negotiate agreement on the scheme with the United States and the Soviet Union. Lie also joined Evatt in sending a letter to the United States, the Soviet Union, the United Kingdom, and France, urging "immediate conversations and . . . all other necessary steps towards the solution of the Berlin Question."[4] The United States did not react positively to the appeal, although the appeal probably helped reduce the tension. This use of the appeal has taken firm hold in the practice of Secretaries-General and was used to great advantage in the Cuban missile crisis.

Lie wrote of his efforts: "None of these efforts brought immediate results, but their effect was greatly to moderate the tension, reduce the danger of war, and gain time for other factors tending to a settlement to make themselves felt."[5] In Arthur W. Rovine's assessment, the effort was important in the context of the Secretary-General's role as a mediator in world politics, "for in the early days of his administration, every move made by Lie served as a precedent for further development and indicated future directions for his office."[6]

U.S. Airmen in China, 1954: In January 1953, a U.S. aircraft with eleven American pilots was shot down over China, and the crew was sentenced to long prison terms as espionage agents. A tense situation ensued between China and the United States. In December 1954, the General Assembly passed resolution 906 (IX) condemning the measures taken against the U.S. airmen and requesting Secretary-General Dag Hammarskjöld to seek their release through "continuing and unremitting efforts" and "by the means most appropriate in his judgment."[7] In a move that became known as the Peking formula, Secretary-General Hammarskjöld chose to rely on his authority under the Charter. In January 1955, Hammarskjöld visited Beijing and held conversations with Chinese premier Zhou Enlai over four days.

According to the communiqué issued at the end of the meetings, the talks were useful and the parties hoped to continue the contact established in the meetings. On 30 May, Beijing released four airmen after a visit by Ambassador Krishna Menon of India. In July 1955, Beijing and Washington announced that they would hold talks in Geneva, and on 1 August 1955, Beijing announced that the remaining airmen would be released, which occurred on 4 August 1955.

Rovine commented on Hammarskjöld's efforts:

> Essentially, Hammarskjöld performed what might be called communications and mediation functions. He served as a kind of substitute for diplomatic relations between Washington and Peking by passing messages and information between the two parties and of course by outlining various bases and possible solutions himself. His diplomatic handling of the problem was superb, as he refrained from commenting on the validity of the legal charges and made no public recommendations for settlement beyond the constant stress on the humanitarian aspects of the problem and the need for peaceful settlement.[8]

Suez, 1956: The story of the establishment of the first peacekeeping force in the aftermath of the Suez crisis of 1956 has been well documented. The idea for establishing the force came from Lester Pearson, a Canadian diplomat and statesman, but Hammarskjöld gave it content and shape. Three features of Hammarskjöld's involvement in the Suez Crisis are noteworthy here.

The first was the nuanced position of principle Hammarskjöld took in the wake of the military actions by the United Kingdom, France, and Israel. Addressing the Security Council on 31 October 1956, Hammarskjöld stated that had the Security Council not been called into session by the United States, he would have called for a meeting under Article 99 of the Charter. He then made the following statement:

> The principles of the Charter are, by far, greater than the Organization in which they are embodied, and the aims that they are to safeguard are holier than the policies of any single nation or people. As a servant of the Organization, the Secretary-General has the duty to maintain his usefulness by avoiding public stands on conflicts between member nations unless and until such an action might help to resolve the conflict. However, the discretion and impartiality thus imposed on the Secretary-General by the character of his immediate task, may not degenerate into a policy of expediency. He must also be a servant of the principles of the Charter, and its aims must ultimately determine what for him is right and wrong. For that he must stand. A Secretary-General cannot serve on any other assumption than that—within the necessary limits of human frailty

and honest differences of opinions—all Member nations honor their pledge to observe all articles of the Charter. He should also be able to assume that those organs which are charged with the task of upholding the Charter will be in a position to fulfil their tasks.

The bearing of what I have just said must be obvious to all without any elaboration from my side. Were the members to consider that another view of the duties of the Secretary-General than the one here stated would better serve the interests of the Organization, it is their obvious right to act accordingly.[9]

The second significant feature of Hammarskjöld's handling of the Suez crisis concerns the orientation that he provided to the United Nations Emergency Force (UNEF). In Hammarskjöld's conception, the force

> would be more than an observer corps but in no way a military force temporarily controlling the territory in which it is stationed; nor, moreover, should the Force have military functions exceeding those necessary to secure peaceful conditions on the assumption that the parties to the conflict take all necessary steps for compliance with the recommendations of the General Assembly.[10]

Rovine highlighted the third important feature of Hammarskjöld's involvement in the Suez crisis:

> Dag Hammarskjöld had opened new vistas in the life of the United Nations and made an enormous contribution to the development of his Office. . . . If the UN is to be a meaningful instrument for the peaceful settlement of international conflict, it must have some independent rights and power of its own, and must be able to take certain initiatives in conflict situations even without the full support of each of the great powers. This was the essence of Hammarskjöld's message as it comes down to us from the Middle Eastern crisis of 1956–57, and it was Hammarskjöld who helped give that perception the shape and vitality essential for the goals of world order.[11]

Cuban Missile Crisis, 1962: In the assessment of historian Arthur Schlesinger, the Cuban missile crisis of October 1962 was the most dangerous moment in history, the moment when the world came closest to destroying itself.[12] The preventive diplomacy of Secretary-General U Thant helped defuse that crisis. In his letter of 28 October to Premier Khrushchev, President Kennedy wrote: "The distinguished efforts of Acting Secretary-General U Thant have greatly facilitated both our tasks."[13] The story of U Thant's efforts is the subject of chapter 5.

Malaysia, 1963: As the Federation of Malaysia was about to be born, Indonesia, the Philippines, and Malaya were in dispute over North Borneo and Sarawak. On 5 August 1963, the heads of state of the three countries asked U Thant to help resolve the dispute, pledging to accept his findings of fact and recommendations. In Rovine's assessment, "It was the first time a Secretary-General had gone beyond simple mediation to the role of arbitrator, and within a context of strongly conflicting claims in which it was not at all clear that any of the parties were willing to lose."[14]

U Thant sent a nine-member team to the area and released his conclusions on 14 September 1963. He reported that a sizeable majority of the inhabitants of North Borneo and Sarawak wished to join the federation. As it happened, Britain and Malaya had gone forward on 29 August and announced the decision to establish the federation of Malaysia, including North Borneo and Sarawak, which was inaugurated on 16 September, two days after U Thant released his report. One can imagine that the British and Malaysian decision to proceed in the matter might otherwise have inflamed opinions in Indonesia and the Philippines. But the release of U Thant's report two days before the inauguration of the federation had a prophylactic effect. U Thant's efforts thus did contribute, in the long term, to a resolution of the dispute involving North Borneo and Sarawak. Both the Philippines and Indonesia came to accept eventually that the two territories would be part of the Malaysian Federation. Indonesia protested for a while but then accepted the outcome. In Rovine's assessment, "Thant's role was valuable as an accommodation device for Indonesia, for if Sukarno was either unwilling or unable to crush Malaysia as he threatened, the Secretary General's conclusion on self-determination served as a useful tool and it would have been politically quite difficult for the Philippines or Malaya to resist the investigation."[15]

Bahrain, 1969–1970: Bahrain was under Iranian sovereignty until 1783, when it was seized by an Arab family. Although it became a British protectorate in the twentieth century, Iran maintained its claim on the islands. With the onset of the independence movement in the 1960s, Iran pressed its claim, which was opposed by the ruler of Bahrain as well as by neighboring Arab states.

In 1969, the British and Iranian governments asked U Thant to exercise his good offices in the dispute, and it eventually fell to Under-Secretary-General Ralph Bunche to lead the effort, which he did brilliantly. For several months, Bunche undertook contacts with diplomats from Iran and the United Kingdom at the UN. Iran pressed for a plebiscite. Bunche thought that the Secretary-General should choose the method of determining the wishes of the people of Bahrain. Bunche applied the same principle when it came to demands of the Bahraini side.

In December 1969, Bunche secured acceptance by the two sides that the Secretary-General would designate a special representative who would be deployed to Bahrain to determine the wishes of the people. Obtaining this acceptance required a heroic effort by Bunche, who was seriously ill at the time. He flew to Geneva, met the Bahraini representatives, and flew back to New York on the same day.[16]

After a formal request by the two sides that the Secretary-General appoint a special representative "to ascertain the true wishes of the people of Bahrain with respect to the future status of the Islands of Bahrain," the Secretary-General designated Winspeare Giucciardi as his representative, who took up his post in Bahrain in March 1970.

The quality and sophistication of Bunche's diplomacy is indicated by the following instructions he wrote to Winspeare:

> There could be disastrous consequences for the mission if there should be the least basis for an allegation that any member of it was seeking to influence the Bahrainian views. Discussions of local politics should likewise be taboo. This is a mission for wise men only, from top to bottom. . . . We approach this exercise with complete impartiality. It will be only the people of Bahrain who will speak conclusively.[17]

Giucciardi stayed in Bahrain until 18 April 1970. He reported to the Secretary-General that the overwhelming majority of Bahrainis wished to gain recognition of their identity in a fully independent and sovereign free state.[18]

Brian Urquhart described these efforts as "a textbook example of settling a dispute by quiet diplomacy before it degenerated into conflict."[19] U Thant wrote that "it was the first time in the history of the UN that the parties to a dispute entrusted it to the Secretary-General's good offices by giving a *prior pledge* to accept without reservation the findings and conclusions of his personal representative."[20]

The Arab-Israeli Conflict, 1973: In 1973, during the tenure of Secretary-General Waldheim, the United States and the Soviet Union faced the possibility of a nuclear confrontation because of the Arab-Israeli War.[21] The Secretary-General's role in dealing with the nuclear face-off was not central, as it was in the Cuban missile crisis, but his efforts and the overall efforts of the UN were useful in containing the situation, preventing it from deteriorating, and helping to bring about solutions.

Four points about this situation are significant regarding preventive diplomacy. First, between 24 and 25 October 1973, the United States placed its forces, including its nuclear forces, on high alert. Efforts by the two countries, members of the Security Council, and the Secretary-General helped defuse the situation. Second, the interposition of UN forces between the Egyptian and Israeli armies helped prevent further fighting at a time when a test of wills was being played out between the United States and the Soviet Union. Secretary-General Waldheim played an important role in ensuring that UN forces were on the ground as soon as possible after adoption of the Security Council resolution. Third, UN peacekeeping forces helped the two sides negotiate and conclude crucial agreements, such as the Kilometer 101 Agreement. Fourth, UN forces helped keep the two countries at arm's length until they concluded the Camp David accords that brought peace between the two countries in March 1979. UN preventive diplomacy assisted greatly in a highly dangerous situation.

The basic facts of the situation were as follows. On 6 October 1973, Egypt and Syria coordinated an attack to regain territories occupied by Israel during the Arab-Israeli War of 1967, and Egyptian forces crossed the Suez Canal to the East Bank. The situation was discussed both in the Security Council and the General Assembly. The Security Council held three meetings on 8 and 9 October that were inconclusive, as neither the Egyptians and Syrians nor the Israelis wanted a cease-fire at that time. Secretary-General Waldheim followed the Security Council deliberations closely, and he was in touch with U.S. secretary of state Henry Kissinger and senior Soviet officials. On 11 October, he appealed to Security Council members to "re-double their efforts" while he continued intensive consultations with all concerned.[22]

A Security Council meeting on 12 October did not make any headway in resolving the crisis. As the situation evolved, the United States airlifted arms to Israel and the Arab countries used the oil weapon. After consultations between Kissinger and Leonid Brezhnev in Moscow, the United States and the Soviet Union urgently requested a meeting of the Security Council to consider a draft resolution they had co-sponsored. The council met on 21 October. Resolution 338 was adopted unanimously on 22 October, calling for a cease-fire within twelve hours in the positions then held by the parties, immediate implementation of Security Council resolution 242 (1967), and negotiations to establish a just and durable peace. Resolution 242 called for the withdrawal of Israeli armed forces from territories occupied in the conflict; termination of all claims of belligerency; respect for and acknowledgement of the sovereignty, territorial integrity, and political independence of every state in the area; the right of those states to live in peace within secure borders; and a just resolution of the refugee problem.

On 23 October, the Security Council reiterated resolution 338 and urged the parties to return to positions at the time it took effect (22 October). The

Security Council called on the Secretary-General for UN observers to supervise the cease-fire, for which the Secretary-General had already made contingency preparations.

The United States was concerned about the possibility that the Soviet Union would insert forces in Egypt and was determined to prevent this. It placed its forces, including its nuclear forces, on high military alert during the night of 24 October. It also warned of grave consequences if Soviet forces were inserted in Egypt. A dangerous face-off, with the possibility of resort to nuclear weapons, took place over the next two days.

Meanwhile, cease-fire violations continued on the ground. On 25 October, on the initiative of nonaligned states, the Security Council adopted resolution 340, demanding a complete cease-fire and a return of both sides to positions of 22 October at 4:50 PM. The council requested an increase in the number of UN observers and set up UNEF and the UN Truce Supervision Organization, an observer group.

Nonetheless, some breaches of the cease-fire continued, and forces were not withdrawn in accordance with Security Council demands. On 11 November, an agreement, supported by Kissinger, was signed at kilometer 101 of the Cairo-Suez Road, providing for strict observance of the cease-fire, nonmilitary supplies for the Egyptian town of Suez, evacuation of wounded civilians, and immediate discussions "to settle the question of the return to the 22 October positions in the framework of agreement on the disengagement and separation of forces under the auspices of the United Nations."[23]

UN checkpoints were established on 15 November, and wounded and prisoners of war were exchanged, but Israel would not contemplate a return to the position of 22 October. On 21 December 1973, Secretary-General Waldheim opened the Geneva Conference on the Middle East, which had been arranged by the United States and the Soviet Union. Egypt, Israel, and Jordan attended, although Syria did not. The Secretary-General pointed out that the return to the 22 October position, which resolution 338 had called for, had not occurred.

Subsequently, a disengagement agreement was reached and signed at kilometer 101 on 18 January 1974 with the UNEF commander general Silasvuo signing as witness. In the agreement, Israel agreed to withdraw across the canal and three parallel strips of six miles were created on the East Bank, with Egyptians nearest the canal, a UNEF buffer in the middle zone, and the Israelis in the eastern strip. The arms and forces in the Egyptian and Israeli strips were to be limited and subject to inspection by UNEF. The plan detailing disengagements was signed on 24 January with provision for the exercise to be completed within forty days. As the disengagement phases progressed, UNEF took over each area for a short period. The process was completed on 4 March 1974.

The parties to the conflict signed a disengagement agreement in Geneva on 31 May 1974, providing for a cease-fire, repatriation of all wounded and prisoners of war, establishment of a UN buffer zone in part of the Golan Heights, and a working group, presided over by General Silasvuo, to work out the details of disengagement. Under a protocol, Israel and Syria agreed to support a Security Council resolution establishing a United Nations Disengagement Force (UNDOF) of 1,250 men for six months. Following Security Council approval, disengagement was put into effect and completed by 25 June, with UNDOF acting as a buffer.

The UN played the leading role in negotiating the disengagement agreement of 18 January 1974; Commander General Silasvuo and Political Affairs officer James Jonah were the architects of the agreement.[24] These UN operatives also played a leading role in the subsequent establishment of UNDOF, which established a buffer zone between Israel and Syria. Without a doubt, these and other UN efforts helped contain the situation and prevent its deterioration. UN peacekeepers and observers acted as a stabilizing and deterrent influence for several years. UN peacekeeping combined with UN peacemaking to resolve conflict and prevent conflict.

As mentioned earlier, on 11 October, Secretary-General Waldheim appealed to Security Council members to redouble their efforts to deal with the situation. The Secretary-General was in a delicate position. Kissinger was undoubtedly the point person in dealing with the crisis, and the Secretary-General lacked the power assets of the American in addressing such circumstances. Even in considering an appeal, the Secretary-General was in a fragile situation. He did, however, make the appeal and led the UN's preparations for deploying peacekeepers and observers. He played the best hand he could.

In 2003, Kissinger published a book that reproduced State Department records of two telephone conversations he had with Waldheim during the crisis. Excerpts from these two conversations are quoted below.

Waldheim and Kissinger
Wednesday, October 10, 1973, 8:27 PM

W: I am sorry to disturb you but I thought I should inform you about the situation here. . . . Zayat informed the Nonaligned countries not to do—to avoid any resolution in the Security Council because they wanted to continue fighting and any resolution would prevent this. That is why the Nonaligned did not insist on working on a draft resolution. As you know, the Israelis are not interested in having a resolution. I talked to Eban and he told me that the Council debate cannot continue. . . .

[. . .]

W: . . . [T]he situation here is that both sides don't want a resolution. They don't want a cease-fire because both think they will gain. . . .

W: I hope to give a brief statement to all parties about stopping the fighting.

K: Let's see what the situation is and I will give you my judgment.

W: I would appreciate it if you could let me know what you are feeling.

K: You're not bound by my views but why don't we talk in the morning?

W: More and more people . . . are asking me what is the Secretary (-General) doing to stop the fighting—why is the Secretary (-General) not trying to stop the fighting and get them back to the negotiating table. That's the psychological background.

K: I understand and I am not objecting. I thought if I could give you my view and then you could do what you want.

W: I am very grateful and I understand. My impression is that they are not interested in doing anything against (the) wish of (the) Arab countries. And I am very worried about the message from Brezhnev to (unclear) and the airlift to Syria is very dangerous—dangerous developments.

K: We agree and we're saying something about this tomorrow.

W: Thank you very much.

K: Please stay in touch and I will take the liberty of contacting you in the morning.[25]

Kissinger was certainly courteous and proper in dealing with the Secretary-General. But one cannot help feeling sympathy for Waldheim, who had few assets at his disposal. Even as he felt the moral need to make an appeal, he needed to make sure that he did not cross the leading power broker in the game. These excerpts provide a vivid picture of the room for maneuver, or lack of it, of a Secretary-General. Kissinger's courtesy would again be seen in the second telephone conversation.

The background to the second conversation is as follows: discussions were under way in the Security Council on the composition of a UN force, and there were objections to the idea that Canada, Eastern European countries, and permanent members of the Security Council would provide troops.

Waldheim-Kissinger
Thursday October 25, 1973, 1:18 PM

W: I am very grateful for (your) returning the call. . . . The situation is that, as you know, the Russians got instructions to accept the new American amendment [which sought to exclude permanent members of the Security Council from providing troops for the force]. Only the French position is reluctant. The

French Ambassador was just here and he said they would ask for a separate vote on the amendment—excludes permanent members. They will vote for the resolution, but ask for (a) separate vote on the amendment in order to show they are not in agreement with this.

K: You are in no doubt, Mr. Secretary-General, that we will veto any resolution which doesn't have it in it?

W: Yes, I was informed of this by Joe Sisco.

K: We will not compromise on this.

W: Yes, that is understood. No problem. . . .

K: Excellent. There is one thing that concerns me, Mr. Secretary-General. We are fundamentally opposed to the introduction of any East European contingents, any Communist countries. There must be enough neutrals in the world to do it. If there were Eastern European countries, it would produce a crisis of confidence here, if any contingents from Communist countries were included.

[. . .]

W: [. . .] I take note of your information and I hope we can proceed on that line.

K: Mr. Secretary-General, when this is all over, and I hope it will be soon, you and I must have a drink together and reminisce.[26]

Again, this conversation illustrates the power realities that a Secretary-General must deal with even as he tries to help contain a dangerous situation. Perhaps these excerpts demonstrate that expectations of the preventive diplomacy role of the Secretary-General must be modest, especially where the great powers are involved.

Even if Waldheim's room for maneuver was restricted, he contributed significantly to managing this crisis. He played an especially important role when it came to preparations for deploying UN peacekeepers. As already mentioned, on 25 October 1973, the Security Council adopted resolution 340 (1973), which asked the Secretary-General to immediately increase the number of UN military observers on both sides and immediately set up a second United Nations Emergency Force (UNEF II) under its authority to be composed of personnel drawn from member states (except the permanent members of the Security Council). It requested the Secretary-General to report within twenty-four hours on the steps taken to that effect.

Immediately after the resolution was adopted, the Secretary-General addressed a letter to the Security Council president, indicating that he would produce the requested report urgently.[27] In the meantime, he proposed to arrange for units of the Austrian, Finnish, and Swedish contingents serving with the United Nations Peacekeeping Force in Cyprus to proceed immediately to Egypt so the emergency force could reach the area of conflict as soon as possible. The Security Council supported the Secretary-General's approach.

In his report to the Security Council, the Secretary-General set out the proposed principles and guidelines for the emergency force.[28] Three essential conditions would have to be met for the force to be effective. First, it needed to have the Security Council's full confidence and backing. Second, it needed to operate with the full cooperation of the parties concerned. Third, it needed to be able to function as an integrated and efficient military unit.

The mandate of UNEF II was to supervise the implementation of Security Council resolution 340 (1973). The force was to use its best efforts to prevent a recurrence of the fighting. Its immediate objective was to help stop the fighting and prevent all movement forward of the troops on both sides. Urgent measures also had to be taken to provide Suez City and the Egyptian third army, which was trapped on the East Bank of the Suez Canal, with nonmilitary supplies.

Troops from Austria, Finland, Sweden, and, later, Ireland, were dispatched to the front line as soon as they arrived and interposed themselves whenever possible between the forward positions of the opposing forces. Observation posts and checkpoints were set up, and patrols were undertaken in sensitive areas.

A meeting between high-level military representatives of Egypt and Israel took place in the presence of UNEF representatives on 27 October 1973 at kilometer 109 on the Cairo-Suez Road to discuss the cease-fire and various humanitarian questions. At this meeting, preliminary arrangements were made to dispatch nonmilitary supplies to Suez and the Egyptian third army. In accordance with these arrangements, convoys of lorries driven by UNEF II personnel were organized under the supervision of the force and the International Committee of the Red Cross to bring nonmilitary supplies through the Israeli-held territory to Suez and the Egyptian third army.

UNEF II organized further meetings to discuss the return of forces of the two parties to the positions they had occupied on 22 October and possible mutual disengagement and the establishment of buffer zones to be manned by UNEF II. Kissinger helped facilitate agreement on these matters during his visits to Egypt and Israel. He transmitted the results of his efforts to Secretary-General Waldheim on 9 November, and on 11 November the Secretary-General requested General Silasvuo to take the necessary measures and make his good offices available to the two sides.

On 11 November, at kilometer 101 on the Cairo-Suez Road, an agreement was signed by Major-General Mohamed El-Gamasy of Egypt and

Major-General Ahron Yaariv of Israel. It was also signed by General Silas-vuo on behalf of the United Nations. The Kilometer 101 Agreement, which entered into force immediately, consisted of six points. First, Egypt and Israel agreed to observe the cease-fire the Security Council had called for. Second, both sides agreed to immediate discussions to settle the question of the return to the 22 October positions. Third, the town of Suez would receive daily supplies of food, water, and medicine, and all wounded civilians in the town would be evacuated. Fourth, there would be no impediment to the movement of nonmilitary supplies to the East Bank. Fifth, the Israeli checkpoints on the Cairo-Suez Road would be replaced by UN checkpoints. Sixth, as soon as these checkpoints were established on the road, all prisoners of war, including wounded, would be exchanged.

This detailed account of the events illustrates the UN in action in a dangerous situation. The lead role in the resolution of the crisis was played by others, but UN personnel were able to avert the escalation of conflict and help manage the details on the ground.

U.S. Hostages in Tehran, 1979: The dispute between Iran and the United States following the Iranian takeover of the American embassy in Tehran was complex and dangerous. The American effort to rescue the hostages through a military operation failed and led to the resignation of U.S. secretary of state Cyrus Vance. The dispute was eventually ameliorated through political methods, notably a deal between the Iranian government and a team of presidential candidate Ronald Reagan. In many ways, the effects of the dispute are still being felt, namely the animosities between the two countries and the current controversy over Iran's alleged pursuit of nuclear weapons.

In the heat of the crisis, Secretary-General Waldheim attempted to defuse the situation. He personally visited Tehran and had a harrowing experience there, during which he felt that his life was in danger. He established a commission to inquire into Iranian grievances, particularly over gross violations of human rights during the shah's regime, and generally sought to do whatever he could to contain the situation and prevent it from escalating.

Waldheim's efforts in this case were not decisive, but they did help calm the situation by being seen to respond to Iranian concerns. The new revolutionary regime was critical not only of the United States but also of the UN for its failure to deal with gross violations of human rights committed under the shah's rule. Waldheim's establishment of the Commission of Inquiry responded to that resentment. Secretariat staff scrambled to gather whatever information they could in the files regarding violations committed during the shah's rule. The commission was rapidly set up and moved into action to illustrate to the new Iranian regime that its concerns were being addressed. When the commission visited Geneva, even its internal methods of work had not been established. The situation was very heated. Secretary-General Waldheim's role in this crisis was not critical, but it was helpful in mitigating tension on the Iranian side by demonstrating the UN's willingness to investigate into a key area of concern within its mandate.[29] Secretary-General Waldheim sought to placate them by establishing the commission, illustrating that the world was body responsive.

Falklands/Malvinas, 1982: At the outset of the war between Argentina and the United Kingdom over the Falkland/Malvinas Islands, U.S. secretary of state Alexander Haig took the lead in seeking to head off a full-blown military confrontation. Secretary-General Pérez de Cuéllar acknowledged the lead role of the United States but was always ready to play a part in helping head off the crisis.

Within the Secretariat, active work was undertaken to prepare options and avenues for the Secretary-General. Careful diplomatic work by Pérez de Cuéllar led to a peace plan that the United Kingdom accepted. But Argentina did not, and the situation escalated to war. Marrack Goulding, a British participant in the talks, has documented Pérez de Cuéllar's efforts.[30]

Secretary-General Pérez de Cuéllar provided a detailed account of his efforts in his memoir:

> Two critical points in my good offices endeavor opened the way to a peaceful settlement. The first was the decision of Argentina not to make agreement dependent on recognition of Argentine sovereignty over the Falklands; the second was British acceptance of an interim administration of the Falklands under a UN Administrator. UN administration would mean the flying of the blue UN flag as the symbol of the Falklands government. . . . [Had] there been more time . . . I myself might have gone to Argentina to increase the leaders' understanding of the value of the proffered agreement. . . . The shortness of time was a fatal enemy.[31]

Bulgaria-Turkey, 1989: In the summer of 1989, a tense situation emerged between Bulgaria and Turkey, and there was a distinct possibility that Turkey would take military action against Bulgaria. Bulgaria had expelled some 300,000 Bulgarian nationals of Turkish ethnic origin to Turkey. Those expelled included mainly women and elderly men; men of military age were retained in Bulgaria. Secretary-General Pérez de Cuéllar established a discreet fact-finding mission to Bulgaria and Turkey led by Assistant Secretary-General James Jonah. This mission was one of the earliest preventive diplomacy missions undertaken within the framework of Pérez de Cuéllar's policy of giving priority to conflict prevention.

In letters dated 16 August 1989 to the permanent representative of Bulgaria and to the chargé d'affaires of the permanent mission of Turkey, the Secretary-General informed them that the mission's task would be:

> to collect and determine the facts with regard to the recent large-scale movement of persons from Bulgaria into Turkey as well as the circumstances surrounding this movement; to ascertain from the Governments of Bulgaria and Turkey the steps they have taken to tackle this situation; and to determine the views of the two Governments as to how the tensions which have emerged as a consequence of this situation may be lessened.[32]

The two governments agreed to receive the mission on these terms. The mission examined the materials that the Secretary-General had earlier received from the two governments and also took into account information obtained from various parts of the UN system. Following its visit to the two countries, the mission submitted a report recommending that the Secretary-General pursue further contacts with the parties. The mission recommended that the Secretary-General help by using his good offices to begin bilateral discussions between the two sides.

The mission emphasized that neither party wanted to lose face over the issues of the agenda and the format of talks between them. The mission suggested that it might be helpful in the Secretary-General's future contacts with the two sides to further explore their thinking on how to reconcile their respective positions on the agenda and format of talks and to use his good offices to promote such bilateral talks.

The mission recalled that the International Covenant on Civil and Political Rights covered the rights of persons belonging to minorities. Bulgaria was a party to this covenant, although Turkey was not. However, Turkey had specifically invoked Article 27 of the covenant in its submissions to the mission and therefore seemed to accept it as a reference point.

The mission recommended that an agenda along the following lines might be explored to meet the two sides' concerns:

> Issues, as appropriate, affecting the exercise by persons belonging to ethnic, religious or linguistic minorities of their right, in community with the other members of their group, to enjoy their own culture, to profess and practice their own religion, or to use their own language.[33]

After the Secretary-General received the report, he began further contacts with the two parties and with the Kuwaiti government, which, in the context of efforts by the Organization of the Islamic Conference, was also seeking to help defuse the issue. The dispute was resolved through these efforts. The Secretary-General's designation of a discreet fact-finding mission and the preventive diplomacy of Assistant-Secretary-General Jonah gained time and helped the parties identify options for resolving the dispute.

South Africa, 1992: As South Africa tackled the dismantling of the apartheid regime and the introduction of democratic governance, the struggle for ascendancy among its political parties presented serious dangers of a descent into anarchy and violence. One such moment occurred in July–August 1992, and the dispatch of UN observers within a matter of a few days helped prevent violent clashes between competing political protagonists.

In certain areas of South Africa, such as KwaZulu-Natal, there was stiff competition between the African National Congress (ANC), led by Nelson Mandela, and the Inkatha Freedom Party (IFP), led by Chief Mangosuthu Buthelezi. The backdrop was Mandela's recent release from prison and South Africa's march to democratic elections. In an effort to show that it was a broad-based political movement and with a view to bolstering its support in KwaZulu-Natal, Buthelezi's home ground, the ANC called for a week of mass action demonstrations throughout the country.

Frederick de Klerk was still in power as president of South Africa, and he and Nelson Mandela were negotiating a political accommodation that would eventually lead to free elections. Fearing the possibility of clashes during the ANC's mass action campaign, Mandela and de Klerk requested Secretary-General Boutros-Ghali to send UN observers to watch over the mass action campaign. Within a matter of days, Boutros-Ghali sent a ten-member team to South Africa.

Part of the team was assigned to observe the exceedingly violent KwaZulu-Natal area, but it had no guidance, no backup, no equipment, and no UN symbols such as flags and insignia. The team made observations by helicopter, a van, personal visits, and through meetings with groups. The daily observation team consisted of five persons: the author of this book, a member of the regional secretariat of the National Peace Accord (NPA), and NPA regional committee members, one each from the South African police, the ANC and the IFP. The ANC member was Jeff Radebe, who had been imprisoned on Robben Island with Nelson Mandela and who subsequently became a government minister. The IFP member was Thomas Shabalala, a militant activist. The South African police member was Captain James Lourens, a professional and brave South African.

The team visited Durban and its townships, Pietermaritzburg and its townships, Empangeni and outlying regions of Durban such as Esikhawini (a place of multiple killings), Ngwelezane, and Kwamsane. During the week, the team visited numerous places of violent action—buses that had been stoned, houses that had been petrol-bombed or were riddled with bullets, cars that were riddled with bullets, and barricades that had been burned or were on fire. Many people were injured during shootings (including one infant who was shot in the leg); in some places over twenty murders occurred during the night.

The team had meetings with groups of chiefs, ANC regional groups, IFP regional groups, and rural groups in various villages. Despite constant tussles, the mission ended harmoniously, with good personal relations on all sides. Both the ANC and IFP representatives thought that the UN should return to the region (which it did). There was no political residue or fallout, and there was deep appreciation for the assistance of the UN on the part of all. The urgent dispatch of UN observers had, without a doubt, helped prevent violent clashes as the ANC pressed ahead with its mass action campaign.

Eritrea-Yemen, 1995–1996: A model case of conflict prevention that involved practically all of the UN's facets of preventive diplomacy took place in August of 1996 when Eritrea and Yemen, which had clashed in December 1995, were on the brink of resuming armed hostilities over the Hanish Islands, which both countries claimed.[34]

In 1995, Secretary-General Boutros-Ghali engaged in strong personal efforts to turn the situation around. He flew to Yemen for conversations with its president, focusing on the search for a peaceful settlement procedure. He also angled for mediation by a major power. The president of Yemen accepted and expressed a preference for French mediation.

Secretary-General Boutros-Ghali then flew to Asmara for conversations with the Eritrean president. He persuaded him to accept mediation by a major power and, without telling him that the Yemeni president had expressed his preference for French mediation, steered him in the direction of French mediation. The president of Eritrea agreed.

When Boutros-Ghali approached the French Ministry of Foreign Affairs, high-level officials were reluctant to become involved, and Boutros-Ghali approached President François Mitterrand personally. The latter agreed to French involvement, and eventually the Secretary-General of the French Foreign Ministry shuttled between the two sides. He secured an agreement from Eritrea and Yemen to refer the dispute over the Hanish Islands to arbitration.[35]

The following year, on 21 May 1996, an agreement was signed in Paris between Eritrea and Yemen, and Secretary-General Boutros-Ghali transmitted the text to the Security Council on 19 June 1996.[36] The agreement required both parties to renounce the use of force and settle their dispute peacefully. They decided to establish an arbitral tribunal and agreed to abide by the tribunal's decision. They also undertook the following specific commitment: "Each Party shall refrain from any form of military activity or movement against the other Party. This commitment shall remain in force until the execution of the final decision of the Tribunal."[37]

On 12 August 1996, the parties were on the verge of resumption of war. That day, Boutros-Ghali's office received an urgent letter from the foreign minister of Yemen informing him that Eritrean troops had been seen on 10 August entering Yemeni territorial waters en route to the Lesser Hanish Island. The Yemeni government had informed the French government of this, pursuant to Article 5 of the agreement of 21 May 1996 between the two countries, and asked the Secretary-General to use his good offices to return the situation to what it had been on 10 August. On 12 August, the Secretary-General also received information from the French permanent mission that indicated that Eritrean armed elements had been observed en route to and on the Lesser Hanish Island. The French authorities kept the Secretary-General informed about the situation.

The Yemeni government informed the Secretary-General that unless Eritrean troops were withdrawn, it would move to expel them militarily within twenty-four hours. Boutros-Ghali, who was away from headquarters, requested Under-Secretary-General Kittani to immediately make contact with the permanent representatives of Eritrea and Yemen; the UN needed updated information about what was actually taking place on the ground. On 13 August, Kittani met with the chargé d'affaires of the Eritrean permanent mission. The following day he met with the permanent representative of Yemen and with the chargé d'affaires of the Ethiopian permanent mission.

On 14 August, Secretary-General Boutros-Ghali addressed identical letters to the presidents of Eritrea and Yemen that conveyed the following information:

- On 13 August, about fifty Eritrean nationals had been observed on Lesser Hanish Island, which had previously been unoccupied.
- A radio navigation antenna had been installed by Eritrea between 7 and 11 August 1996 on another of the disputed islands, Law Island.
- Eritrean vessels had been observed en route to Lesser Hanish Island.

The Secretary-General urgently appealed to the presidents of the two countries to exercise the utmost restraint and to cooperate fully with French authorities to address these developments so that efforts to implement the agreement of 21 May would not be affected. The Secretary-General wrote to each president: "I should like to appeal to Your Excellency to exercise maximum restraint in the situation and to facilitate efforts to normalize the situation."[38]

On 15 August, the Secretary-General spoke to the president of Yemen by telephone and appealed for maximum restraint. The same day, the Secretary-General tried unsuccessfully to reach the president of Eritrea by telephone. At the request of the Secretary-General, Under-Secretary-General Kittani met with the ambassadors of Egypt and Ethiopia, co-signatories of the 21 May agreement, requesting them to use their influence to resolve the situation peacefully.

On 15 August, Ambassador Gnehm of the U.S. permanent mission contacted Under-Secretary-General Kittani and told him that the United States supported the French efforts and was making its own effort in support. Under-Secretary-General Kittani briefed Ambassador Gnehm on the efforts of the Secretary-General. On 15 August, the French authorities informed the Secretary-General that they had again spoken to the president of Yemen, who had told them that the situation was extremely serious and that Yemen would use force to expel the Eritreans if they were not out of Lesser Hanish Island by 17 August.

On 15 August 1996, the Secretary-General issued the following statement:

> Secretary-General Boutros Boutros-Ghali has been following the situation between Eritrea and Yemen closely. The Officer-in-Charge of the Department of Political Affairs, Ismat Kittani, has held a series of meetings with representatives of Eritrea and Yemen, as well as that of France, during the past three days.
>
> The Secretary-General supports the diplomatic efforts that France is currently undertaking at both capitals. Yesterday, he also addressed letters to the Presidents of Eritrea and of Yemen, in which he appealed for maximum restraint on both sides and appealed for their full cooperation in order to calm the situation and to facilitate the implementation of the agreement of 21 May, in letter and spirit.[39]

In the afternoon of 16 August, Assistant Secretary-General Rosario Green briefed the Security Council in informal consultations. Following the briefing, council members agreed that the council president would make a statement to the press containing the following points:

- The Security Council has been briefed by the representative of the Secretary-General on the latest developments in the Red Sea and appreciated the efforts being deployed by the Secretary-General and his staff.

• The Security Council notes that Lesser Hanish Island has been occupied by the Eritrean armed forces.

• Council members are concerned by these developments and call on the two parties to abide by the 21 May agreement, which obligates them not to use force.

• The council members call on the two parties to exercise the utmost restraint and refrain from the use of force and to take advantage of the mediation efforts being offered by the international community, in particular France.

• The Security Council urges the two parties to return to the status quo ante, and it is closely following further developments.

• The Security Council members request the president to call in representatives of the two countries.[40]

German ambassador Tono Eitel, president of the Security Council, conveyed these points to the media after the meeting.

As requested by council members, Ambassador Eitel met that same evening, 16 August, with the deputy permanent representatives of Eritrea and Yemen. He informed them about the developments on Lesser Hanish Island and expressed the council's grave concern and its decision to meet on short notice if the situation necessitated that. He urged both sides to take advantage of the forthcoming visit of the French envoy, Ambassador Gutman, to Asmara and to Sanaa on 17 August and told them that the council was giving Ambassador Gutman its full support.

In his meeting with the deputy permanent representative of Eritrea, Ambassador Eitel especially underlined the demand—which he directed to both representatives—to reestablish the status quo. In his meeting with the deputy permanent representative of Yemen, he especially underlined the demand—also directed to both representatives—to refrain from using force after the deadline of the ultimatum of 17 August, 2:00 AM local time, which had been set by the Yemeni government.

Mindful of the efforts of the Secretary-General and the Security Council, and acting within the framework of the agreement of 21 May, Ambassador Gutman shuttled between the two countries. On 19 August, the French Foreign Ministry confirmed that Eritrea had agreed to withdraw from Lesser Hanish Island to avoid further conflict. Secretary-General Boutros-Ghali's spokesman noted that he "welcomed the fact that the tension which had arisen between Yemen and Eritrea during the past week had been defused" and thanked Ambassador Gutman for his mediation efforts.[41] Secretary-General Boutros-Ghali hoped that both sides would continue to respect the agreement of 21 May. French mediation efforts continued, and eventually an arbitration commission was established to decide the fate of the Hanish Islands. The arbitration eventually awarded the disputed islands to Yemen, although it recognized the historic rights of fishermen in the adjacent waters. The dispute was thus peacefully resolved.

The dispute between Eritrea and Yemen over the Hanish Islands was on the verge of erupting into war. The Secretary-General, his senior officials, the Security Council, its president, and the French mediator all contributed to preventing war. Under-Secretary-General Kittani presented the matter to the representatives of the two countries very carefully. The Secretary-General acted behind the scenes through personal contacts and in letters to the presidents of the two countries. In addition, the Secretary-General and the president of the Security Council made public statements to urge restraint on the parties. Major powers supported all of these efforts. Together, these actions succeeded in preventing the outbreak of war.

Cameroon-Nigeria, 2002: Nigeria and Cameroon share a 1,600-kilometer land boundary.[42] In 1981, the two neighbors were on the brink of war over ownership of the Bakassi Peninsula, which forms the border area between the two countries. Armed clashes recurred in the early 1990s, and Cameroon responded by taking the matter to the International Court of Justice on 29 March 1994.[43]

Anticipating the court's decision, Secretary-General Annan invited the presidents of both countries to a meeting in Paris on 5 September 2002. At that meeting, Annan secured a commitment from Presidents Paul Biya and Olusegun Obasanjo to respect and implement the court's judgment. He also obtained their agreement to establish a mechanism to implement the decision. The two presidents recognized that the border dispute needed to be seen in the "wider context of the overall relationship" between the two countries.[44] The Secretary-General made sure that the United States, Britain, and France were on board with his initiative.

The court handed down its judgment on 10 October 2002, finding that sovereignty over Bakassi rested with Cameroon.[45] It asked Nigeria to withdraw its administration and forces and to transfer possession of the peninsula to Cameroon. Simultaneously, the court asked Cameroon to withdraw its administration and forces from areas that, in terms of the judgment, fell within the sovereignty of Nigeria.

The verdict occasioned sharp comments from Nigerian officials and commentators alike. The situation was tense, and there was a distinct danger of a clash between the two countries. However, the government of Nigeria did not reject the judgment, instead calling for an agreement that would provide peace with honor. The Secretary-General, meanwhile, reiterated his call on both parties to respect and implement the court's decision, and he reaffirmed his readiness to assist the two countries.[46]

Once again, Secretary-General Annan called the two presidents to meet him, this time in Geneva. At a meeting on 15 November, the two leaders agreed to ask the Secretary-General to establish a Cameroon-Nigeria mixed commission that was comprised of representatives of the two countries and was chaired by a representative of the Secretary-General, Ahmedou Ould-Abdallah, to consider ways of following up on the court's ruling and moving the process forward. Both parties also agreed to identify a number of confidence-building measures.[47]

The commission's mandate covered:

- Demarcation of the land boundary
- Withdrawal of civil administration and military and police forces and the transfer of authority
- Eventual demilitarization of the Bakassi Peninsula
- Protection of the rights of the affected population
- Promotion of joint economic ventures
- Reactivation of the Lake Chad Basin Commission[48]

The commission's first meeting took place in Yaounde on 1 December 2002, with several other meetings following. The parties agreed to reestablish the Lake Chad Basin Commission.[49] The commission established two subcommissions and four working groups to carry out various aspects of its work, which was based in Dakar, Senegal.

The commission also began making field visits to the land boundary, and it decided to deploy its observer personnel group in the area, which would provide a report one month after the final handover. The observers were provided by both Cameroon and Nigeria.[50]

The first and second phases of the commission's work were completed on 18 December 2003 and July 2004, when both countries completed their withdrawal of civil administration and military and police forces in the Lake Chad and the land boundary areas. A UN civilian observer team was deployed in the two areas to ascertain the transfer of authority and observe that the rights of the affected populations were protected. At the same time, relations between Chad and Nigeria continued to improve, and cordial relations were established between the two leaders through visits to each other's capitals. The commission also made progress that included the demarcation of the land boundary between the two countries and issues related to the protection of the rights of the affected population.[51] The commission also addressed the question of the maritime boundary.[52] In January 2004, just over one month after the withdrawal from the Lake Chad area, the two presidents met the Secretary-General in Geneva to review progress. They agreed to consider a treaty of friendship and nonaggression.[53]

The good offices process functioned along two tracks: the political work undertaken by the Secretary-General and the chair of the commission and the more procedural track manifested in the technical work of the commission. The process was rewarded with success when Nigeria completed its withdrawal from the Bakassi Peninsula in 2006. The preventive diplomacy of Secretary-General Annan had been used to good effect.

Public Controversy and Quiet Diplomacy

Secretary-General Lie's public criticism of what he considered to be communist aggression during the Korean War had negative consequences, ultimately ending his effectiveness at the United Nations. Subsequent Secretaries-General have also been criticized for taking certain positions. Hammarskjöld was criticized by the Soviet Union, unfairly in the light of history, for his handling of the Congo crisis. U Thant was criticized by the United States for some of his stances on the Vietnam War. Secretaries-General Waldheim and Pérez de Cuéllar, careful diplomatic operators, did not suffer much open criticism for their public positions. But Secretary-General Boutros-Ghali came under fire from the United States because of his strong stances on some issues and was eventually pushed out from office. Issues of policy and public controversy were at the root of his difficulties. In his second term, Secretary-General Annan came under severe criticism on a variety of grounds, as is discussed later. How does public controversy affect quiet diplomacy by the Secretary-General? This question was put directly to Secretary-General Hammarskjöld.

At a press conference on 29 May 1961, a reporter asked him:

> Sir, in recent months, we have had, just checking the record, a plethora of charges and accusations in this building, some of them directed against yourself. To some extent we can ascertain the effect these charges and accusations may have on the solution of a problem, by the past developments and what is yet to come. But I am curious for some information, some indication, concerning the extent to which these charges and accusations affect the day-to-day operations of quiet diplomacy.[54]

Hammarskjöld replied:

> If the question is put in the way you now put it, I would say that such accusa-
> tions, etc., do not affect quiet diplomacy at all. All the contacts I have to pursue
> have been pursued in very much the same atmosphere, in very much the same
> way as if we had not had the discussions in public which have been going on. As
> to the day-to-day work, I think you can see very clearly that this kind of debate
> takes a lot of time from other tasks, because you must reply, you must do this,
> you should do that because of it. But, otherwise, I do not think that you should
> fear that it influences either the direction of action or the spirit in which action
> is undertaken.[55]

The reporter persisted:

> To pursue just one point further, when public opinion in a particular country
> seems influenced by these matters, does it not have some sort of effect on the
> position and the problems of the diplomats with whom you must discuss these
> problems?[56]

Hammarskjöld answered:

> I would say less than you believe, because public opinion and direct private
> diplomacy are somewhat separate. There is a more stable trend in diplomacy
> than you can have in public opinion, which may be carried away by emotion or
> carried away by propaganda statements which do not apply behind closed
> doors.[57]

Hammarskjöld was attacked on policies and positions. U Thant also
came under fire for the positions he took on the Vietnam War. But these
were disagreements on issues of policy. In Annan's case, the problems went
beyond policy. After a smooth first term, Annan found himself caught up in
controversies prior to and after the invasion of Iraq in his second term.
Eventually he declared the invasion illegal. Around this period, scandals
emerged concerning the administration of the UN Oil-for-Food Programme and in the UN Procurement Office. Annan and a close member of
his family came under scrutiny in the media, and Annan was publicly criticized by the Volcker reports for serious mismanagement of the Oil-for-
Food Programme.[58] On 10 March 2006, the UN's staff council passed a motion of no confidence in him and his administration.[59]

How might all of this have affected the Secretary-General's capacity to
engage in preventive diplomacy? Trust and confidence in the UN's leader
are crucial for the discharge of his functions regarding the maintenance of
international peace and security.[60] The available evidence suggests that

Annan continued to exercise good offices to contain or prevent conflicts in situations involving Third World countries. We recounted his successful efforts on the Cameroon-Nigeria situation. In the aftermath of the Israeli counterattacks on Hezbollah and Lebanon in the summer of 2006, he made intensive efforts to help stabilize the situation and put together the building blocks of peace. His efforts were appreciated.

Yet his leadership style at the UN itself raises other questions. During his tenure, Annan sought to lead through a series of public reports on UN reforms and other topics, sometimes advancing proposals on which the membership had not been consulted beforehand and on which there were widely differing views. The membership had to grapple with his proposals after they were published. The Secretary-General came out explicitly in favor of humanitarian intervention. He led the charge to abolish the Commission on Human Rights and replace it with the Human Rights Council,[61] which came under critical scrutiny once it began functioning. No Secretary-General before Annan sought to prescribe policy to the membership to such an extent. Prescription followed prescription during his ten-year tenure. It was an era of permanent reform proposals. It may have been bold, but was it wise?

An important policy issue is involved here: Should a Secretary-General seek to lead and advance ideas after contacts, consultations, and careful diplomacy or through public statements or reports launched, in many instances, without prior consultation with the membership? Further, the Secretary-General who repeatedly criticizes the membership needs to be in a position to command respect and trust to exercise influence on the issues or situations of the day. Where is the balance point between public leadership and considered diplomacy? This question requires careful reflection. The Secretary-General must always strive to be wise even while being principled.

5

Preventive Diplomacy during the Cuban Missile Crisis

The Cuban missile crisis created an unprecedented danger, a first in the UN's history. President Kennedy was particularly concerned about the danger of a miscalculation or a mistake in judgment by either side. Even after he ordered a naval quarantine of Cuba, he sought to avoid physical contact between American and Soviet vessels to keep open the possibility of a negotiated solution.[1] When, at one stage, there was a danger of a clash with a Russian submarine, he asked, "Isn't there some way we can avoid having our first exchange with a Russian submarine—almost anything but that?"[2] At a particularly dangerous moment, he turned to U Thant to buy twenty-four to forty-eight hours of accident-free negotiating time.

U Thant believed in preventive diplomacy, which he saw as the exercise of good offices to settle disputes or difficulties at the request of the states concerned, even without specific authorization from the Security Council or the General Assembly: "I believed," he wrote, "that preventive diplomacy of this kind is far more effective—and incidentally much cheaper—than attempting to resolve a conflict that has been allowed to reach an acute stage."[3] He placed a premium on total discretion on the part of the Secretary-General and the cooperation, restraint, and good will of the parties concerned.

For him, two considerations were key in matters relating to international peace and security. First, the Secretary-General must always be prepared to take an initiative if he believes this might mean the difference between peace and war. Second, the Secretary-General must maintain an independent position.[4]

The Timeline of the Cuban Missile Crisis

The heart of the Cuban missile crisis lasted from 16 to 28 October 1962. President Kennedy addressed the nation on 22 October, announcing that he had ordered a naval quarantine around Cuba that would come into force on 24 October. The Organization of American States (OAS) convened in Washington on 23 October and unanimously resolved that "the Member States . . . take all measures individually and collectively, including the use of armed force, which they may deem necessary to ensure that the Government of Cuba cannot continue to receive from the Sino-Soviet powers military material and related supplies which may threaten the peace and security of the Continent."[5]

U Thant first heard of the impending crisis on 20 October from his military adviser, who probably had picked it up from the U.S. permanent mission. His main source of information was the media. At the request of Cuba and the United States, the Security Council convened on the evening of 23 October 1962. U Thant received representatives from several member states on the morning of 24 October. He wrote his first letter to the two sides on his own initiative that day. Prior to the entry into force of the quarantine and following an American idea put to him discreetly behind the scenes, he wrote to the two sides again on 25 October, seeking to obtain an agreement that Soviet vessels would not enter the quarantine area. American and Soviet naval vessels had been in close proximity with a Soviet submarine captain authorized to use nuclear weapons in defense of Soviet ships or in self-defense.[6]

After the Soviets accepted U Thant's second appeal on 26 October, efforts behind the scenes to find a way out of the crisis took place in Washington. Attorney-General Robert Kennedy met with Soviet ambassador Anatoly Dobrynin in Washington, and a Soviet intelligence agent passed messages to the White House through a Washington correspondent.

Premier Khrushchev wrote a hard-line letter to President Kennedy on 26 October. An American plane was shot down over Cuba on 27 October. Khrushchev wrote Kennedy a more conciliatory letter on 27 October, which he followed with another hard-line letter. It was believed that Khrushchev's conciliatory letter was written by himself and that the more formal, harsher letter was written by the collective leadership in the Soviet Union. The contents of Khrushchev's conciliatory letter were broadcast over Radio Moscow on 28 October. In a highly dangerous situation, President Kennedy wrote to Premier Khrushchev accepting the terms of his conciliatory letter as broadcast over Radio Moscow. This effectively defused the crisis.

Premier Fidel Castro had to be brought on board to implement the agreement to dismantle the nuclear installations and weapons and return them to the Soviet Union, and U Thant visited Cuba from 30 to 31 October to discuss implementation issues. American and Soviet representatives met in New York during the fall to discuss these issues, and on 7 January 1963, they wrote to U Thant to say that all matters had been resolved and that the item should be removed from the Security Council's agenda. The letter stated: "On behalf of the Governments of the United States of America and the Soviet Union, we desire to express to you our appreciation for your efforts in assisting our Governments to avert the serious threat to peace which recently arose in the Caribbean area."[7]

Information and Analysis Available to the Secretary-General

U Thant first learned of the missile crisis on 20 October 1962 from his military adviser, General Indar Jit Rikhye, who was probably tipped off by a contact in the U.S. permanent mission. Later that day, the UN representative in Washington, Philip Dean, telephoned to say that something important was brewing in Washington. The resources available to the UN for information-gathering and analysis have always been meager, and this was the case here. In his memoirs, U Thant wrote that the Secretary-General often lacked the first-hand resources of information on which governments could base their plans.[8] He had to act on information and analysis that was publicly available.

The desperate situation of the UN regarding lack of information was painfully brought out in *Eyeball to Eyeball*, Dino Brugioni's account of the Cuban missile crisis. Brugioni, an American security analyst, wrote that neither U Thant nor his military adviser had much idea of where the missile sites were located or even what constituted a missile site. American intelligence experts sent one of their numbers, Colonel Parker, to the UN to brief General Rikhye. Brugioni and his colleagues compiled a three-ring binder containing forty-two aerial photographs, and maps were compiled for this purpose. The U.S. authorities asked Rikhye not to take the binder with him on U Thant's eventual visit to Cuba out of concern that it might fall into the hands of the Cubans or the Russians and reveal to Russia the extent of U.S. knowledge of the military installations in Cuba. Rikhye took aerial photos of the missile sites that he had clipped from the *New York Times* to Cuba. Brugioni wrote: "We suspected that he also took the binder with him but never had the opportunity to use it."[9]

The Role of the Security Council

In his televised address on 22 October 1962, President Kennedy announced that the United States had requested that an emergency meeting of the Security Council be immediately convened to take action against "this latest Soviet threat to world peace. Our resolution will call for the prompt dismantling and withdrawal of all offensive weapons in Cuba, under the supervision of United Nations observers, before the quarantine can be lifted."[10] The Soviet Union and Cuba also asked for an urgent meeting of the Security Council, which met the night of 24 October.

Moral Pressure from the UN Membership

On the morning of 24 October, U Thant received representations from more than fifty member states calling on him "to intervene in the titanic conflict, in order to avert the coming catastrophe."[11] He replied that he intended to speak in the Security Council meeting that evening. In his statement before the Security Council, on 25 October 1962, Alex Quaison-Sackey, the Ghanian representative, explained what had taken place. He disclosed that a demarche had been made to U Thant by the representatives of Cyprus, the United Arab Republic, and himself in the name of fifty member states. Those representatives had authorized an approach to U Thant, the acting secretary-general, suggesting that in the interest of international peace and security, he might ask the parties concerned to refrain from any action that might aggravate the situation.[12]

In the debates in the Security Council during the four meetings held to discuss the crisis, the U.S. representative, Ambassador Adlai Stevenson, denounced the Soviet Union for introducing the missiles that were threatening the United States and the Western hemisphere. When the Soviet representative, Ambassador Valerian Zorin, denied the existence of the missiles, Stevenson made dramatic presentations detailing their existence that included photographs. The Soviet representative defended his government, but he probably had not been briefed about the missiles and was plainly at a disadvantage in the debate. The Cuban representative vehemently attacked the United States for aggression against his country.

The representatives of the United Kingdom and France backed the United States, as did the representative of China (then the representative of nationalist China). Among the nonpermanent council members, countries such as Ireland, Venezuela, and Chile backed the United States, while the Romanian representative supported the Soviet Union. The representative of Ghana supported Cuba on the grounds of respect for Charter principles and of peoples' rights to determine their own political, economic, and social system. He also invoked the principles and precepts of the Non-Aligned Movement.

In the midst of all of this, it was the voice of Ambassador Quaison-Sackey that came across as the voice of moderation. After discussing the principles of international law applicable to the situation, he stated:

> In conclusion, I must say that the delegation of Ghana cannot apportion blame for this grave crisis. What is important, and what a very large number of Member States of this Organization representing millions of people want now, is that the danger of war should be arrested quickly. Time is of the greatest essence at this momentous moment. We all call upon the leaders of the United States, the Soviet Union and Cuba to understand the yearning of humanity for peace at this critical period.[13]

He also stated that the Security Council had overwhelming responsibility regarding the situation and asserted that negotiation was required to solve the crisis on the basis of mutual respect for each other's sovereign rights. He urged the Security Council to authorize the acting secretary-general to immediately confer with the parties to facilitate negotiations and a draft resolution to this effect.[14]

U Thant's Statement to the Security Council

U Thant spoke to the Security Council immediately after the Ghanian representative spoke, underlining the gravity of the situation. The United Nations, he stated, faced a moment of grave responsibility. It was not just the interest of the parties involved that was at stake or the interest of all member states, but the very fate of humankind. "If today the United Nations should prove itself ineffective, it may have proved itself so for all time."[15] He expressed a profound hope and conviction that moderation, self-restraint, and good sense would prevail.

He informed the Security Council of appeals that he had sent to the leaders of the three countries directly involved and cautioned that in the seventeen years since World War II, there had never been a more dangerous confrontation between the major powers. He recalled the principles enunciated by Secretary-General Hammarskjöld when he addressed the Security Council during the Suez Crisis and concluded:

> I hope that at this moment, not only in the Council Chamber but in the world outside, good sense and understanding will be placed above the anger of the moment or the pride of nations. The path of negotiation and compromise is the only course by which the peace of the world can be secured at this critical moment.[16]

The Appeal and the Proposal

U Thant called for urgent negotiations, informing the Security Council that he had sent identical messages to Kennedy and Khrushchev appealing for a two- to three-week moratorium. For the Soviet Union, this would entail the voluntary suspension of all arms shipments to Cuba. On the part of the United States, it would require the voluntary suspension of the quarantine, especially the searching of ships bound for Cuba. He also offered to make himself available to all the parties for any services he might be able to perform. U Thant had also appealed to the president and the prime minister of Cuba to suspend the construction and development of major military facilities and installations in Cuba during the period of negotiation.[17]

It is important to underline that U Thant issued his appeals to the powers involved without having consulted them beforehand, and he maintained his independence about the content and timing of his actions. When Stevenson heard that U Thant was about to take an initiative, he called U Thant for an appointment, and they spoke at 2:30 PM. U Thant informed him that he would be sending out his appeals by 6 PM that day. When Stevenson asked him to wait twenty-four hours, U Thant declined.[18]

At about 5:00 PM that day, after reporting to President Kennedy and Secretary of State Dean Rusk, Ambassador Stevenson called on U Thant to request that he change his appeal regarding the construction of the missile sites. U Thant said it had already been sent at about 3 PM by commercial telegram. According to Stevenson's biographer, the United States received it at approximately 5:30 and the Soviet Union at approximately 6:30. On Stevenson's urging, U Thant agreed to include a sentence about stopping military construction inside Cuba in his statement to the Security Council that night. "He declined to include a reference to the missiles already in place."[19]

On 25 October, Premier Khrushchev wrote to U Thant: "I agree to your proposal, which is in the interest of peace."[20] The United States was concerned that a moratorium of the quarantine would leave open the possibility of continued construction of the missile-launching sites in Cuba. President Kennedy, however, opted for a more nuanced reply. He wrote on 25 October that he appreciated the spirit that had prompted U Thant's message and underlined that the key to solving the crisis lay in removing the weapons from Cuba. In response to U Thant's ideas and suggestion of preliminary talks to determine whether satisfactory arrangements could be assured, Kennedy informed U Thant that Ambassador Stevenson was "ready to discuss promptly these arrangements with you."[21] While he did not withdraw his demand for the removal of the missiles, President Kennedy was keeping the door open to a negotiated solution.

U Thant immediately replied to Khrushchev and Kennedy that he hoped to begin discussions with Ambassadors Zorin and Stevenson the following day and that he trusted that the outcome of the discussions would advance the cause of peace.[22]

Later that day, U Thant followed up with a third message to the two leaders because he was concerned that Soviet ships already on their way to Cuba might challenge the quarantine and produce a confrontation between Soviet and U.S. vessels, threatening the possibility of negotiations. He asked Khrushchev to instruct any Soviet ships already sailing to Cuba to stay away from the interception area for a limited time only. He also asked Kennedy to instruct U.S. vessels in the Caribbean to do everything possible to avoid direct confrontation with Soviet ships. To each, he stated that if he received the assurance sought he would inform the other side.

U Thant later wrote that President Kennedy "immediately accepted my proposal, contingent upon acceptance by the Soviet Government."[23] Kennedy pointed out, however, that the matter was one of great urgency, since Soviet ships were still proceeding toward the interception area and work on the missile system was continuing. Premier Khrushchev also accepted the moratorium. He informed U Thant that he had ordered Soviet vessels bound for Cuba to stay out of the interception area but stressed that his order was temporary since he could not keep ships immobilized on the high seas.[24]

The next day, 26 October, U Thant sent a message to Fidel Castro, informing him of the encouraging responses he had received and asking that the construction of major military installations in Cuba, especially those designed to launch medium- and intermediate-range ballistic missiles, be suspended during the negotiations.[25] Castro sent a forceful response complaining about the United States, but he extended an invitation to U Thant to visit Cuba for direct discussions.

While these contacts were taking place, Kennedy and Khrushchev were having their own exchange, through letters and messengers, and managed to reach an agreement on the formula that eventually ended the missile crisis.

The Diplomacy behind U Thant's Third Message to Kennedy and Khrushchev

There is no doubt that the conversations between American and Soviet diplomats and U Thant were a central part of the process that eventually resolved the crisis. Reports from the U.S. mission to the UN to President Kennedy provide insights into the content of the American meetings with U Thant.

According to President Kennedy's biographer, Barbara Leaming, as the moment of the entry into force of the quarantine approached at 10 AM on 24 October, President Kennedy searched for a means to permit Premier Khrushchev to back down without sacrificing his dignity:

> Kennedy hit on the idea of asking UN Secretary-General U Thant to intervene in such a way as to give the Soviets "enough of an out to stop their armaments without looking like they completely crawled down." Thant, awakened in the night, agreed to convey to the Soviets that if they would consent to halt their shipments for the time being, the United States wanted to talk. "Otherwise," Kennedy said sadly at the close of a late-night phone conversation with [Under-Secretary George] Ball, "we just have to go with this thing."[26]

Adlai Stevenson's biographer wrote that at 8:30 AM on 25 October, Stevenson received instructions from Under-Secretary Ball to tell U Thant that the United States hoped that Premier Khrushchev would keep his ships out of the quarantine interception area for a limited time to permit discussion. The United States did not want any incidents. Ambassador Stevenson promptly saw U Thant to transmit this message to him.[27]

At the UN archives, in a file containing U Thant's papers on the missile crisis, there is a note with the handwritten inscription: "Handed to A/SG by Stevenson, 25 October '62—10:30 AM" that reads as follows:

I. An expression of concern that Soviet ships might be under instructions to challenge the quarantine and consequently create a confrontation at sea between Soviet ships and Western Hemisphere ships, which could lead to an escalation of violence.

II. An expression of concern that such a confrontation would destroy the possibility of the talks such as you [U Thant] have suggested as a prelude to a political settlement.

III. An expression of hope that Soviet ships will be held out of the interception area for a limited time in order to permit discussions of the modalities of an agreement.

IV. An expression of your confidence, on the basis of Soviet ships not proceeding to Cuba, that the United States will avoid a direct confrontation with them during the same period in order to minimize chances of an untoward incident.[28]

U Thant transmitted his appeal to the two sides and continued to play an indispensable calming role.

On 26 October, U.S. secretary of state Rusk sent a telegram to Ambassador Stevenson on the subject "Cuba: Talks with Acting Secretary-General," giving him the following instructions:

> At beginning of first meeting with SYG you should take occasion restate basic US position that early removal nuclear missiles and other offensive weapons from Cuba is the essence of the matter. We understand that the Secretary-General is proposing first a discussion of some form of standstill or freeze (covering arms shipments to Cuba, the build up of offensive weapons in Cuba, and our quarantine action), to be followed by broader talks on peaceful settlement of the larger issue created by Soviet introduction of missiles and other offensive weapons into an island just off our shores.
>
> While we are willing to handle matter in two stages, we would emphasize at the start that the build up must stop, and the weapons must be removed before too long and that these things must be done under inspection arrangements that insure against secrecy and cheating. We would emphasize further that the OAS quarantine action will not be lifted until the threat which provoked it is removed.[29]

In a telegram on 26 October, the U.S. mission reported on the meeting that Stevenson and his colleagues, John McCloy, Charles Yost, and George Plimpton, had had with U Thant and his colleagues at 4:30 PM that day. Paragraph 10 of the telegram reported that regarding the dismantling of the sites, the Secretary-General had said that he would appeal to Castro that night to suspend construction of the sites and would also speak to Soviet ambassador Zorin about them. Regarding the ultimate dismantling of the sites, the Secretary-General had said that he would insist on a UN team to oversee compliance.

In paragraph 16 of their telegram, the mission stated:

> SYG again raised question of solving whole problem through assurance by US that it would not attack Cuba and would prevent others from doing so, with resulting dismantling of all Soviet installations, and reiterated that this should be a starting point. He suggested the possibility of the President's writing him a letter to the effect that the US willing to make such a guarantee, if offensive weapons withdrawn, which he would use in negotiations.[30]

The American diplomats reported that they had told U Thant that the OAS would have to be consulted in any such connection, "which the SYG said he understood." In a general assessment of the meeting, the American diplomats reported:

> General atmosphere was quite relaxed and friendly. SYG much less concerned with blockade than at earlier meeting with Yost and Plimpton and seemed much more aware of site construction and missile operability problems and need for inspection. He clearly putting principal emphasis in his mind on possibility of US guarantee to Cuba as short circuit solution of whole problem.[31]

A telegram from the U.S. mission to the United Nations to the State Department in Washington dated 27 October, 2 PM, reported on a meeting with U Thant at 11:45 that morning. Paragraphs 10 and 11 reflected U Thant's concerns:

> 10. SYG mentioned the great concern all over world as to seriousness of situation. He said he had received 620 telegrams, most from US, as to his proposals, only 5 of which were negative.
> 11. SYG said he had urged both Castro and Zorin to have work on sites stopped immediately. Cuban Rep had said he would communicate SYG's request to his govt. Zorin had turned request aside asking how anyone could rely on US intelligence.[32]

On 27 October, Ambassador Stevenson wrote to U Thant, transmitting the following urgent message from President Kennedy:

> A number of proposals have been made to you and to the United States in the last 36 hours. I would appreciate your urgently ascertaining whether the Soviet Union is willing immediately to cease work on these bases in Cuba and to render the weapons inoperable under United Nations verification so that various solutions can be discussed.[33]

During the evening of 27 October, still seriously worried about the situation, President Kennedy asked Secretary Rusk to secretly contact the former UN chef de cabinet, Andrew Cordier, and provide him with a state-ment that U Thant might issue if necessary in dire circumstances calling for the removal of American Jupiter missiles in Turkey and the Soviet missiles in Cuba. Rusk contacted Cordier, and they agreed that if Rusk received a further message, he should contact Secretary-General U Thant to issue the statement. In this way, President Kennedy would be seen to agree to a UN proposal rather than a Soviet one regarding the removal of the Jupiter mis-siles.[34] Ultimately, this was not needed, but this initiative illustrates another way the Secretary-General can be useful in a dangerous crisis.

While U Thant's efforts were under way, he received significant support from the leaders of the Non-Aligned Movement, including supportive mes-sages from President Josip Broz Tito of Yugoslavia, Prime Minister Jawa-harlal Nehru of India, and Emperor Haile Selassie of Ethiopia. The text of these and other messages are in the UN archives.[35]

Visit to Cuba

U Thant traveled to Cuba from 30–31 October 1962 for conversations with Cuban leaders. By this time, the nuclear confrontation was over, and U Thant was concerned about implementation issues, including verification of the dismantling of the missile sites and the return of the missiles to the Soviet Union. U Thant's visit was important because as it gave the Cuban leaders an opportunity to let off steam to him, but there was not much prac-tical action to be discussed since the idea of UN verification was not ac-ceptable to the Cuban leadership and was, in any case, being superseded by then.[36] While the idea of UN verification had been raised by the United States and U Thant had looked into options, the idea did not survive. The Soviet Union had expressed a preference for verification by the Interna-tional Committee of the Red Cross, and the United States had accepted this. The idea of verification was not acceptable to the Cuban government, how-ever, and, in the final analysis, it was not followed up at the United Nations.

Conclusion

U Thant received lavish praise inside and outside the Security Council for his part in helping defuse the crisis. In the Security Council on 25 October, Ambassador Quaison-Sackey expressed appreciation to U Thant for his "tremendous show of statesmanship and initiative." He commended the suggestions that U Thant had put forward that, he was confident, would "greatly ease the situation and give time for the necessary discussions and negotiations to get under way."[37] When all the details had been settled, and the crisis was over, the American and Soviet negotiators, Ambassador Stevenson and Vasili V. Kuznetzov, sent a joint letter to U Thant:

> The Governments of the United States of America and of the Soviet Union express the hope that the actions taken to avert the threat of war in connection with this crisis will lead toward the adjustment of other differences between them and the general easing of tensions that could cause a further threat of war.[38]

U Thant thanked them but continued to press the point of continued vigilance: "I am also confident that all Governments concerned will refrain from any action which might aggravate the situation in the Caribbean in any way."[39] Preventive diplomacy thus continued.

6

The Practice of Preventive Diplomacy
by Representatives of the Secretary-General
and UN Subregional Offices

- Missions of Special Representatives of the Secretary-General
- An Under-Secretary-General for Preventive Diplomacy?
- Preventive Diplomacy in UN Subregional Offices
- Conclusion

Missions of Special Representatives of the Secretary-General

Special representatives or envoys of the Secretary-General play an important role in the practice of preventive diplomacy.[1] The use of special representatives for preventive purposes was a key part of Secretary-General Hammarskjöld's concept of preventive diplomacy; he envisioned the deployment of representatives in leading crisis spots where the Secretary-General might be able to play a role in heading off conflict.

The presence of representatives of the Secretary-General in trouble spots predated Hammarskjöld. Famous examples were Count Folke Bernadotte and Ralph Bunche. Count Bernadotte was appointed by Secretary-General Trygve Lie as mediator in the conflict between Arabs and Israel over Palestine in 1948. He was assassinated in Jerusalem on 17 September 1948 while performing his mandate. Ralph Bunche succeeded him and negotiated an armistice between the Arabs and Israel in 1948–1949, for which he received the Nobel Peace Prize in 1949. Hammarskjöld's innovation was the idea of deploying a ring of representatives in trouble spots, which he did in Guinea in 1958–1959, Jordan in 1959, Laos in 1959–1960, and Somalia in 1961. Hammarskjöld's idea was that these representatives would report to him on developments and conditions that might be important in the light of the obligations of the Secretary-General.[2]

Recent Secretaries-General have called on the services of trouble-shooting envoys or under-secretaries-general. They have also drawn on the services of regional troubleshooters who have undertaken diplomatic missions for the Secretary-General in trouble spots. There is room for the diplomacy of such representatives to grow in the future, particularly the use of regional envoys. This chapter looks at the preventive diplomacy role of representatives and envoys of the Secretary-General.

Efforts to Defuse Crises

In his study *The Ways of the Peacemaker*, Venkata Raman noted that the deployment of representatives of the Secretary-General to Cambodia and Thailand in 1958 and 1962 to help them resolve their differences illustrated the potential of the UN system to induce states to turn to the Secretary-General for assistance in settling their disputes peacefully. In that situation, which involved accusations of intimidation, border violations, and piracy by one side and denials by the other, the two countries asked the Secretary-General to inquire into the difficulties that had arisen between them. In 1958, the Secretary-General designated Johan Beck-Fries of Sweden as his special representative to assist the parties. In 1962, he designated Nils G. Gussing, also of Sweden, as his special representative for one year. Gussing's mandate was to place himself at the disposal of the parties to assist in solving the problems that had arisen or might arise between them. According to Raman, "the outcome of these good offices was a reduction of tension between the parties."[3]

Raman also pointed to the efforts of Luis Weckmann-Muñoz of Mexico, special representative of Secretary-General Waldheim, in defusing tensions between Iran and Iraq in 1974. The Security Council had recommended that the Secretary-General investigate a violent border conflict between Iran and Iraq and report back to the council. Following the efforts of Weckmann-Muñoz, the parties accepted a suggestion for the prompt and simultaneous withdrawal of their armed forces along the border. Since the border had not previously been demarcated, Weckmann-Muñoz suggested that this be an item of negotiations between the parties. The parties accepted his suggestion that they create a favorable climate for an early resumption of talks to achieve a comprehensive settlement of all issues between them. Weckmann-Muñoz's efforts helped defuse tension between the two countries.[4]

The use of special representatives to defuse crises continues today. In an interview with this author on 14 July 2006, one of the Secretary-General's representatives related a recent mission he had undertaken at the request of Secretary-General Annan to a country facing a possible internal crisis, including the possibility of civil war. Following contested elections, the country, a large one in Africa, had experienced riots, killings, and imprisonment of opposition leaders. Amidst this continued internal unrest and protests, the government was taking a hard line toward the opposition.

Secretary-General Annan had spoken with the prime minister and asked him to receive an envoy on a very discreet basis. Although the government was resistant to any suggestion of external interference, the Secretary-General persuaded it to receive his envoy and accept that the envoy would meet with opposition leaders.

The envoy visited the country at the beginning of July 2006, held meetings with the prime minister and other government members, and encouraged them to turn the crisis around and be receptive to a dialogue with opposition leaders. The envoy held similar meetings with leading opposition members, encouraging them to avoid an internal explosion. He also succeeded in bringing key government and opposition figures together for discussions, encouraging them to continue such discussions. The talks set the basis for a dialogue between the opposition and the government.

The envoy reported to the Secretary-General and expected to undertake further similar missions to the country in the future. This is an example of a situation where the Secretary-General and his envoy acted discreetly behind the scenes to help prevent a situation from deteriorating into civil war. Even if the outcome of the effort was not known, it bought some time for dialogue.

Efforts to Prevent an Explosion

In *Burundi on the Brink 1993–1995: A UN Special Envoy Reflects on Preventive Diplomacy*,[5] Ahmedou Ould-Abdallah provides a revealing account of his efforts to prevent a crisis in Burundi in 1994 following the plane explosion over Kigali Airport that killed the presidents of Burundi and Rwanda. Six months earlier, the assassination of a previous president of Burundi had resulted in the massacre of more than 50,000 people. Ould-Abdallah feared another outbreak of violence or, worse, another putsch in the political vacuum that had been produced by the explosion over Kigali Airport.

Ould-Abdallah met with the speaker of Burundi's parliament and later with the speaker, the prime minister, the minister of defense, and the army chief of staff—all of whom were Tutsis.

> The five of us decided upon and organized my first official live appearance on Burundian television. I wanted to show my support for Ntibantunganya, who,

as President of the National Assembly, was the constitutional successor to the deceased Cyprian Ntaryamina. . . . This backing, and through me that of the international community, was vital to show the Hutus—whose second President in six months had just been killed—that the speaker was the hostage neither of the Tutsi-dominated army nor of the Prime Minister, also a Tutsi.[6]

Surrounded by those four political figures, the speaker of parliament read the speech (on which Ould-Abdallah had worked) on the national television station (which Ould-Abdallah had telephoned so that it would not shut down as it normally did at 10:30 PM). Ould-Abdallah emphasized the importance of communicating that the Burundian president's death had been an accident.

From the television station, the five men went to the army headquarters to show that the government and the army were unified at a time of crisis. The army chief of staff called the heads of the different military camps to tell them about the situation and ask them to work with the civilian governors. The speaker of parliament simultaneously called the civilian governors to ask them to work with the military. Ould-Abdallah summed up the situation:

> We stayed at the military headquarters until around 3 am and managed to reach all the governors except one or two who had run away. The entire exercise proved to have been of vital importance: less than twelve hours after the assassination the situation was under control throughout the country. During the following days there were no massacres anywhere. People were stunned by the brutality of the events and the tragic fate of the second Frodebu president, but at the same time they were relieved to feel that the country was being taken care of by a national team. . . . The decision that night to let a fearful nation know that someone was in control was a key preventive action.[7]

Containing a Crisis: Peacemaking and Peacekeeping

Toward the end of 1991, the situation in the former Yugoslavia was of great concern to the international community and had been the subject of Security Council resolutions. Secretary-General Pérez de Cuéllar had designated former U.S. secretary of state Cyrus Vance as his personal envoy, and during November–December that year, Secretary Vance and Marrack Goulding, under-secretary-general for special political affairs (peacekeeping operations), discussed a peacekeeping plan called the "Concept for a United Nations Peacekeeping Operation in Yugoslavia" with Yugoslav leaders.[8] That concept paper, as eventually acted on by the Security Council, led to the establishment of the United Nations Protection Force in the Former Yu-goslavia (UNPROFOR), an innovative effort to contain the war in Croatia and prevent its further spread and intensification. As an exercise in pre-ventive diplomacy, it was instructive. UNPROFOR helped contain the situ-ation for some two and a half years until the geopolitical landscape changed and the government of Croatia, with support from the United States, moved to expel the Serb population en masse from Croatia.

The concept paper called for a UN peacekeeping operation in Yugoslavia that was an interim arrangement to create the conditions of peace and se-curity required for negotiating an overall settlement of the Yugoslav crisis. It did not prejudge the outcome of negotiations.

The concept paper envisioned that UN troops and police monitors would be deployed in certain areas in Croatia, designated as United Nations Protected Areas (UNPAs). Those areas would be demilitarized; all armed forces in them would be either withdrawn or disbanded. The UN troops would ensure that the areas remained demilitarized and that all persons re-siding in them were protected from armed attack. The UN police monitors ensured that the local police forces carried out their duties without dis-criminating against people of any nationality or abusing anyone's human rights.

UNPAs would be areas in Croatia where the Secretary-General judged that special arrangements were required during an interim period to ensure that a lasting cease-fire was maintained. They would be areas where Serbs constituted the majority or a substantial minority and where intercommu-nal relations had led to armed conflict in the recent past. There would be three UNPAs: Eastern Slavonia, Western Slavonia, and Krajina.

In the proposed peacekeeping plan, the UN force's infantry units and its civilian police monitors would protect the inhabitants of the UNPAs and the infantry would ensure that the UNPAs remained demilitarized. The po-lice monitors would ensure that the local police carried out their duties without discrimination and with full respect for human rights. The UN force would also include a group of military observers who would be un-armed, in accordance with normal UN practice.

On the basis of agreed timetables, demilitarization of the UNPAs would be implemented as rapidly as possible. At the same time that the UN force assumed its protective functions in the UNPAs, any Yugoslav army units deployed elsewhere in Croatia would be relocated outside that republic.

The concept of the UNPAs succeeded for several months in protecting the Serb population of Croatia by separating them from the Croatian army. To that extent the concept proved successful. However, protection was meant to be temporary while political solutions were negotiated. In the end result the situation of the Serbs in Croatia was related to the broader conflict among Bosnians, Serbs, and Croats in Bosnia-Herzegovina as well. In Bosnia-Herzegovina itself, the UN declared six "safe areas" but these also could be protected only if large troop deployments were possible while political solutions were negotiated. It is now a matter of history that contributing states were unwilling to provide the 33,000 troops judged necessary, and the Bosnian Serbs overran some of the safe areas such as Srebrenica and committed atrocities there. In the UNPAs in Croatia, the Croats eventually expelled most of the Serb population with the support of some western governments.

The fact that the concept of the UNPA and of safe areas in Bosnia failed in the end does not detract from the creativity of the original idea of the UNPA. It was a bold concept that the UN should act to protect populations at risk. The intellectual heir of this idea is that of the responsibility to protect, which was endorsed by the General Assembly on the occasion of the sixtieth anniversary of the UN. It is a matter of common knowledge that the UN is rarely able to uphold the responsibility to protect. This, however, does not diminish the power of the idea which, one hopes, will be vindicated in the future. Seen from these perspectives, the idea of the UNPA was an historic innovation.

Emergency Political and Humanitarian Intercession: The Panel of Eminent Persons to Algeria

Since 1992, Algeria had experienced severe internal violence. Hundreds of people had been killed in terrorist attacks. The roots of the situation and the reasons for the violence were complex. The question for the Secretary-General was how to use his influence to mitigate the conflict and reduce the violence. As the situation evoked more and more international concern and anguish, Secretary-General Annan maintained contact with the Algerian president, and in June 1998 he made the following announcement:

> At the invitation of the Government of Algeria, the Secretary-General has today established a panel of eminent persons to visit that country. The purpose of this mission will be to gather information on the situation in Algeria and present a report to him, which he will make public. The Government of Algeria has assured the Secretary-General that it will ensure free and complete access to all sources of information necessary for the panel to exercise its functions, in order to have a clear vision and a precise perception of the reality of the situation in all its dimensions in Algeria today.[9]

The panel consisted of Mário Soares, former president of Portugal (chair); Inder Kumar Gujral, former prime minister of India; Abdel Karim Kabariti, former prime minister and minister of defense of Jordan; Donald McHenry, former U.S. permanent representative to the UN; Simone Veil, former state minister of France and former president of the European parliament; and Amos Wako, attorney-general of Kenya. The panel, which visited Algeria from 22 July to 4 August 1998, heard from a cross-section of Algerian government leaders, representatives of political parties (including the opposition), members of civil society, members of human rights and women's organizations, media representatives, representatives of religious institutions, members of the families of victims of terrorism and of disappeared persons, and other Algerian citizens. It also visited different regions of Algeria, sites where massacres had occurred, and a prison.

According to the panel, over the previous two years, the civilian population had been targeted by terrorists in an unprecedented manner. A pattern of mass killings in rural areas had resulted in the death or injury of many women and children. In 1997 and early 1998 the massacres had been especially widespread; they were often a daily occurrence. Villagers had been massacred in the most brutal ways. Some were decapitated or mutilated with knives, machetes, and saws; some were shot dead; and others were burned alive when their homes were set on fire. Several thousand people had been killed in these massacres.

In its observations to the Secretary-General, the panel underlined that efforts to combat terrorism must take place within the framework of legality, proportionality, and respect for human rights. Law enforcement, security and self-defense forces should be held to the highest standards of accountability so that the Algerian population and the international community would feel confident that the rule of law prevailed in Algeria. More democracy and more respect for human rights would fight terrorism. The panel felt that Algeria deserved the support of the international community in its efforts to consolidate democratic institutions, address economic challenges, defeat terrorism, and establish security, all with scrupulous respect for the rule of law and respect for human rights in daily practice. Further, the panel believed it was essential that democratic pluralism be strengthened and that the civilian element in government be reinforced. The panel believed that energetic efforts should be made to entrench in society and all public institutions a state of legality and respect for the rule of law and encourage more political openness.[10]

The panel recommended that the international community consider avenues or programs of cooperation and support in solidarity with Algeria in its efforts to deal with the pressing problems facing it. Algeria would need the support of the international community because deterioration of the situation there would have a negative impact on the Mediterranean region, Europe, and the international community. The panel called for the further strengthening of the Algerian institutions responsible for promoting and protecting human rights and expeditious attention to complaints of arbitrary detention, extrajudicial execution, and disappearances. Finally, the panel recommended that Algerian authorities examine measures to improve the transparency of their decisions and the dialogue with and the flow of information to the Algerian citizenry. In plain language, the panel recommended a more open and transparent democracy.

The significance of this panel lay in its composition, the fact that it was able to enter Algeria and have conversations with the Algerian government, and the contacts that subsequently took place between Secretary-General Annan and the Algerian government. The panel consisted of a former president of Portugal, a former prime minister of India, a former prime minister of Jordan, a former French cabinet minister, a former U.S. permanent representative to the United Nations, and the serving attorney general and minister of justice of Kenya. The government of Algeria, which insisted that the violence taking place in that country was a matter belonging to its internal affairs, agreed to receive and talk to the panel in part because of the authority of its members and also because of the delicate negotiations between Secretary-General Annan and the president of Algeria.

During its visit, as could be seen from its report, the panel broached many sensitive issues with the Algerian government, such as the fate of the hundreds of people who had "disappeared." The panel pressed the Algerian authorities to help clarify the fate of these missing persons, and there were some indications of willingness on the part of the authorities to help in this area. The Algerian authorities were able to benefit in a discreet way from the insights and suggestions of the members of the panel.

Following the publication of the panel's report, Secretary-General Annan and other senior officials continued to make representations on issues such as the clarification of the fate of disappeared persons. At the end of the day, the panel recognized that the Algerian government was dealing with the actions of terrorists, and it recognized that the government had a responsibility to protect the security of the Algerian people. It insisted, however, that this be done within the law and with respect for the principle of proportionality.

The efforts of the panel stand as a pathbreaking example of how the UN might be able to establish a dialogue with a government dealing with terrorism on the sensitive question of the protection of human rights in the pursuit of security.

Special Missions of Senior Officials

Like his predecessors, Secretary-General Annan drew on the services of his senior colleagues as de facto regional envoys in some situations of international concern. He sent a Latin American under-secretary-general on discreet missions to two Latin American countries that were experiencing severe internal unrest; the Secretary-General's emissary sought to provide advice in helping defuse those situations. As was discussed earlier, a senior official traveled to a major African country experiencing similar internal unrest to foster dialogue and help prevent the situation from deteriorating. Senior UN officials, including the under-secretary-general, the assistant secretaries-general, and the political directors in the Department of Political Affairs have discreetly undertaken special missions to different parts of the world in the exercise of preventive diplomacy. The annual reports of the Secretary-General sometimes provide skeletal references to such missions.

Good Offices in a Long-Running Boundary Dispute

The good offices of the Secretary-General and that of his representative in the boundary dispute between Guyana and Venezuela is a noteworthy case of discreet preventive diplomacy. The border between British Guiana and Venezuela had been the subject of an arbitral award in 1899. As British Guiana approached its independence in 1966, Venezuela reopened its claim to large tracts of the territory that had been awarded to British Guiana in 1899. In the boundary arbitration between Great Britain and Venezuela in 1899, a panel of arbitrators led by the great Russian jurist F. de Martens settled the boundary; this was accepted and implemented by Great Britain and Venezuela after 1899. A posthumous letter written by a lawyer involved in the arbitration on behalf of Venezuela alleged that de Martens might have influenced some members into assenting to the final decision as president of the arbitral tribunal. In 1962, Venezuela declared that it would no longer abide by the 1899 arbitration.

To facilitate the independence of the colony, on 17 February 1966, representatives of Britain, Guyana, and Venezuela signed an agreement establishing a border commission consisting of two Guyanese and two Venezuelans. The commission did not reach agreement, and both countries agreed to resolve their dispute by peaceful means. From 1967 to 1970, the two countries experienced difficulties in their relations over the border issue, and in 1970, they concluded the Protocol of Port-of-Spain, in which they agreed to a twelve-year moratorium on the dispute. In 1981, Venezuela indicated that it would not renew the moratorium, and relations between the two countries again became strained. Subsequently, the two countries agreed to accept the good offices of the Secretary-General.

Successive Secretaries-General have since maintained contacts between the two countries, meeting with their representatives usually on an annual basis. Between these meetings, a representative of the Secretary-General has kept in contact with the two sides, exploring ideas for moving forward toward a resolution of the issue. The substance of these contacts is not in the public domain, and thus they cannot be assessed. What can be said, however, is that the Secretary-General and his representative have provided a channel for the parties to communicate with each other and that this process has had an overall calming effect on the situation.[11] Before the process was instituted, there had been vexing incidents: Venezuelan forces occupied a border island, Ankoko, in 1966, and an uprising by some ranching families on the Guyana side of the border on 2 January 1969 led to recriminations between the two sides and increased tension, with Guyana fearing an armed Venezuelan incursion into the disputed parts of its territory. The good offices process has—at least—resulted in fewer incidents between the two countries even though Venezuela issued a new flag in 2006 with an additional star representing the disputed portions of Guyana's territory.

An Under-Secretary-General for Preventive Diplomacy?

In a report submitted to Secretary-General Annan on 30 June 1997, Under-Secretary-General Marrack Goulding recommended the appointment of a full-time special representative for preventive diplomacy based in New York.[12] Goulding wrote the report based on his experience as under-secretary-general for political affairs and under-secretary-general in charge of peacekeeping operations. He felt that such an appointment would underline the Secretary-General's commitment to prevention rather than cure and would provide him with the services of a senior official who would be better able than any head of department to devote time to individual cases. The special representative's relations with the departments, especially the Department for Political Affairs and the Office of the High Commissioner for Human Rights, would have to be carefully defined, and he or she would need political sensitivity to make those relationships work.

Goulding saw this concept as a variant of the mandate of the Organization for Security and Co-operation in Europe (OSCE) high commissioner on national minorities, who had, according to him, "succeeded in playing a preventive role in a low-key but often effective way."[13] According to the proposal, the special representative's mandate would be to initiate preventive action at the earliest possible stage of a potential conflict, using his or her good offices to persuade the parties to ease tensions and seek compromises. He or she would act discreetly and, as much as possible, without publicity. The usual principles of impartiality and confidentiality would be respected. He or she would intercede in situations that had been identified by the Secretariat as being potentially conflictive or which he or she, on his or her own initiative, judged to require preventive attention.

In Goulding's proposal, the Secretary-General's approval would be sufficient authorization for such intercession. Before giving such authorization, the Secretary-General or the special representative would consult the parties; the special representative's services would not be imposed on them. The Secretary-General would keep the member states as informed as possible without compromising the confidentiality and discretion that would be key to the special representative's success.

The proposal specified that the special representative would work closely with the under-secretary-general for political affairs, who would continue to have lead responsibility for advising the Secretary-General on preventive action; the special representative would be the operational arm, especially in the very early stages of potential conflict, when a low-key and discreet approach is required. The office of the special representative would be small and would be staffed and financed by the Department of Political Affairs. The special representative would normally report to the head of the Department of Political Affairs but, like other special representatives, would have direct access to the Secretary-General on major policy issues.

Goulding recommended that the Secretary-General appoint a full-time special representative for preventive diplomacy, initially on an experimental basis, which would make the post eligible for funding from the Trust Fund for Preventive Action. Secretary-General Annan apparently planned to appoint such a special representative but never did. The follow-up to the report of the High-level Panel on Threats, Challenges and Change in 2004 would have been a good opportunity to return to this idea. That panel made significant recommendations to strengthen the organization and resources of the Department of Political Affairs for preventive diplomacy.[14] Among the ideas advanced within the department to follow up on the panel's recommendations was that one of the two assistant secretaries-general in the department be made assistant secretary-general for preventive diplomacy. Unfortunately, the Secretary-General's 2005 report *In Larger Freedom,* which followed up on the recommendations of the high-level panel, did not contain any proposals to strengthen the organization and resources of the Department of Political Affairs for preventive diplomacy.[15] This was a missed opportunity that the incoming Secretary-General will probably try to remedy.

Preventive Diplomacy in UN Subregional Offices

The Subregional Office for West Africa

Dag Hammarskjöld had the idea of placing a ring of representatives of the Secretary-General in different trouble spots for the purposes of preventive diplomacy. A related experiment that has recently been under way is the establishment of subregional political offices to engage in preventive diplomacy and preventive work on the ground. One such office, for West Africa, has been in existence for five years and another, for Central Asia, is on the drawing board.

Addressing the Security Council at a meeting devoted to West Africa on 9 August 2006, Ahmedou Ould-Abdallah, special representative for West Africa, reviewed the evolution of conflicts in West Africa over the preceding five years, pointing out urgent issues that he felt would warrant the council's attention from the point of view of preventive diplomacy in the region. These included the following:

- Unemployment among the young and its impact on regional peace and stability
- Irregular migration and its consequence on governance, local and international
- The need for peaceful change of power as an approach to conflict prevention
- Galloping urbanization and its contribution to increased insecurity in West African capitals (38 to 40 percent of West African populations live in cities)
- Problems of free circulation of people across borders, notwithstanding subregional agreements[16]

These issues illustrate the interrelatedness of political, economic, social, and human rights and humanitarian factors in conflict prevention generally and preventive diplomacy in particular. But how had Ould-Abdallah come to appear before the council?

On 25 June 2001, Secretary-General Annan informed the president of the Security Council of his intention to establish a United Nations Office for West Africa (UNOWA). On 26 November 2001, he informed the council that the office would be known as Office of the Special Representative of the Secretary-General for West Africa and would be entrusted with four functions (to which a fifth was added in 2005):

- Enhance linkages in the work of the UN and other partners in the subregion through promoting an integrated subregional approach and facilitating coordination and information exchange, with due regard to specific mandates of UN organization as well as peacekeeping operations and peacebuilding support offices
- Liaise with and assist, as appropriate, ECOWAS and the Mano River Union, in consultation with other subregional organizations and international partners
- Carry out good offices roles and special assignments in countries of the subregion on behalf of the Secretary General, including in the areas of conflict prevention and peacebuilding efforts
- Report to UN headquarters on key developments of subregional significance
- Carry out additional tasks assigned by the Secretary-General and the Security Council, including support to the work of the Cameroon-Nigeria Mixed Commission and following up on relevant recommendations contained in the report of the June 2004 Security Council mission to West Africa (S/2004/525 of 2 July 2004) and the council's recommendations on cross-border issues in West Africa (S/PRST/2004/7 of 25 March 2004)[17]

The office was based in Dakar, Senegal. The first special representative was Ahmedou Ould-Abdallah of Mauritania, a former director in the Secretariat and special representative in Burundi as well as former minister for foreign affairs and cooperation of Mauritania and the Mauritanian ambassador to the United States. The office of the special representative, who was appointed at the level of under-secretary-general, had an initial international staff of seven. It was established for an three-year period from January 2002 and has since been continued; its current mandate lasts until 31 December 2007.[18] In the summer of 2006, its staff included officers with responsibility for political, humanitarian, human rights, information, and development issues. UNOWA participates in Security Council and other missions from UN headquarters to West Africa.

Recent economic studies have cautioned that unless the incidence of civil war is reduced, a substantial group of the poorest countries are likely to be caught in a conflict trap. The typical civil war in a low-income country, one study has concluded, lasts for nearly a decade, and the typical cost is at least $50 billion. On average, two civil wars break out each year around the world. One study has identified a threefold strategy for reducing the global incidence of civil war: preventing conflict, shortening the duration of conflict, and improving the prospects of sustaining post-conflict peace.[19]

The same study examined civil wars during 1965–1999 and found that a typical low-income developing country faced a 14 percent risk of civil war in any five-year period. The most important risk factors were the level of per capita income, the country's rate of growth, and the country's government structure. Doubling the level of income halved the risk of conflict. Increasing the growth rate by one percentage point reduced the risk of conflict by roughly a percentage point. Reducing dependence on natural resource exports significantly reduced the risk of conflict.[20] The author concluded that countries with all three of the high-risk economic characteristics—low income, low growth, and dependence on natural resources—"are in effect playing Russian roulette."[21]

A perusal of the documents on UNOWA's Web site brings out forcefully the economic and social root causes of conflict and the interrelatedness of these issues with political, electoral, human rights, and humanitarian questions. UNOWA's background documents point out that large parts of the subregion have known instability and conflict for several years. As a result, four countries—Côte d'Ivoire, Guinea-Bissau, Liberia, and Sierra Leone—were hosting UN peace missions, "while the UN system as a whole is active in a wide range of political, development, human rights and humanitarian activities."[22] The cross-border impact of conflict in West Africa has sometimes been further exacerbated by ethnic, cultural, and historical links, and conflicts have often spread from one country to another. A full 60 percent of the population in many West African countries is under the age of twenty, and youth issues require serious consideration. Youth unemployment in particular is a major source of concern in the subregion.[23] On top of this, porous borders and neglected border areas call for a regional border approach. Too often, security forces in West Africa have been a source of insecurity rather than a factor of democratic stability.

On 9 August 2006, in preparation for the Security Council's discussion of West Africa, Ghana, which held the presidency for that month, circulated a concept paper identifying the following "broad cross-cutting themes re-lating to peace consolidation . . . the outcome of which should provide an important contribution to the work of the newly established Peacebuilding Commission (PBC)":

- How can we manage conflicts to prevent further escalation and achieve expedited resolution?
- What measures should be taken to prevent the outbreak of new con-flicts?
- Given that several peace agreements have collapsed within five years, how do we prevent the relapse into conflict of countries emerging from conflict?
- How can we promote human security and economic development in order to sustain peace in the region?
- How can we develop a more complementary relationship between ECOWAS/AU/UN and other regional organizations?[24]

The Secretary-General of ECOWAS, Mohammed Ibn Chambas, told the Security Council during its meeting on 9 August:

> Peace consolidation for West African countries will include the following four major components: the rebuilding of democratic institutions, including the ju-diciary, parliament and the civil service; security sector reform to establish com-petent, truly national security forces that are well equipped and can adequately protect lives and property; support for the economic capacity of the Govern-ment to rebuild destroyed infrastructure and deliver social services to the peo-ple; and private sector development to create jobs and economic opportunities for the large army of unemployed people, especially youth.[25]

In its preventive strategies, UNOWA has had to address these and related issues, which were well reflected in a framework of action for peace and se-curity that it agreed with ECOWAS in 2005. On 18 May 2005, following ear-lier preparatory work, ECOWAS, the European Union (EU), and UNOWA adopted a framework of action for peace and security with the following content:

- Addressing structural causes of conflict: A shared conflict prevention strategy would include the use of development instruments to address structural causes of conflict such as inadequate governance and hu-man rights violations, environmental degradation, economic stagna-tion and youth unemployment and demographic trends, including massive urbanization.

- Border issues: The three organizations planned to focus on some priority clusters of border areas: (i) southern Guinea and neighboring areas of Sierra Leone, Liberia and Côte d'Ivoire; (ii) southern Mali, southern Burkina Faso and northern Côte d'Ivoire; northern Mali and neighboring countries. Work would also be done to strengthen cross-border security cooperation, especially to address illegal trafficking of children, weapons, drugs, conflict resources and the movement of armed bands and mercenaries.
- Free movement: Particular attention would be paid to the facilitation of freedom of movement as a fundamental part of the economic integration agenda of the sub-region.
- Improving governance and protecting human rights: Programs would include the democratic control of the armed forces, their re-structuring and downsizing, improving living conditions in barracks, training and developing alternative occupations.
- Electoral assistance and observation: Support would be provided for the strengthening of ECOWAS's electoral capacity, especially its Electoral Assistance and Observation Unit and the provision of technical assistance for observance missions.
- Transparency: ECOWAS would be supported in the elaboration of an annual report on transparency and the fight against corruption in member states.
- Human rights: The three organizations would promote the ratification of and respect for international and regional human rights agreements, the sensitization of populations about their benefit and their integration into national legislation.
- Conflict management coordination: Efforts would be made to improve joint planning processes for crisis management.
- Mediation and facilitation: Support would be provided to enhance ECOWAS's capacity for mediation and negotiation training and the provision of mediation support to ECOWAS special representatives
- Peace agreements: Cooperation would be pursued to support African efforts to develop realistic, inclusive and enforceable peace agreements that take account of the protection of civilians.
- Peace-support operations: Support would be provided for the creation of the ECOWAS standby force and the harmonization of procedures for peace-support operations, as a part of the efforts of the African Union on these matters.
- Disarmament, demobilization, and reintegration (DDR): DDR processes were recognized as critical to post-conflict stabilization. The

importance of securing timely resources and undertaking sufficient planning for rehabilitation and reintegration of former combatants would require particular emphasis, as would the need for a regional approach to DDR that also took account of the needs of countries affected by neighboring conflicts.[26]

At the request of the Security Council or the Secretary-General, UNOWA is currently engaged in preparing and implementing several projects related to the peace and security of the subregion. These include cross-border challenges; the regional impact of the crisis in Côte d'Ivoire; cooperation with ECOWAS; disarmament, demobilization, and reintegration; youth unemployment; reform of the security sector; and integrated strategies for sensitive border areas in West Africa.

UNOWA closely follows the internal developments in several countries of the subregion. One of its major concerns is to help minimize instability relating to elections or the transfer of power, and the special representative maintains close contacts with West African leaders on this issue.

Against the background of years of war in the West African subregion and multiple conflicts and bearing in mind the complex political, economic, social, and military backgrounds of these conflicts, Special Representative Ahmedou Ould-Abdallah had to develop approaches to exercise preventive diplomacy that matched the challenges of the situation. He did this with conviction and discernment.

The special representative is in frequent contact with leaders in the region, the leadership of ECOWAS, and with the heads of the other UN peace operations in the Côte d'Ivoire, Liberia, Sierra Leone, and Guinea-Bissau. He chairs the high-level meetings of heads of UN peace operations in West Africa. He represents the Secretary-General at important peace negotiations such as the Linas-Marcoussis negotiations on Côte d'Ivoire in 2003 and the ECOWAS-led peace negotiations on Liberia in Accra in July–August 2003.

In an interview, a member of Ould-Abdallah's staff, who had worked with him closely for nearly three of the five years he had been in the position, stated that one of his leading contributions had been to serve as a bridge to ECOWAS and to national leaders in the subregion in dealing with situations and emergencies. She also considered that his role as facilitator had been important—for example, his participation in meetings of EU/ECOWAS. Third, he had also rendered a great service in his ability to talk candidly to leaders in the region, pointing out dangers to them and calling them to their responsibilities.

In a separate interview, Ould-Abdallah stated: "My action has been to speak to the parties and often to tell them the plain facts, to engage in plain speaking to them and inform them about the risks."[27] He commented, wistfully, that to do this, it is important for him to be briefed with the latest information but that this is not often forthcoming within the United Nations.

His approach emphasizes information-sharing among parties. He tries his best to stay informed about particular situations, notwithstanding the difficulties of getting information support within the UN, and to share information among parties concerned. He realizes that parties who mistrust one another can easily escalate the situation unless information is shared with them to give them a common understanding of the essential facts. He also attaches great importance to active consultations with all the parties. "Before making a proposal you have to make sure not to lose face," he explained. One should also help ensure that participants do not lose face.

Ould-Abdallah thinks it is important to help set the agenda in the subregion. He has arranged for the publication of a series of issues papers, one of which covers youth unemployment and regional insecurity in West Africa.[28] Another is a courageous and fascinating publication called *Life After State House: Addressing Unconstitutional Changes in West Africa.*[29] The paper is meant to promote orderly transitions of power. As Ould-Abdallah stated in the preface: "This Issue Paper seeks to address the question of how to prevent unconstitutional changes of government in West Africa and, related to this, to encourage incumbent leaders to leave office peacefully at the end of their term."[30]

Ould-Abdallah explained the practical importance of this issue. He was particularly concerned about a country where the head of state was considered to be no longer in charge, a situation that is unpredictable for many reasons and a cause for great concern. As special representative, he helped encourage the cabinet to function as a cabinet. There were rumors of a possible coup, and the senior army leaders feared a countercoup by junior officers. In this volatile mix, the external partners were threatening to impose sanctions, and there was a great danger of civil war. The special representative, who was seeking to stave off a possible war, explained part of his approach, which he already applied in Burundi: "When there is a crisis you should be on people's backs. You should stay on the situation and speak to the main actors. Make sure that it does not go out of control."

Ould-Abdallah applied some elements of this approach in another situation involving two countries whose leaders greatly disliked each other. In this situation, the risk that each leader would take action against the other was high. He sought to be a bridge between them, educating both leaders about the relevant facts and making sure that neither acted hastily on the basis of misperceptions or miscalculations. In addition to being a bridge, he had to stay on the case and stay on the facts, sharing key information with both parties.

He has also made considerable efforts in situations involving elections, which, he explained, can lead to serious violence. He has compiled a list of upcoming elections and regularly visits the countries involved. He feels that it is important to talk to the leaders, encourage orderly elections, and be in contact with the parties, the local actors, and the diplomatic community. It is particularly important that the electoral process be transparent and be viewed as such by all sides.

In May 2005, as part of his good offices in Togo, and following visits to that country, Ould-Abdallah attended the Mini-Summit on the Situation in Togo, during which heads of state and government held extensive discussions with the government of Togo and the leaders of Togolese political parties. The summit discussed the functioning of Togolese institutions, especially establishing an all-inclusive national reconciliation government, increasing respect for human rights, facilitating the return of refugees, and preparing new legislative elections.

In a statement to the Security Council on 9 August 2006, Ould-Abdallah stated that "the Security Council should discuss how to find the best way to support the presidential and parliamentary elections to be held in 2007 in Benin, Côte d'Ivoire, Mali, Nigeria, Senegal and Sierra Leone. It is a period of tensions—tensions that must be prevented."[31]

In his interview with the author, Ould-Abdallah referred to his office's role in facilitating a peaceful outcome of the boundary dispute between Cameroon and Nigeria. The implementation of the Secretary-General's good offices initiative was entrusted to UNOWA, and the process culminated with an agreement in June 2006. Ould-Abdallah chaired the Cameroon-Nigeria Mixed Commission that the Secretary-General established in November 2002 to facilitate implementation of the October 2002 International Court of Justice ruling on their border dispute. He drew particular attention to his innovation of placing observers along the border. He arranged for twenty-two nonmilitary observers to be deployed along the border and for Cameroon and Nigeria to pay the costs of their deployment.[32] He feels that this initiative in watching over the final implementation phase is very important and thinks that there was great room for the UN to consider the deployment of observers in more situations, at far less cost than formal peacekeeping operations.

The special representative noted that controversy often develops when people travel from country to country because of border controls. This has been, and still is, an explosive issue. He facilitated efforts to promote smoother border crossings, and, as part of the discreet efforts of his office, he had a senior official periodically travel to sensitive crossing points to observe the process and signal the UN's interest in the matter. In short, preventive diplomacy was working on the ground in innovative and practical ways.

A Subregional Office for Central Asia

In October 2003, in cooperation with the OSCE and the government of Turkmenistan, the UN organized the Forum on Conflict Prevention and Sustainable Development for Central Asia. For four years, the establishment of a regional center for preventive diplomacy was on the drawing board. In an article published in the *UN Chronicle* in August 2004, President Saparmurat Niyazov stated that Turkmenistan was ready to host the regional center and provide resources, including office space, infrastructure, and living facilities. In an address to the High-Level Plenary Meeting of the General Assembly on 16 September 2005, Turkmenistan's foreign minister, Rashid Meredov, stressed that "the Regional Centre for Central Asia on Preventive Diplomacy in many respects will promote comprehensive consideration and resolution of questions related to prevention of contentious situations, fight against terrorism and illegal drug trafficking as well as to the all-round sustainable development in the central region."[33]

In his 2005 annual report, Secretary-General Annan reported that the idea had moved forward, and in his 2006 annual report, he stated that he had "initiated the establishment of a regional United Nations centre for preventive diplomacy, an initiative that enjoyed the support of the five countries of the region."[34] The UN Regional Centre for Preventive Diplomacy for Central Asia came into existence during the tenure of his successor. At the center's inauguration on 10 December 2007, Ban Ki-moon offered a message asserting that preventive diplomacy was not an option but rather a necessity.

Conclusion

This chapter has provided glimpses into the practice of preventive diplomacy through special representatives and other envoys of the Secretary-General. In each instance, preventive diplomacy was undertaken with the consent of the governments concerned and was pursued discreetly with the aim of helping these governments or other parties on the ground talk among themselves, defuse situations, and help minimize human suffering. At the end of the day, the UN can only assist those who wish to be assisted. When called on to assist, however, the UN can be quite sophisticated in the practice of preventive diplomacy. The proposal for a special representative for preventive diplomacy is one that deserves renewed consideration.

UNOWA has been in existence for five years and is continuing proof of the interrelatedness of political, economic, social, electoral, human rights, and humanitarian factors in the exercise of preventive diplomacy on the ground. The efforts of the Secretary-General, the special representative, and the Cameroon-Nigeria Mixed Commission have played a valuable role in managing relations between the two countries and promoting their peaceful evolution. In a presidential statement of 9 August 2006, the Security Council emphasized the regional dimension of peace and security in West Africa and asked the Secretary-General, in consultation with the ECOWAS secretariat, to submit a report with recommendations on cooperation between the UN missions in the region and on cross-border issues in West Africa by the end of 2006.[35] Preventive diplomacy in West Africa thus received encouragement from the preeminent UN organ of peace and security.

Hopefully the regional center for Central Asia will be launched in the near future. Interviews with the Department for Political Affairs indicate that consideration is also being given to establishing a subregional center for the Association of Southeast Asian Nations (ASEAN) region. The West African model has proven its worth, and plans are afoot to emulate it elsewhere.

7

The Preventive Role of UN Peacekeepers and Observers

- Preventive Peacekeeping in Macedonia
- The Idea for the Establishment of a Rapid Reaction Force
- UN Observers in South Africa
- Conclusion

The idea of an international police force has its roots in the post–World War II era. In 1947, the first Secretary-General, Trygve Lie, called for the establishment of a corps of UN guards.[1] In the Reith lectures on the BBC in 1957, Canadian Lester Pearson, who was awarded the Nobel Peace Prize that year for his role in using the UN to defuse the Suez crisis, advocated establishing an international police force that could be rapidly deployed.[2] It was an idea that had in view prevention, containment, settlement, and transformation, all core elements of conflict resolution.[3] In his Nobel Prize acceptance speech, Pearson referred to UNEF as the "first genuinely international police force of its kind."[4] Because of Pearson's close association with the UN and his role in developing peacekeeping, his ideas belong to the intellectual stream of the world organization.

The preventive role of peace observation and peacekeeping forces in the UN's history is important not only because it has historical significance but because it is very relevant to the future of the UN and of peacekeeping. In his 1960 annual report, Hammarskjöld presented the concept of preventive diplomacy for the first time, explicitly mentioning the Suez operations and the establishment of UNEF within the intellectual stream of preventive diplomacy.[5] The first and second generation of peacekeeping activity emphasized containment and prevention. Peacekeepers were meant to monitor cease-fire lines, thereby having a calming and preventive effect. Nowadays, in what is deemed the third generation of peacekeeping or peace support operations, the preventive dimension of this activity is emphasized. The British doctrine of peace support operations states the issue thus:

For the foreseeable future United Kingdom (UK) foreign policy is likely to underpin its conflict prevention activities with the regeneration or sustainment of fragile states. The UK Government usually undertakes such operations as part of United Nations (UN) led operations or as part of multilateral endeavours. . . . The generic title of Peace Support Operations (PSOs) is given by the military to these activities. Typically, the UK's Armed Forces are given responsibility for preventing or suppressing any conflict so that others can undertake activities that will alleviate the immediate symptoms of a conflict and/or a fragile state. Usually, there are associated activities to ensure stability in the long term.[6]

This structural approach is particularly important in view of the findings of Paul Collier's study on civil wars, which found that around half of all civil wars are due to post-conflict relapses. Given the reality that some military force is needed in post-conflict situations but that force provided by the post-conflict government is often counterproductive, there is a need for an external military force, which typically are UN peacekeeping forces. Seen from this perspective, peacekeeping and peacebuilding can be strong preventive elements.[7]

The first-ever preventive deployment of UN peacekeepers, which took place in the former Yugoslav republic of Macedonia, demonstrated its worth and remains a model that can be emulated to advantage in future situations.

Preventive Peacekeeping in Macedonia

The initiative for a preventive deployment first came from the co-chairs of the International Conference on the Former Yugoslavia. They had discussed this idea with Macedonia's president, Kiro Gligorov, who wrote to the Secretary-General on 11 November 1992 requesting a preventive deployment. In a letter of 18 November 1992 to the Secretary-General, the co-chairs, former U.S. secretary of state Cyrus Vance and former British foreign minister Lord David Owen, reported the growing need to take preventive measures to avoid the outbreak of violence in Macedonia and Kosovo. They also mentioned their warning to the Security Council a few days earlier that had spoken of the dreadful tragedy that could occur if conflict broke out in Macedonia and Kosovo. Such a conflict had the potential to spread to neighboring countries. The letter was carefully written to ensure that it would be positively received in the Office of the Secretary-General and in the Department of Peacekeeping Operations. It suggested that the Secretary-General send an exploratory mission to the Former Yugoslav Republic of Macedonia to look further into the feasibility of the idea of a preventive deployment.

Elaborating on their idea, the co-chairs stated that it would be desirable to put UN personnel, under the aegis of UNPROFOR, in Macedonia to provide a calming influence for all sides and give a sense of stability. They recommended that the Secretary-General deploy "a contingent of UNPROFOR personnel within Macedonia, who could have their headquarters in Skopje and be distributed in the main population centres, as well as on the Macedonian borders with Serbia (including Kosovo) and Albania. Their efforts would be complemented by those of the CSCE, which already had a small 'spill-over mission' in Skopje."

The co-chairs suggested that as a start, about a dozen UN military and police officers and supporting political staff be sent. They could be stationed in Skopje and could travel to the border areas. In the light of their experience and recommendations, the UN presence could be built up as needed. The co-chairs were conscious of the scarcity of UN resources, and they were seeking a way to implement their recommendation even in the face of that scarcity.

Secretary-General Boutros-Ghali sent an exploratory mission to the Former Yugoslav Republic of Macedonia to look into the possibility of establishing a preventive deployment of peacekeepers in the country. Following its visit, the exploratory mission made the following recommendations:

- That a small UNPROFOR presence be established on the Macedonian side of the Republic's borders with Albania and the Federal Republic of Yugoslavia (Serbia and Montenegro) with an essentially preventive mandate of monitoring and reporting any developments in the border areas which could undermine confidence and stability in Macedonia or threaten its territory
- That a small group of United Nations civilian police be deployed in the border areas to monitor the Macedonian border police[8]

The rationale for the deployment to the border areas was that incidents arising from illegal attempts to cross the border had increased tension on the Macedonian side. The mission believed that the presence of a small UN civilian police detachment would have a calming effect.

In December 1992, the Secretary-General reported to the Security Council on the findings of the exploratory mission, together with his recommendations.[9] On 11 December 1992, the Security Council authorized the Secretary-General to establish a presence of UNPROFOR in Macedonia.[10] The council requested that the Secretary-General immediately deploy the military, civil affairs, and administrative personnel he had recommended in his report, as well as police monitors.

In mid-December 1992, a UN team discussed practical arrangements with the government in Skopje. The first United Nations Civilian Police monitors arrived on 27 December 1992 and were eventually deployed along the northern and western borders. On 28 December, a reconnaissance team went to the country to make arrangements for the interim deployment of a Canadian company. On 7 January 1993, a Canadian company arrived in the country pending the arrival of a joint battalion from Finland, Norway, and Sweden. On 25 January, Brigadier-General Finn Saermark-Thomsen of Denmark, who had been designated commander of the Macedonia command of UNPROFOR, arrived in Skopje. On 18 February, the Nordic battalion took over the operation from the Canadian company.

The Nordic battalion was 434 strong and was composed of three rifle companies. It was deployed on the western border from Debar northward and on the northern border up to the border with Bulgaria. At the beginning, there were nineteen UN military observers in the area of operations. The western border south of Debar was covered solely by UN military observers.

From early January 1993, the northern border and the western border north of Debar were constantly monitored from observation posts and by regular patrols. The UN military observers conducted regular patrols to look for activities that might increase tension or threaten peace or stability. They also visited border villages to gain the confidence of their inhabitants so that they could help defuse possible interethnic tensions.

While carrying out their border-visiting program, the UN military observers were approached by different ethnic groups, who lodged various complaints about alleged discriminatory practices by the authorities. In cases where the complaints were relevant to the mission's mandate, they were brought to the attention of the appropriate authorities. Some were also brought to the attention of the international bodies, such as the International Conference on the Former Yugoslavia.

United Nations civilian police also conducted regular daily patrols to specific crossings and to the border areas in general. In the course of doing so, it received a number of complaints concerning the local border police through mayors. In cases where there appeared to be a basis for the complaint, United Nations civilian police took up the matter with the relevant police authorities.

From the outset, the civil affairs component of the mission established an information program to explain the role of UNPROFOR in the country. UNPROFOR maintained close coordination with the mission of the Conference on Security and Co-operation in Europe that was in the country.

By the middle of 1993, UNPROFOR's assessment was that it had been successful in its preventive mandate. It was concerned, however, about the internal situation and the possibility of instability if interethnic tensions increased, a possibility that was repeatedly mentioned by local and international sources. Another concern of UNPROFOR related to the deterioration of the economic situation stemming from the sanctions, which could exacerbate interethnic tensions.

In July 1993, the Secretary-General reported to the Security Council that the UNPROFOR command in the Former Yugoslav Republic of Macedonia consisted of 1,190 military and civilian personnel, including United Nations civil police.[11] A Nordic battalion was based in Kjojila, east of Skopje, and a U.S. contingent of 315 troops had arrived in Skopje in early July, deploying to the Former Yugoslav Republic of Macedonia side of the border with the Federal Republic of Yugoslavia. United Nations military observers, civilian police, and civil affairs officers also continued their activities. UNPROFOR reported: "This first venture in the field of preventive peace-keeping on the part of UNPROFOR continues to be successful, and to enjoy an excellent cooperative relationship with the FYROM Government, and to be fully supported by the people of the country."[12]

In May 1993, following the signing of the Vance-Owen peace plan for Bosnia-Herzegovina in Athens, Secretary-General Boutros-Ghali designated Cyrus Vance's successor, Thorvald Stoltenberg, as his special representative in charge of all UN operations in the former Yugoslavia. Stoltenberg combined the functions of co-chair of the International Conference on the Former Yugoslavia and special representative for the former Yugoslavia.

The commander in charge of the preventive deployment, General Saermark-Thomsen, was a wise and thoughtful general who proceeded in confidence-building mode. When he took command of the deployment, he was part of the larger UNPROFOR force, which had other contingents in Bosnia and Croatia. The situation in those two countries was tense, and thus the overall force commander, who was based in Zagreb, had his hands full. It was left to Saermark-Thomsen to give shape to the preventive deployment.

From the beginning, it was clear that the preventive deployment should become an independent peacekeeping operation so that the force commander on the ground could have direct access to the special representative and, through him, to the UN leadership in New York. The new force required step-by-step shaping. It needed political and other backup. General Saermark-Thomsen drafted an ideas paper on the future development of the force and shared it with the special representative. In this way, General Saermark-Thomsen, who received feedback from the special representative's office, knew that he was getting backup from the Office of the Special Representative. That was important to him in the formative period.

In those early months, the commander and members of the deployment faced an issue of considerable delicacy. As the civilian police officers went about their rounds, they were being approached by the local population who had grievances of one sort or another. At the beginning, it was not within their mandate to respond to such questions. But the civilian police officers explained that it made no sense for them simply to observe the local police in action, ignoring the concerns of the local population. They therefore made their own decision, outside the mandate, to listen to the local population and communicate their concerns to the authorities. On early visits to Skopje, the special representative encouraged the officers to respond to the local population, using their judgment.

The leadership of the preventive deployment ultimately concluded that the "increasing internal instability in the FYROM could prove to be more detrimental to the stability of the country than outside threats." UNPROFOR would therefore need "to consider what its role should be, if any, in the event that internal stability results in some form of civil conflict."[13]

Thus, the operation developed the second of its three pillars, good offices and political action. (The other two pillars were troop deployment and the human dimension.) The mission developed and maintained active contacts with political forces and ethnic groups to promote domestic stability. Efforts were made to reduce the level of mistrust among the country's political and ethnic actors, and the United Nations Preventive Deployment Force (UNPREDEP) set in place a dialogue on questions regarding the rights of ethnic communities and national minorities.

> UNPREDEP was recognized as a significant instrument for facilitating dialogue, restraint and practical compromise between the different segments of Macedonian society. UN troop patrols along the northern and western borders of the country effectively complemented such activities; this outreach had a calming and stabilizing effect throughout the area. The contingent of UN military observers and the team of civilian police monitors rendered equally invaluable services.[14]

Henryk Sokalski has written about the human dimension of UNPREDEP's efforts.[15] At the beginning of the deployment and well before a human dimension was explicitly authorized by the Security Council, members of the Nordic battalion provided a spectacular example of the human dimension through voluntary service. The Nordic troops were stationed on a mountain overlooking Kosovo and Macedonian Albanian villages connected by dirt roads. In the rainy seasons, the roads became impassable, and the villages were almost cut off from one another. Members of the Nordic battalion undertook Operation Mongoose as a private initiative: In their spare time, they constructed proper roads linking the villages so they would not be isolated during the rainy seasons.

The preventive deployment in the Former Yugoslav Republic of Macedonia worked effectively, externally as well as internally. The model in which UN observers patrolled sensitive areas where ethnic tensions were high, received complaints, transmitted them to the authorities, and served as an intermediary and confidence builder clearly has great relevance to situations of ethnic and religious tension, situations with minority populations, or situations where internal strife or conflict could result in gross violations of human rights. The establishment of a UN rapid reaction force would certainly help facilitate the dispatch of preventive deployment of UN peacekeepers in situations of urgent need.

The Idea for the Establishment of a Rapid Reaction Force

The possible establishment of a rapid reaction force has been under discussion in UN circles for some time but has so far seen only partial implementation. It is, however, an important preventive idea that has great relevance to the future of the world organization.

In the 1990s, the Friends of Rapid Deployment worked with the Department of Peacekeeping Operations to secure support for developing a rapidly deployable mission headquarters.[16] In 1994, the Department of Peacekeeping Operations organized the United Nations Stand-by Arrangement System to expand the quality and quantity of resources that member states might provide. To complement this arrangement, the Danish government, in cooperation with thirteen regular troop contributors, organized a multinational Stand-by High Readiness Brigade in 1995.

In 1995, the Netherlands published *A UN Rapid Deployment Brigade: A Preliminary Study,* which argued that developing crises necessitated a rapidly deployable "fire brigade" and called for a permanent rapidly deployable brigade.[17] That same year, the Canadian government published a study—*Towards a Rapid Reaction Capability for the United Nations*—that proposed an early warning mechanism, an effective decision-making process, reliable transportation and infrastructure, logistical support, adequate finances, and well-trained and equipped personnel.[18]

The principal idea of the Canadian study is the "vanguard concept," according to which the UN could assemble a multifunctional force of up to 5,000 military and civilian personnel from member states and rapidly deploy it under the control of an operational-level headquarters on the Security Council's authorization. The operational-level headquarters, a new unit in the UN system, would be responsible for the planning and advance preparation that is crucial for rapid response. The vanguard concept emphasizes the importance of making significant changes at the operational level of the UN system and with the troop contributors who would provide the trained equipped forces essential to rapid reaction. Forces would be provided through enhanced standby arrangements which the Secretariat would conclude with member states that offered personnel to participate in peace operations. The report also includes recommendations to enhance training, explore more efficient systems for logistics and transportation, and bolster the planning efforts of the entire UN system.[19]

In the academic writings on the subject, Howard Peter Langille has made the case for a UN Emergency Peace Service: "The development of a UN Emergency Peace Service, or of a mechanism similar to it, is . . . a progression of the idea of the collective human security agenda to which the UN is committed. . . . This does indeed require new ways of thinking about the nature and roles of peacekeeping and about the function of peace operations in the emerging global order."[20]

The High-Level Panel on Threats, Challenges and Change made the following recommendation in December 2004,

> Deploying military capacities—for peacekeeping as well as peace enforcement—has proved to be a valuable tool in ending wars and helping to secure States in their aftermath. But the total global supply of available peacekeepers is running dangerously low. Just to do an adequate job of keeping the peace in existing conflicts would require almost doubling the number of peacekeepers around the world. The developed States have particular responsibilities to do more to transform their armies into units suitable for deployment to peace operations. And if we are to meet the challenges ahead, more States will have to place contingents on stand-by for UN purposes.[21]

A UN rapid reaction force, which has yet to materialize, would certainly contribute to the UN's ability to act urgently and preventively in situations of need. Pending its establishment, the ad hoc deployment of UN observers for preventive purposes could be of great service. This is what occurred in South Africa in 1992–1993.

UN Observers in South Africa

Chapter 4 discussed how the dispatch of UN observers to South Africa in August 1992 helped contain a dangerous situation and prevented a decline into violence. This ad hoc mission was followed by the United Nations Observer Mission in South Africa (UNOMSA), which arrived with thirteen staff members on 13 September 1992, after the settlement process had run into problems.[22] The number of UNOMSA observers grew to 100 in the mission's first year; in the final stage of the operation, 2,500 people were part of the mission. It was deployed first to the spots with greatest violence —the Vaal, Johannesburg, and KwaZulu-Natal—and eventually spread to forty-five locations. Its mandate was carried out by teams of two or three in various locations, who were in daily contact with headquarters in Johannesburg.

The presence of international observers did not end political violence, but it created favorable conditions for democratic transition. According to Angela King, the head of the mission:

> UNOMSA was one of the UN's first experiences of a preventive diplomacy mission as defined in the *Agenda for Peace.* It became a model rich in lessons in how to develop community involvement and national ownership of a peace process. Although the mandate of the mission was to observe and to be the Security Council's eyes and ears, the teams rapidly developed quiet supportive diplomacy in harmony with the peace accord counterparts, and once they had gained trust and confidence took a much more proactive role in negotiating, persuading, nudging and sometimes shaming South Africans to return to the peace tables at all levels and though often characterized as low-key, has been followed by the United Nations in other areas.[23]

From the first day, UNOMSA's teams reached out to all eleven regions of the country. Its monitoring of demonstrations, marches, political funerals, and other types of public protests were often planned in concert with OAU, EU, and Commonwealth teams. The aim was to keep these events free of political violence. Channels of communication were established across the political spectrum with all twenty-five political parties and entities. The head of mission met and had regular consultations with the leaders of all parties and entities as well as, more importantly, heads of the police and military in the various provinces. This ensured that the mission had inside information about political developments, knowledge of where new unrest was likely to break out and where bombs were likely to be placed, and early warning on both sides of impending outbreaks. For the most part, this information-gathering ensured the safety of the mission's personnel—the South African counterparts as well as UNOMSA staff—though some received wounds from bullets, strafing, and stone-throwing.

The e contacts were useful in carrying out the mandate, particularly in explaining the importance of the design of political institutions for a sustainable democratic settlement, getting peace negotiations back on track, and defusing violence and tensions between the security forces and the population as well as between various political and ethnic factions.

Nongovernmental organizations and religious and tribal leaders played a useful role in the political process. UNOMSA staff attended numerous caucuses and meetings and provided legal and logistical support to independent watchdog organizations, among them the Goldstone Commission. South Africans grew accustomed to seeing the UN's face—women and men dressed in blue caps and smocks, carrying the UN flag proudly.

In the view of Angela King, the primary lesson of UNOMSA was what Lakhdar Brahimi, who had come to watch over the successful elections, later called a "light footprint" in national reconciliation. According to this concept, instead of sending an international mediator or military peacekeepers, the international community encouraged local parties and then observed their direct negotiations, intervening only at vital junctures. This included assisting in the creation of the Transitional Executive Council and the Independent Electoral Commission and furthering the election process that culminated in the holding of the first democratic nonracial elections in April 1994.

Through all of this, UNOMSA's main ally was the framework of the peace accord signed by all parties. Its structures at the national, regional, and local levels gave entry points to all parts of the country and to different strata of society and access to all disputes and settlements. It gave the mission access to the courts so it could ensure that judges were being fair; to hostels, where migrant workers had been kept, often in dire conditions; to prisons; and to the seat of power in Ulundi, Bophutaswana, Ciskei, Western Cape, and elsewhere. The peace accord South Africans drew up before the arrival of the UN was implemented under UNOMSA.

Another key lesson learned from UNOMSA, according to King, was the critical role of women in political processes. From the beginning, a special effort was made to select UNOMSA staff on the basis of gender balance, ethnic diversity, and varied occupational experience. The presence of so many women in leadership positions in UNOMSA, over 50 percent in the first fourteen months, acted as a catalyst to change the views and attitudes of many local women irrespective of their party affiliation. International and local women proved to be successful negotiators, capable of proposing non-traditional approaches to establishing dialogue between polarized groups.[24]

With the assistance of UNOMSA, South African women participated in peace committees, church groups, and nongovernmental organizations. Through traditional mediation means such as family ties, oral narratives, prayers, and songs, women raised awareness of the need for reconciliation and the restoration of trust between communities. With compassion and understanding, they explained the benefits of peace and the futility of violence and conflict, contributing to a peaceful environment. During electoral campaigns, women advocated increased integration of a gender perspective into decisions and policies concerning their communities.

Conclusion

This chapter has illustrated that the establishment of the first formal preventive peacekeeping force in the Former Yugoslav Republic of Macedonia, UNPREDEP, was a conceptual and operational breakthrough that has great significance for the future. This is the case even if, almost a decade and a half later, formal preventive deployments have not occurred. The idea of establishing a rapid reaction force is an important one that should be kept on the negotiating table. There is also a question of whether the idea should be enlarged to include establishing a corps of UN observers who could be deployed at short notice. Even in 1947, Secretary-General Lie foresaw such a possibility in his idea of establishing a corps of United Nations guards. The establishment of a mission of UN observers in South Africa helped stabilize that country in the run-up to its first independent elections. Like UNPREDEP, UNOMSA was a great success.

8

Preventive Diplomacy in the Economic, Social, Human Rights, and Humanitarian Fields

- The Economic Commission for Europe as an East-West Bridge
- Early Warning and Urgent Response Systems
- Identifying and Heading Off Economic and Social Emergencies
- The Articulation of Development Policy: The Millennium Development Goals
- Preventive Human Rights and Humanitarian Strategies to Date
- The Promotion of Democracy and the Rule of Law
- Preventive Strategies for the Future
- Conclusion

This chapter looks at whether the idea of preventive diplomacy has been put to use in the economic and social fields in the past and whether there might be room to draw on it in the future. To the extent that the UN has consistently sought to give priority to development and to alleviating the plight of the poor, it has been engaged in advocacy for human progress and has sought to address the economic and social roots of conflicts.[1]

The Economic Commission for Europe (ECE) has played a role in this process, specifically regarding building confidence between capitalist and communist countries in the dangerous period of the Cold War. Although this was not done as an exercise in preventive diplomacy, the ECE rendered an invaluable service in helping promote dialogue and cooperation between the two sides.

A number of UN agencies have early warning and urgent response systems. Agencies such as the International Atomic Energy Agency (IAEA), the Food and Agriculture Organization (FAO), the United Nations Environment Programme (UNEP), the United Nations High Commissioner for Refugees (UNHCR), the United Nations Children's Fund (UNICEF), and the World Health Organization (WHO) have developed and operated such systems for a long time. The Department of Economic and Social Affairs has also made substantial efforts to identify, analyze, and monitor emerging problems in the world economy.

The Economic Commission for Europe as an East-West Bridge

The ECE was created in 1947 with the primary task of dealing with problems of postwar reconstruction in Europe. Following the period of reconstruction, the commission increasingly became a major instrument for regional economic cooperation between countries of the East and West. Much of the ECE's past activities involved a search for solutions to problems of common concern to these two groups of countries, for appropriate forms of contact between them, for methods of exchanging experiences, and for techniques and procedures through which their diverging interests could be reconciled.

The ECE concentrated on promoting facilities for trade between centrally planned and market economy countries, particularly through the standardization and unification of trade practices and the development of legal and technical norms applicable to trade relations among Eastern European countries. ECE committees thus performed "clearinghouse" functions and engaged in efforts to eliminate obstacles to trade among countries with different socioeconomic systems.

In the ECE's early years, a major source of difficulty between market economy and centrally planned countries was the complaint by East European countries that trade and export-licensing policies discriminated against them. In 1949, the ECE established the Committee on the Development of Trade, which initially experienced problems because of the Cold War. However, with the thaw in East-West relations after 1954, the committee began to gain ground and meet regularly.

In 1963, the ECE established an ad hoc working group of experts to study certain policy problems of East-West trade, including 1) the role of customs tariffs in the trade of member countries with different economic systems and how pricing and taxation policies affected external trade; 2) the most-favored-nation principle and nondiscriminatory treatment as applied in the different economic systems and problems concerning reciprocal obligations under the different systems; and 3) the possibility of further multilateralization of trade and payments.[2]

The consideration of these issues took time and was quite painstaking, but the discussion provided a useful opportunity for each side to better understand the other's positions. In the end, there was a general consensus that detailed talks on the concept of the most-favored-nation clause and its application in trade between countries with different economic systems would be less profitable, and it was agreed that the general objective should be to achieve an equitable and mutually advantageous balance in trade and an increase in trade on the basis of the most-favored-nation concept. The discussion thus led to the pursuit of practical ideas in relations between the two groups of countries.[3]

ECE experts from participating countries agreed that the goal should be to achieve effective reciprocity or mutual advantage by means of realistic and practical approaches. They also agreed that effective reciprocity and mutual advantage should be measured in terms of concrete results, namely the increase in the volume and composition of trade between countries with different systems. They favored concrete mutual commitments of the trading partners intended to result in the maximum increase of the volume of imports and the widening of the composition of imports. This would require removing discriminatory obstacles to trade, the conclusion of long-term trade agreements, and a more flexible payments system.

On 2 May 1968, the ECE adopted a resolution inviting member countries to take all possible measures to permit a broad expansion of intra-European trade that could bring them economic advantages "and would be likely to contribute to the strengthening of peaceful and friendly relations."[4] In 1976, ECE delegations emphasized the great importance attached to action to reduce or progressively eliminate obstacles to the development of trade.[5]

In their study of the ECE, Berthelot and Rayment assessed that its major achievement was to keep the idea of a larger Europe alive between 1947 and the end of the Cold War. "It did so by building and preserving a bridge between its western and eastern halves when no one else was willing or able to do so and when the prospect of reuniting them was so distant."[6] This was preventive diplomacy in action.

Early Warning and Urgent Response Systems

A number of UN agencies have established and operated early warning and urgent response systems for some time now, and they have undoubtedly made important contributions in the economic, social, environmental, and nuclear fields. UNEP's environmental assessment program, Earthwatch, established in 1972, aims to study the interaction between humans and the environment, provide early warning of potential environmental hazards, and determine the state of natural resources. The Global Environmental

Monitoring System, which began in UNEP in 1975, collects data on topics such as renewable resources, climate, health hazards, long-range transport pollutants, integrated monitoring of pollutants and ecosystems, and the oceans. To convert the data into information usable by decision makers, a global resource information database was set up in 1985. UNEP's Global Environmental Information Exchange Network (INFOTERRA) provides national focal points for the exchange of environmental information.[7]

The FAO's Global Information and Early Warning System was established at the request of the 1973 FAO conference and the 1974 World Food Conference. Governments and international agencies participate formally while nongovernmental organizations cooperate closely. The system monitors global food supply stocks, monitors the food supply outlook at the national level, alerts governments to emerging problems, and provides assistance to strengthen national early warning capacities in developing countries.[8]

UNDRO, whose work is now performed by the Office for the Coordination of Humanitarian Affairs (OCHA), sought to develop early warning and urgent response systems for natural disasters since 1972. In December 1989, the General Assembly proclaimed the 1990s the International Decade for Natural Disaster Reduction. The assembly called on all governments to adopt policies to achieve disaster mitigation. It also called on scientific and technological institutions, financial institutions, foundations, and national and international nongovernmental organizations to participate fully in efforts to prevent natural disasters.[9] These and other efforts continue to be spearheaded by a specialized section of the Office for the Coordination of Humanitarian Affairs.[10] The Asian tsunami disaster vividly demonstrated the need for better early warning and alerts about impending natural disasters.

The IAEA has contributed to studies on handling nuclear emergencies and has conventions on early notification and assistance in the case of a nuclear accident. For some time now, the WHO has operated an emergency preparedness and response system. UNHCR and UNICEF also have emergency preparedness and response systems.[11]

Identifying and Heading Off Economic and Social Emergencies

Under Article 55 of the Charter, the UN is expected to promote solutions to international economic, social, and health problems. Responsibility for discharging these functions lies with the General Assembly and with ECOSOC.

The latter has a mandate to initiate studies and reports on international economic, social, cultural, educational, and health matters and to make recommendations on them to the General Assembly, member states, and relevant specialized agencies. Under Article 65, ECOSOC may furnish information to the Security Council and assist the Security Council on its request.

Since its establishment, ECOSOC has served as a forum for discussing global economic and social problems and for developing policy recommendations for tackling them. It has undoubtedly encountered many problems in fulfilling its role. But it has also made some contributions in highlighting the plight of the poorest and vulnerable. There are inherent preventive dimensions in this.

In 1989, ECOSOC reviewed a survey of the mechanisms and means available within the UN system for early identification, analysis, and monitoring of world economic developments.[12] The survey discussed conceptual issues and provided a summary of the systems, reports, and activities the UN system uses for the early identification, analysis, and monitoring of emerging problems in the world economy.

Following its consideration of the survey, ECOSOC adopted resolution 1989/85 of 26 July 1989, which acknowledged that the UN needed to improve its analytical and forecasting activities on a coordinated basis and requested that the Secretary-General present proposals to improve the UN's work in this area. The council stressed that the UN should strengthen information links within the UN system, improve existing mechanisms and means of providing socioeconomic data in a comprehensive and readily available form, further develop links and increase the flow of information between the UN and national research and information centers, and expand the analysis of options and possible actions that might be taken in connection with emerging problems in the world economy, with a view to encouraging member states to improve their own analytical work and forecasting activities.

In response to the council's request, the Secretary-General submitted a report to the council in 1990 reviewing the role of the UN and presenting a number of proposals to improve existing analytical and forecasting activities on a coordinated basis and strengthen the flow of information for the analysis and forecasting of world economic developments, both within the UN and between it and national research units.[13] One proposal stated that the assessments of organizations regarding the immediate prospects for the world economy should be strengthened in the context of available global, sectoral, and regional models. There was a corresponding need to strengthen modeling frameworks used to study the potential of the world economy over the longer term. Where possible, models should be designed to incorporate the impact of technological change and the availability and yield of resources relevant to predicting economic growth. To that end, the proposal stated that organizations and bodies should intensify their efforts at long-term global modeling as a matter of priority and should attempt to establish, within the framework of a variety of econometric models, means for the international community to explore alternative paths for world economic, environment, and social developments.[14]

Subsequent to the publication of these recommendations and the deliberations of ECOSOC, the Department of Economic and Social Affairs sought to enhance cooperation with partners for the early identification, analysis, and monitoring of emergency problems in the global economy. Later in the 1990s, however, the Asian economic crisis took the world by surprise with its disastrous economic and social consequences. There is still a need for global monitoring and forecasting to detect and possibly head off economic and social crises. One example is the SARS epidemic and what might ensue if the virus were to infect humans on a large scale.

The Articulation of Development Policy: The Millennium Development Goals

Successive UN policy documents have set development goals and pursued strategies to tackle the massive economic and social problems, particularly the extreme poverty of two-thirds of the world's population. While these documents fall largely in the category of policy development and advocacy, they also have a preventive dimension to the extent that they draw attention to economic and social problems.

The Millennium Declaration, which was adopted on 8 September 2000, is the latest example of such a policy document.[15] In it, heads of state and government reaffirmed their commitment to the purposes and principles of the UN Charter and expressed their determination to establish a just and lasting peace. They believed that the central challenge was to ensure that globalization became a positive force for all the world's peoples. They considered certain fundamental values to be essential to international relations in the twenty-first century, including freedom, equality, solidarity, tolerance, respect for nature, and shared responsibility.

They declared their intention to spare no effort to free people from war and strengthen the rule of law in international and national affairs and make the UN more effective in maintaining peace and security. They solemnly declared that they would spare no effort "to free our fellow men, women and children from the abject and dehumanizing conditions of extreme poverty."[16] In particular, they resolved to halve the proportion of the world's people whose income was less than one dollar a day as well as to save the same proportion of people from hunger by the year 2015. Further, they resolved to halve the proportion of people unable to reach or afford safe drinking water by the same date. They also committed themselves to ensure that all children—both boys and girls—would be able to complete a full course of primary schooling. Similar goals were set in relation to reducing maternal mortality, tackling HIV/AIDS and malaria, and improving the lives of slum-dwellers.

Supporters of the declaration declared their solemn intention to protect vulnerable populations and to protect and assist children and civilian populations that disproportionately suffer the consequences of natural disasters, genocide and armed conflicts, and other humanitarian emergencies. They promised to spare no efforts to make the UN a more effective instrument for pursuing the fight for development for all people; the fight against poverty, ignorance, and disease; the fight against injustice; the fight against terror and crime; and the fight against the degradation and destruction of "our common home."[17]

The heads of state and governments made specific commitments regarding human rights, democracy, and good governance. They resolved to strengthen the capacity of all their countries to implement principles of democracy and respect for human rights, including minority rights. They also resolved to eliminate all forms of violence against women; take measures to protect human rights of migrants, migrant workers and their families; eliminate the increasing acts of racism and xenophobia in many societies; and promote greater tolerance in all societies.

The signatories further resolved to strengthen cooperation between the UN and national parliaments and to give greater opportunities to the private sector, nongovernmental organizations, and civil society to help realize UN goals and programs. They asked the General Assembly to review the progress made in implementing the provisions of their declaration and asked the Secretary-General "to issue periodic reports" for the General Assembly and as a basis for further action.[18]

The Millennium Declaration thus entrusts the Secretary-General with important responsibilities to identify issues requiring urgent action. Might there be room for the Secretary-General to make a discreet contribution to alleviating the plight of the poor and protecting the vulnerable? The Secretary-General could raise these issues in his annual reports and as part of the process of cooperation with regional organizations. If, for example, economic analysis indicates that a country might be able to alleviate poverty by taking remedial actions, could the Secretary-General, through the head of the regional economic and social commission concerned and in cooperation with the head of the relevant regional intergovernmental organization, intercede discretely to help activate remedial measures? Likewise, could discreet diplomacy behind the scenes, again involving the relevant regional economic and social commission and regional intergovernmental organization, help vulnerable parts of the population, such as minorities or indigenous populations? This would be a departure in the practice of Secretaries-General, but discreet preventive diplomacy should certainly be considered —not only with respect to political crises and emergencies but also with respect to economic and social crises and emergencies.

UN bodies have provided hard evidence and valuable insights into the nexus between economic and social problems and violence and conflict. A case in point is the Committee on Economic, Social and Cultural Rights, a body established by ECOSOC, which operates under the International Covenant on Economic, Social and Cultural Rights. The committee adopted a statement on poverty in 2001 that noted that poverty can arise when people lack access to resources because of who they are, what they believe, or where they live. Discrimination may cause poverty, just as poverty may cause discrimination.[19]

Preventive Human Rights and Humanitarian Strategies to Date

Preventive strategies have been a part of UN efforts to deal with human rights and humanitarian issues from the earliest days of the organization, although the extent of such policies has been limited. Every Secretary-General has exercised humanitarian good offices.[20] The Office of the United Nations High Commissioner for Refugees was created in 1950 to deal with refugee situations and, to a certain extent, help avert new refugee outflows.[21] This preventive dimension was given particular emphasis in the 1970s when Canada proposed an item on human rights and mass exoduses in the Commission on Human Rights. The rationale was that the human rights root causes of refugee outflows should be addressed. This initiative eventually led to one of the experimental early warning processes in the UN whereby the Centre for Human Rights received a mandate to consult partner departments and organizations and to advise the Secretary-General of situations where he could act to head off mass exoduses.[22]

At that same time, Germany launched an initiative in the General Assembly on international cooperation to avert new flows of refugees. This initiative led to the creation of what is now the Office for the Coordination of Humanitarian Affairs. The head of this office engages in ongoing preventive diplomatic efforts, as does the representative of the Secretary-General on internally displaced persons and the United Nations Inter-Agency Unit on Internally Displaced Persons.[23]

The efforts of the International Committee of the Red Cross to promote and disseminate international humanitarian law and help protect those at risk have an implicit preventive rationale. The work of Red Cross delegates in the field and at headquarters includes a significant dimension of preventive diplomacy. The Red Cross's "right of initiative," by which it can initiate action it deems necessary to help victims of conflict, is a classic case of the exercise of mitigatory preventive diplomacy.[24]

UN Human Rights Actors

The Convention on the Prevention and Punishment of Genocide, adopted on 9 December 1948, the day before the Universal Declaration of Human Rights was proclaimed by the General Assembly, has an express preventive goal. So does the Universal Declaration itself, which opened with the recognition that human rights had to be respected under the rule of law if human beings were not to be forced to resort to rebellion against tyranny and oppression.

The Sub-Commission on the Prevention of Discrimination and Protection of Minorities, a subsidiary body of the former Commission on Human Rights, was one of the early human rights organs. It was later known as the Sub-Commission on the Promotion and Protection of Human Rights. The subcommission implemented the prevention mandate through a series of global thematic studies followed by recommendations for norms and policies to address discrimination. The subcommission's work made the world aware of situations of discrimination, and it provided the basis for many global norms and policies. It is unfortunate that the preventive aspect of this subcommission's work has been dropped.

In 1967, the agenda of the Commission on Human Rights included an item on violations of human rights. The public discussion of the item was a significant move in the exercise of public diplomacy intended to react against gross violations and prevent their recurrence. The commission began designating fact-finding rapporteurs and working groups on particular country situations or on global problems such as arbitrary, summary, and extrajudicial executions; torture; and involuntary disappearances. The urgent action procedures of these fact-finders, their visits to countries, and their reports on thematic and country situations had significant elements of mitigatory and preventive diplomacy.[25]

In 1970, ECOSOC resolution 1503 established a procedure for responding to petitions (called communications) alleging gross violations of human rights. This procedure had a built-in dimension of human rights diplomacy in the form of dialogue and direct contacts with governments. Though the process was reactive, it did have a preventive dimension inasmuch as it was intended to mitigate violations and, hopefully, help bring them to an end. Since 2003, the use of the "right of initiative" by the UN High Commissioner for Human Rights provides another example of the exercise of preventive diplomacy.[26]

Exploratory early warning and urgent action procedures have been developed by some of the human rights treaty bodies such as the Human Rights Committee, which operates under the International Covenant on Civil and Political Rights, and the Committee on the Elimination of Racial Discrimination, which operates under the Convention on the Elimination of Racial Discrimination. During the 1990s wars in the former Yugoslavia, the Human Rights Committee called for special reports from all the successor republics to signal its concern over human rights violations and to begin a dialogue with the governments on human rights questions. The competence of the Committee against Torture (which operates under the Convention against Torture) to undertake country visits has elements of early warning, preventive action, and preventive diplomacy.

In 1992–9393, the preventive role of human rights treaty bodies was discussed in various treaty bodies, as reflected in the following consideration taken from the fourth meeting of the chairs of human rights treaty bodies:

> The treaty bodies have an important role in seeking to prevent as well as to respond to human rights violations. It is thus appropriate for each treaty body to undertake an urgent examination of all possible measures that it might take, within its competence, both to prevent human rights violations from occurring and to monitor more closely emergency situations of all kinds arising within the jurisdiction of States parties. Where procedural innovations are required for this purpose, they should be considered as soon as possible.[27]

Taking into account the procedures adopted by other treaty bodies,[28] the Committee on the Elimination of Racial Discrimination followed this recommendation and decided to create an early warning and urgent action procedure. To this end, it adopted a working paper in 1993 that presented the legal basis of the procedure.[29] The working paper is instructive about the indicators and approaches of the treaty bodies and is summarized in what follows.

Early warning measures: Aim at addressing existing structural problems to prevent them from escalating into conflicts and include confidence-building measures to identify and support structures to strengthen racial tolerance and solidify peace in order to prevent a relapse into conflict. The criteria for the adoption of such measures include:

- Lack of an adequate legislative basis for defining and criminalizing all forms of racial discrimination
- Inadequate implementation or enforcement mechanisms, including the lack of recourse procedures
- The presence of a pattern of escalating racial hatred and violence or racist propaganda or appeals to racial intolerance by persons, groups, or organizations, particularly by elected or other officials
- A significant pattern of racial discrimination evidenced in social and economic indicators
- Significant flows of refugees or displaced persons as the result of a pattern of racial discrimination or encroachment on the lands of minority communities[30]

The working paper proposed the following measures to remedy such a situation:

- Offer to send to state parties one or more of its members to facilitate the implementation of international standards or technical assistance to establish an institutional human rights infrastructure.
- Recommend that state parties avail themselves of the advisory services and technical assistance program of the OHCHR.
- Submit information to the Secretary-General as a contribution to his early warning mechanism.
- Recommend greater cooperation at the regional level.[31]

Urgent procedures: Aim at responding to problems requiring immediate attention to prevent or limit the scale or number of serious violations of the convention. Possible criteria for initiating an urgent procedure include "the presence of a serious, massive or persistent pattern of racial discrimination; . . . or that the situation is serious and there is a risk of further racial discrimination."[32]

The working paper proposed these measures to enhance the effectiveness of urgent procedures:

- Request the urgent submission of a special report concerning measures taken to prevent a serious a pattern of racial discrimination.
- Designate a special rapporteur to act as a focal point for monitoring critical situations and consult with the committee chair to initiate the urgent action procedure and follow up when decisions have been taken.
- Express concern and recommendations for actions to:
  - The state party concerned;
  - The special rapporteur on contemporary forms of racism, racial discrimination, and xenophobia and related intolerance;
  - The UN Secretary-General;
  - The Security Council through the Secretary-General;
  - Other relevant human rights bodies.[33]

In her annual report to the Commission on Human Rights in 2000, High Commissioner Mary Robinson wrote that the quest to prevent gross violations of human rights and of conflicts was a defining issue of our times. The universal implementation of human rights—economic, social, and cultural as well as civil and political—was the surest preventive strategy and the most effective way to avoid conflict. Unfortunately, the commission did not take any action on this important report.[34]

In her 2006 report to the General Assembly, Louise Arbour, the current high commissioner, emphasized country engagement, which, in its various forms, aims to address gaps in protection through a consultative process involving governments, civil society, and other relevant international and national counterparts. The OHCHR, she emphasized, is not an arbiter or judge; its work is an ongoing dialogue that brings duty-bearers and rights-holders together in order to more effectively promote and protect human rights. To this end, the monitoring of human rights developments at the country level and the relevant collection of information are indispensable tools for an objective analysis of the human rights situation, which, in turn, is fundamental for devising the most adequate forms of technical cooperation.[35]

The high commissioner considers national human rights institutions a key element of the OHCHR strategy to engage countries. According to Arbour, the OHCHR will be able to achieve its greatest impact though an expanded presence in the field at both the country and regional levels.[36] She is planning to expand country offices and increase support to the human rights components of UN peace missions. Cooperation with the UN resident coordinator system and UN country teams is, in her assessment, becoming more structured and systematic.

Arbour's office is strengthening its capacities and consolidating its expertise in the right to development and the Millennium Development Goals (MDGs). It is pursuing a human rights approach to migration, the rule of law and transitional justice, and the protection of human rights. It is also countering terrorism and is supporting the UN Global Compact initiative on human rights cooperation with business organizations. It is supporting confidence-building measures among special procedures and governments.

Arbour attaches high importance to the Human Rights Council's planned establishment of a universal periodic review (UPR) that will subject all states to a periodic review of their fulfillment of their human rights obligations and commitments. According to Arbour, the review process should be inclusive, results-oriented, well-structured, and transparent. She emphasized the following key elements:

> The willingness of countries under review to open themselves to genuine scrutiny which, in turn, might prompt remedial action, is crucial for the success and effectiveness of the UPR.[37] Countries should be assessed on the basis of human rights instruments to which they are parties and other obligations, as well as the 2005 Summit Outcome Document and States' voluntary pledges and commitments to the Council, if any. The result should both yield a full picture of a country's human rights situation, and help to identify gaps that may require concerted action to improve protection capacity.[38]

It is clear that significant human rights diplomacy could be involved in implementing these ideas. It remains to be seen whether, and to what extent, this diplomacy will have preventive effects.

UN Humanitarian Actors

Over the six decades of the UN's history, preventive humanitarian diplomacy has been exercised by the Secretary-General, the High Commissioner for Refugees, senior officials such as the executive director of UNICEF, and more recently created offices, such as the special representative of the Secretary-General for internally displaced persons.

Successive UN high commissioners for refugees have long exercised their good offices to prevent and ameliorate refugee situations, and the office has arrangements and procedures for urgent response to crisis situations. However, because it is a humanitarian organization, the office has looked to the political parts of the UN for help on preventive actions and diplomacy.

The good offices of the UNHCR have been used in cases when a situation fell outside of its mandate but people still required protection. In 1957, the General Assembly called on the high commissioner to deal with the problems of Chinese refugees in Hong Kong. One problem was that a refugee had to be unable or unwilling to avail himself or herself of the protection of a recognized government in order to come under the mandate of the UNHCR. But at the time, there were two Chinas in existence, and the People's Republic of China had not yet taken the Chinese seat at the UN. To overcome the difficulty, the General Assembly asked the high commissioner for refugees to exercise his good offices to assist the refugees. Out of this action, the concept of the good offices of the high commissioner was born.

In a course of lectures at the Hague Academy of International Law in July 1965, a former high commissioner for refugees, Felix Schnyder, characterized the good offices of the high commissioner as "action to promote, stimulate and, where necessary, coordinate external assistance with a view to enabling a government to deal with a refugee problem within its frontiers."[39] Commenting on the classical concept of good offices involving an intermediary role, he noted that the high commissioner played the role of an intermediary "sometimes in a purely voluntary capacity and sometimes by virtue of his obligations under the mandate."[40]

In the past, the UN high commissioner for refugees has also deployed good offices to help head off problems. Prince Sadruddin Aga Khan, another former high commissioner for refugees, has identified three criteria for action by the high commissioner's office. First, the needs to be met and the necessary action to be undertaken should be of strictly humanitarian and nonpolitical. Second, there should be a request to the high commissioner from the government or governments directly concerned. Third, the persons for whom the assistance program is to be implemented must qualify as refugees or be in a situation analogous to that of refugees.[41]

He discussed the concept of good offices and noted that beyond the original conception introduced by the General Assembly, the institution remained useful

for contingencies and situations on the fringe of the normal activities of the High Commissioner's Office. These may relate more to diplomacy and the role of "intermediary of good will" which the High Commissioner is sometimes called upon to play. For example, discreet approaches are sometimes made by the UNHCR in the hope of easing a situation involving refugees or displaced persons. Similarly, using the tool of "quiet diplomacy" the High Commissioner is often required to ease the tensions that arise inevitably between the country of origin and the country of asylum. His task then consists in depoliticizing refugee situations and putting them into a purely humanitarian context so that they do not continue to be contentious.[42]

Appeals by the UN high commissioner for refugees and visits by the high commissioner or senior officials can be, and have been, part of the good offices or preventive diplomacy the UNHCR exercises. A good example of this is a UNHCR appeal on the issue of the Vietnamese boat people in Hong Kong in December 1989. The UNHCR asked Hong Kong to refrain from forcibly returning more people to Vietnam until an international conference met the following month to consider new approaches to the problem.[43] Hong Kong attenuated its policy of forcible return pending the conference.

In its more recent history, the UNHCR has used international conferences and action plans to respond to crises related to refugees and displacement, to help contain such crises, and to help avoid or contain situations that could lead to refugee outflows. The UNHCR has used these strategies regarding situations such as that of the Indo-Chinese refugees, refugees and displaced persons in Central America, and refugees and displaced persons in Central Africa. A UNHCR plan of action helped successfully address the refugee situation following the breakup of the former Soviet Union and the fears of refugee movements in the countries of the Commonwealth of Independent States.[44]

During its decade and a half of existence, OCHA, previously the Department of Humanitarian Affairs, has had some experience in the early detection of humanitarian crises and in acting behind the scenes to head them off. During the tenure of Yasushi Akashi in the 1990s, the Department of Humanitarian Affairs operated the Humanitarian Early Warning System, which built on UNICEF's experience with emergency forecasting and preventive action. In the mid-1990s, Ambassador Teferra Shiawl-Kidanekal, UNICEF's field operative in Africa, covered twenty-three West and Central African countries, conducting on-the-ground forecasting for UNICEF and alerting its regional office to situations that required attention. After that, in 1999, Shiawl-Kidanekal ran the Humanitarian Early Warning System for the Department of Humanitarian Affairs, a system that functioned until it was reformed into an information service by Akashi's successor, the late Sergio Vieira de Mello.

Humanitarian Early Warning System personnel conducted briefing papers and analyses of countries of concern and likely scenarios using a set of indicators the early warning system had developed. The Department of Humanitarian Affairs discreetly sent teams to countries of concern, such as Albania, Indonesia, Bulgaria, and the Democratic Republic of the Congo. In 1998, Shiawl-Kidanekal participated in a mission to Bulgaria to discuss a developing humanitarian situation of concern. Based on the evidence the mission supplied, the Department of Humanitarian Affairs canvassed donors and UN agencies for $10 million for Bulgaria to use to defuse a deteriorating humanitarian situation. This succeeded in containing a situation of concern. In some instances, as in the case of the Democratic Republic of the Congo in 1998, the head of the department went to a country to advise its leaders discreetly of a situation of concern and to help them head it off.[45]

Another innovative step in the Department of Humanitarian Affairs was sponsorship of the Integrated Regional Information Networks (IRIN) service, which has issued a number of public reports about humanitarian situations of concern and contributed to the consolidated appeals system. The public reports of IRIN provide early warning and help generate humanitarian responses.

Since the abolition of OCHA's early warning system described above, OCHA has been experiencing a need for early warning and alert arrangements. An OCHA director discretely indicated in an interview with the author in September 2006 that there had been contacts between the office and some Security Council members with a view to sharing information on advance detection of humanitarian emergencies and the preparation of urgent responses.

Jan Egeland, head of OCHA until the end of 2006, acted in mitigation as well as preventive mode. His efforts in 2004–2006 to generate international attention to the situation in northern Uganda, where the Lord's Resistance Army had perpetrated atrocities over many years, and to help promote a solution there had elements of humanitarian response as well as prevention of future atrocities. Egeland's public statements on a number of situations highlighted the plight of people in distress and headed off further atrocities. From the outset of the crisis in Darfur, he led the search for solutions, and his was one of the few voices that publicly protested Israel's extensive bombardments of civilians in Lebanon in July 2006.

At the beginning of the Darfur crisis, Egeland spoke out against atrocities being committed there, prompting the government of Sudan to threaten to withdraw cooperation from him, which would have immobilized him and his department. He had to tone down his public comments and look to the high commissioner for human rights to take the lead in speaking out on the situation and deploying observers there. The lesson here was that a bold humanitarian actor seeking to perform an advocacy or protection role has to be ready to bear the consequences of noncooperation and nonviability on the ground.

Finally, the efforts of the Secretary-General's special representative on internally displaced persons and the Inter-Agency Unit on Internally Displaced Persons should be noted. The special representative's role in drafting a set of guidelines for the protection of internally displaced persons, securing broad-based agreement on these guidelines, and promoting the application of the guidelines is an example of systemic or structural preventive diplomacy, to use the categories of Secretary-General Annan. The special representative, to some extent, has also engaged in operational preventive diplomacy in some instances.[46]

The Promotion of Democracy and the Rule of Law

Article 21 of the Universal Declaration of Human Rights proclaimed that the will of the people shall be the basis of the authority of government. This will is expressed in periodic and genuine elections that should be based on universal and equal suffrage and be held by secret vote or by equally free voting procedures.

Article 25 of the International Covenant on Civil and Political Rights states that everyone has the right and the opportunity without any of the distinctions mentioned in Article 2 and without unreasonable restrictions (a) to take part in the conduct of public affairs, directly or through freely chosen representatives; (b) to vote and to be elected at genuine periodic elections that are by universal and equal suffrage and held by secret ballot, guaranteeing the free expression of the will of the electors; (c) to have access, on general terms of equality, to public service in his or her country.

Likewise, the European Convention on Human Rights and Fundamental Freedoms calls for an effective political democracy. In its decisions, the European Court of Human Rights has acknowledged that the notions of pluralism, tolerance, and broadmindedness should be characteristics of a democratic society and that one of the fundamental principles of a democracy is the rule of law.[47] Justice is best served by constitutional democracy under the rule of law. In the case of *Peter Chiko Bwalya v. Zambia*, the Human Rights Committee held that a violation of Article 25 of the covenant had been committed when Bwalya had been prevented from participating in a general election campaign as well as from preparing his candidacy for his party.[48]

There are those who make the claim that democracy should be recognized as a basic human right. The World Conference on Human Rights (1993) declared that democracy, development, and respect for human rights were interdependent and mutually reinforcing. It emphasized that the "international community should support the strengthening and promoting of democracy, development and respect for human rights and fundamental freedoms of the entire world."[49] Louis Henkin has argued that

> human rights ideology and the law of human rights represented in the International Covenant [on Civil and Political Rights] include . . . a right to democracy in the sense of constitutional democracy and its elements—authentic popular sovereignty, respect for individual rights, the rule of law, due process of law and commitment to the principle of justice. I think that these principles of justice were what those who drafted the Covenant contemplated and what states that became parties to the Covenant committed themselves to abide by.[50]

If the UN is to succeed in preventing conflict and gross violations of human rights in the future, it is imperative that the Secretary-General use his influence to reinforce democratic governance. The following considerations should guide the Secretary-General. First, the aim is to bring about constitutional democracy, namely governance, in accordance with a constitution that is supported by the people and represents their hopes and aspirations. Second, people's rights to freely determine their own political, economic, and social systems should be respected. Third, the importance of democratic legitimacy for peace, human rights, and development should be underlined. Fourth, democratic governance should be recognized as a basic human right. Fifth, the role that constitutional democratic governance can play in preventing conflicts should be emphasized. Sixth, the role that constitutional democratic governance can play in spurring development should be underlined. Seventh, the role that constitutional democratic governance can play in preventing terrorism is important. Finally, the role of constitutional democratic governance in advancing justice and equity locally and internationally is of great importance.

Bruce Russet highlighted the significance of Secretary-General Boutros-Ghali's *Agenda for Democratization,* noting: "Internationally as well as nationally, institutions must be seen as legitimate, not just as immediately effective. In the long run, effectiveness depends on legitimacy. Democracy is an instrument for achieving both."[51]

Recently, the principle of democratic legitimacy has been recognized and applied in significant ways. In a recent resolution on Bosnia, the Security

Council referred to the standards of a modern democracy.[52] A recent study found that from 1993 through 2000, the Security Council referred to "democracy" in fifty-three resolutions. According to the study, the council has praised democratic governance for its role in fostering national reconciliation, ensuring security in states recently emerging from civil war, and assisting in reconstructing governing infrastructures.[53]

The council has refused to recognize as legitimate regimes that have overthrown elected leaders. It has also authorized the use of armed force to depose the usurpers and return the elected leaders to office. The Security Council and the African Union have stated that they will not accept the violent overthrow of a democratically elected government.

Democracy is an important factor in preventing conflicts. As Kevin Cahill argues, the "building of democratic institutions would be one of the greatest conflict prevention measures that could be taken, especially if one thinks in terms of both political and economic democratic structures."[54]

In *An Agenda for Democratization,* Boutros-Ghali emphasized the role of democracy in conflict prevention:

> Lacking the legitimacy or real support offered by free elections, authoritarian Governments all too often take recourse to intimidation and violence in order to suppress internal dissent. They tend to reject institutions such as a free press and an independent judiciary which provide the transparency and accountability necessary to discourage such governmental manipulation of citizens. The resulting atmosphere of oppression and tension, felt in neighbouring countries, can heighten the fear of war. It is for this reason that the Charter declares that one of the first purposes of the United Nations is "to take effective collective measures for the prevention and removal of threats to the peace." Threatened by the resentment of their own people, non-democratic Governments may also be more likely to incite hostilities against other States in order to justify their suppression of internal dissent or forge a basis for national unity.[55]

In his second comprehensive report on preventing conflict, Secretary-General Annan stressed the importance of democracy as a universal value. Countries prone to armed conflict merit special assistance with respect to democratization. Democratic governance depends on a legal framework that protects basic human rights and provides a system of checks and balances. It also depends on functioning institutions that operate by rule of law. It is the absence of precisely these characteristics that often leads people to feel they must resort to violence. Individual governments must find their own path to democracy, but the UN and its partners offer a variety of important services that are available at the request of member states. These include assistance with elections, assistance in forming constitutions, human rights capacity-building, support for good governance, anti-corruption initiatives, and reforms in key sectors, including the security and judicial sectors.[56]

Democratic legitimacy is furthermore a key requirement for the prevention and suppression of terrorism. Human rights monitoring bodies have made an important distinction between democracies and dictatorships in their evaluations of whether an emergency exists and is threatening the nation. Regional and international supervisory human rights bodies have granted democratic governments a wider "margin of appreciation" (more latitude for their policy judgments) than unrepresentative governments in determining whether a state of emergency exists—be it an external or internal threat. However, national courts and regional or international supervisory bodies hold themselves competent to supervise the application of emergency measures. In scrutinizing the application of such measures, the principles of legality, proportionality, nonderogability of certain fundamental rights, and the principle of nondiscrimination are kept in mind.

At the UN, attention to the issue of new and restored democracies began to be emphasized in 1988 in Manila, where thirteen countries participated in the first international conference on this topic. By the time the last conference was held in Qatar in 2006, 120 countries were present, together with a large number of participants in the parliamentarian and civil society forums.[57]

The UN has extensive experience with monitoring popular plebiscites, referenda, and elections in colonies and trust territories. The intent is to ensure that people can freely exercise their choice. UN supervision has varied according to the circumstances of the case and the mandate established by the General Assembly, the Trusteeship Council, or other appropriate UN organs. The UN drew a distinction between supervising popular consultations and observing them. Supervision was wider in scope and covered the organizational aspects as well as the observation stage.

Prior to the 1990s, the UN had observed elections in a few independent countries.[58] However, from the 1990s, there was a determined push for more UN involvement in promoting democracy and free elections. When President George H. W. Bush addressed the UN General Assembly at its 45th session in 1990, he stated that free elections were the foundation of democratic government and could produce dramatic successes, as had recently been seen in Namibia and Nicaragua. He argued that the time had come to structure the role of the UN in such efforts more formally. He proposed that the organization establish a special coordinator for electoral assistance, to be assisted by a UN electoral commission comprised of distinguished experts from around the world.[59]

The proposal did not go forward without controversy, but the upshot was the establishment of a unit for electoral assistance within the Department of Political Affairs. The activities of this body, which later became a division, must be included in the catalogue of UN preventive diplomacy. The division provides advice and technical assistance at the request of governments and has helped organize and observe elections. All three facets of the division's activities—advice and assistance, organization, and observation—aim to help countries conduct free elections and, in some instances, avoid conflict that could be caused by compromised elections.

Since 1989, the UN has received over 150 requests for electoral assistance from member states. In 1991, following General Assembly resolution 46/137, the Secretary-General designated the under-secretary-general for political affairs as the focal point for electoral assistance activities. According to the Web site of the Department of Political Affairs, member states most often seek advice and assistance on the legal, technical, administrative, and human rights aspects of organizing and conducting democratic elections or they seek the organization's assistance in supporting the international observation of an electoral process.[60]

Since the establishment of the Electoral Assistance Division in 1992, the UN has provided various forms of electoral assistance to over seventy member states, including the coordination and support of international observers. This form of assistance is most commonly used when several governments and organizations have been invited by a member state to observe an election. The Electoral Assistance Division establishes a small secretariat in the requesting country, in cooperation with UNDP, to help coordinate and provide logistical support to international election observers. Throughout the operation, the UN maintains a clear public position of neutrality. The international observer groups normally issue a joint statement of their findings in the pre- and immediate post-election period in addition to issuing their own reports. This type of assistance was first tested in Ethiopia and Kenya in 1992 and was subsequently provided to support the international observation of elections in Niger, Lesotho, Malawi, Tanzania, Armenia, Azerbaijan, Sierra Leone, Mali, and Algeria, among others. As might be expected, a great deal of careful diplomacy is required throughout the process.

In special cases, a small UN observer team, usually composed of political affairs officers, may be sent to a country to follow the final phase of an electoral process and issue an internal report to the Secretary-General. Support is also provided for national election monitors. This form of assistance emphasizes the importance of building observation capacity within the requesting country by supporting members of civil society who monitor elections on a nonpartisan basis.

The UN also regularly provides advice and assistance to electoral authorities in areas such as electoral administration and planning, voter registration, election budgeting, review of electoral laws and regulations, training of election officials, logistics, voter and civic education, procurement of election materials, coordination of international donor assistance, electoral dispute resolution, computerization of electoral rolls, and boundary delimitation.

Preventive Strategies for the Future

As early as the 1970s, it was clear that humanitarian workers were experiencing difficulty because of the need for parallel work by political and human rights actors on root causes of refugee outflows. At the time, faced with growing numbers of refugees and displaced persons, the UNHCR held a forum at the International Institute of Humanitarian Law in San Remo to discuss the root causes of refugee outflows and to stress the need for political and human rights actors in the UN to deal with those root causes. A number of papers were authored by UNHCR officials on this topic, and they raised the issue with the Centre for Human Rights repeatedly.[61] At the time, the UNHCR thought there should be a senior official in the Office of the Secretary-General to deal with issues of root causes and engage in political representations where needed—the UNHCR felt it needed political backup.

Governmental discussion on the root causes led to governmental initiatives. Canada made one initiative in the Human Rights Commission. It called for reports from the Secretary-General on human rights and mass exoduses, an item that was still on the commission's agenda when it passed out of existence in 2006. At one stage, the Commission on Human Rights requested a report from Special Rapporteur Saddrudin Aga Khan. In a pathbreaking document, he called for a program of preventive action and the establishment of a corps of humanitarian observers, among other things.[62]

Prince Saddrudin advocated creating an early warning system based on regular collection of information from all the relevant and reliable sources. This data would be used to provide the Secretary-General with reports on situations likely to produce mass displacements. After studying those reports, the Secretary-General would determine whether and what action might be required from the UN system. The Secretary-General might initiate discussions at an early stage with the governments concerned as well as with the relevant regional organizations.

In the next stage, an executive designated by the Secretary-General could bring the situation to the attention of states in a position to take preventive action. Humanitarian agencies would also be alerted, enabling them to respond quickly if mass movements of people did occur. The executive might also be entrusted with monitoring and warning others about a situation and might carry out functions that other agencies could not assume because of institutional or mandate constraints. The executive might be assisted by a small ad hoc corps of humanitarian observers who could monitor situations in the field and, through their presence, help de-escalate tension.[63] Prince Saddrudin's study led to the first experimental early warning procedure in the fields of human rights and humanitarian aid.[64]

The report of the International Commission on Intervention and State Sovereignty launched the concept of the responsibility to protect. In the commission's view, the responsibility to protect embraced three specific responsibilities:

- The responsibility to prevent: to address both the root causes and the direct causes of internal conflict and other man-made crises putting populations at risk.
- The responsibility to react: to respond to situations of compelling human need with appropriate measures, which may include coercive measures like sanctions and international prosecution, and in extreme cases military intervention.
- The responsibility to rebuild: to provide full assistance with recovery, reconstruction and reconciliation, particularly after a military intervention addressing the causes of the harm the intervention was designed to halt or avert.[65]

The commission was firm in its view that prevention was the most important dimension of the responsibility to protect: prevention options should always be exhausted before intervention was contemplated and more commitment and resources must be devoted to it. The exercise of the responsibility to both prevent and react should always involve less intrusive and less coercive measures before more coercive and more intrusive measures are applied.

At the UN summit to mark the organization's sixtieth anniversary, world leaders created the Human Rights Council to replace the Commission on Human Rights. They gave the new council the responsibility to promote universal respect for the protection of all human rights and fundamental freedoms for all without distinction of any kind and in a fair and equal manner. They felt that the council should address situations of human rights violations, including gross and systematic violations, and make recommendations thereon. It should also promote effective coordination and the mainstreaming of human rights within the UN system.

Because the international community now emphasizes preventive actions, one should expect the Human Rights Council to use its best endeavors to prevent gross violations of human rights. The council should detect potential violations before they occur and act to head them off in cooperation with regional and other partners. The prevention of genocide is a case in point.

The council is establishing a system of universal periodic reports under which all countries will be reviewed from the point of view of their implementation of international human rights norms. The system will need a thematic focus to be viable. The council would do well to focus on the concept of the national protection system.[66] This would entail looking at the constitution, laws, and courts of a country to examine the extent to which they reflect international human rights norms. The council will also need to ascertain whether the country has specialized human rights institutions such as a national human rights commission or an ombudsman, whether the country is providing for the instruction of human rights in primary and secondary schools, and whether the country has monitoring arrangements to detect grievances from groups of the population to head off those grievances. A discussion of the national protection system of each country would be a good start to orient the council toward preventive work.

As part of a preventive approach that would involve national, regional, and international efforts to prevent gross violations of human rights, the council could include an item entitled "Prevention of Gross Violations of Human Rights" on its agenda each year. Under this item, the council could consider situations of gross violations of human rights. Diplomatic contacts and other appropriate forms of action could be used to help a government end gross violations, prevent their recurrence, and provide relief and redress as required. In situations where the council considers that the government is not cooperating in good faith in dealing with a situation of gross violations, it should take measures intended to discharge its responsibility to protect. Where warranted, the council should refer situations of concern to the General Assembly from the point of view of the discharge of the responsibility to protect.

Conclusion

The UN system has paid attention to the early identification, analysis, and monitoring of emerging problems. Early warning and urgent response systems are operating in many parts of the system. The UN has also sought to highlight the plight of the poor, the importance of development, and the situation of the vulnerable and to develop policies for tackling these problems. The world body has provided leadership and advocacy on these issues.

With the exception of Hammarskjöld's identification of the importance of development as part of preventive diplomacy and the de facto contribution of the ECE during the Cold War, there is only limited evidence of preventive diplomacy in the economic and social sector. Other sections of this book have illustrated examples when the Secretary-General or his senior officials helped defuse national crises caused by economic and social problems. This is preventive diplomacy in crisis management mode more than economic and social preventive diplomacy as such. Should the Secretary-General engage in targeted preventive diplomacy in the economic and social sectors? Yes. There is room for preventive diplomacy in dealing with the problems of the vulnerable and the poorest. Such preventive diplomacy would show that the UN is concerned about the plight of people, its ultimate constituency, and that people look to the Secretary-General for care and support.

The goal of the effort to develop and implement international human rights and humanitarian law is to prevent gross violations of those laws. Prevention is thus intellectually at the core of the human rights and humanitarian endeavors. But the harsh reality is that human rights and humanitarian laws are violated on massive scales around the world. While it will not be easy in the short and medium terms, the policy direction should move toward more and more preventive strategies and preventive diplomacy. This chapter has sought to advance some ideas for ways to place greater emphasis on preventive approaches in the future.

Human rights work at the UN is riddled with political controversy. In the future, it will be important to be guided by four principles: the principle of universality, the principle of respect among nations and peoples, the principle of confidence-building around norms and methods of response, and the principle of protection. Preventive diplomacy to advance a universal culture of human rights must be based on the solidarity and support of people across the globe. This is a true diplomatic challenge.

After fourteen years of experience at the UN with democracy and electoral assistance, one must wonder whether it is time to return to the proposal of the senior President Bush to establish a special coordinator for electoral assistance supported by a UN electoral commission comprised of distinguished experts from around the world.

9

Preventive Diplomacy in an Age of Genocide, Terrorism, and Nontraditional Threats to Security

- Preventing Genocide
- Preventing Terrorism
- Nontraditional Threats to Security
- Conclusion

Preventing Genocide

The international community has consistently reiterated its determination to prevent the recurrence of genocide, yet genocide continues to take place. The Summit Outcome Document adopted by world leaders at the UN in 2005 affirmed the determination of the world community to protect against genocide, ethnic cleansing, mass killings, and crimes against humanity.[1] An intriguing question that has been posed in recent times is whether the international community can marshal efforts to prevent genocide and what role the Secretary-General might be able to play in this regard. In 2004, Secretary-General Annan moved to establish a position of special adviser on the prevention of genocide, an action that has attracted much attention. The origins and progress of this initiative are discussed below.

On 11 December 1946, the General Assembly declared that genocide was a crime under international law that the world condemned. It declared that those guilty of genocide were punishable, whoever they were and for whatever reason they had committed the crime. The assembly invited member states to enact the necessary legislation to prevent and punish this crime and called for international cooperation toward this end.[2]

On 9 December 1948, the day before it adopted the Universal Declaration of Human Rights, the General Assembly approved the Convention on the Prevention and Punishment of the Crime of Genocide, which entered into force on 12 January 1951. Article I of the convention states that genocide is a crime under international law, in times of peace and in times of war. The International Court of Justice has subsequently affirmed that the principles underlying the convention have the character of *jus cogens.*

Article II of the convention defined genocide as acts aimed at destroying a national, ethnical, racial, or religious group. Article IV provides that guilty persons shall be punished, whether they are constitutionally responsible rulers, public officials, or private individuals. Article VI provides that persons charged with genocide shall be tried by a competent tribunal of the state in the territory where the act was committed or by an international penal tribunal that has jurisdiction because the contracting parties have accepted its jurisdiction. In this regard, it is worth noting that the statute of the International Criminal Court also covers genocide.

Article VIII provided that any contracting party may call on competent organs of the UN to take such action under the Charter that they consider appropriate to prevent and suppress acts of genocide or any of the proscribed acts enumerated in the convention.

Since the General Assembly adopted the convention in 1948, many genocides have taken place.[3] To what extent—if any—did the member states, the Security Council, the General Assembly, or the Secretary-General marshal diplomatic resources to highlight the crime of genocide and prevent it from taking place? The unfortunate answer to this question is that during the Cold War and even for most of the post–Cold War period there is little evidence of special diplomatic activity to warn of the dangers of genocide. In Rwanda and Darfur, mass killings have taken place under the very eyes of the international community.

To be fair, the human rights program of the UN did attempt to place the spotlight on the dangers of genocide. This was done within the Sub-Commission on Prevention of Discrimination and Protection of Minorities, which issued a global study on genocide in 1978 and a second study two decades later.[4] The author of the first study recommended that that the Commission on Human Rights set up ad hoc committees to inquire into allegations of genocide supported by sufficient prima facie evidence. He also called on the General Assembly to continue considering international criminal jurisdiction.

There has been the occasional inquiry into allegations of genocide such as the one prepared by Abdelwahab Bouhdiba, a member of the subcommission, into the crimes committed under the Pol Pot regime in Cambodia. Three decades later, the Extraordinary Chambers in the Courts of Cambodia for the Prosecution of Crimes Committed during the Period of Democratic Kampuchea was established in Cambodia to try some of those responsible for what Bouhdiba has described as "auto genocide."

After years of efforts, the Rome Statute of the International Criminal Court was adopted on 17 July 1998 and is now in force. The statute gives the International Criminal Court jurisdiction to deal with accusations against persons charged with genocide. Accusations of genocide have been brought before the international criminal tribunals on the former Yugoslavia and Rwanda, and the Rwanda tribunal even handed down a verdict of genocide in one case.

When it comes to diplomacy per se, there is not much practice to go on. However, a spectacular case of preventive diplomacy in the form of mitigatory action took place under Secretary-General U Thant in relation to events in what was then known as East Pakistan in 1971.[5] The scale of the killings and other atrocities committed there was of such magnitude that many considered it comparable with a genocidal situation. U Thant designated a special representative who led diplomatic efforts and relief efforts to stop the killings and decrease the human suffering.

In 2004, hopes that diplomacy could prevent genocide were raised when Secretary-General Annan proposed "establishing a Special Rapporteur on the prevention of genocide . . . who would report directly to the Security Council—making clear the link . . . between massive and systematic violations of human rights and threats to international peace and security."[6]

In a follow-up address to the Commission on Human Rights on 7 April of that year, Annan announced that he would create a somewhat different post of special adviser on the prevention of genocide, who would report through the Secretary-General to the Security Council and the General Assembly as well as to the commission. This adviser's mandate would refer not only to genocide but also to mass murder and other large-scale human rights violations, such as ethnic cleansing. His or her functions would be:

- First, to work closely with the high commissioner to collect information on potential or existing situations or threats of genocide and their links to international peace and security
- Second, to act as an early warning mechanism to the Security Council and other parts of the UN system
- Third, to make recommendations to the Security Council on actions to be taken to prevent or halt genocide[7]

On 12 July 2004, the Secretary-General appointed Juan Mendez as his special adviser.[8] The basis for establishing the post was Security Council resolution 1366 (2001), particularly paragraph 10, in which the council invited the Secretary-General to refer to it information and analyses from within the UN system on cases of serious violations of international law, including international humanitarian law and human rights law and on potential conflicts arising from ethnic, religious and territorial disputes, poverty, and lack of development.[9] The special adviser would collect existing information from within the UN system on massive and serious violations of human rights and international humanitarian law of ethnic and racial origin that might lead to genocide. The adviser functions as mechanism of early warning to the Secretary-General and through him or her to the Security Council. Other tasks include making recommendations to the Security Council, through the Secretary-General, on actions to prevent or halt genocide; liaising with the UN system on activities to prevent genocide; and working to enhance the UN's capacity to analyze and manage information relating to genocide.

The special adviser must carefully verify facts and engage in serious political consultations in order to provide his or her analysis, and this must be done discreetly. This will help the Secretary-General define the steps necessary to prevent existing situations from deteriorating into genocide. The special adviser does not make a determination on whether genocide— within the meaning of the convention—has occurred. The purpose of his or her activities, rather, is practical and is intended to enable the UN to act in a timely fashion.[10]

Two years after the post of special adviser was created, the Secretary-General submitted a report to the Commission on Human Rights on his activities. It contained a list of possible warning signs that could indicate situations which, if not prevented or halted, might lead to genocide:

- The existence of a national, ethnic, racial or religious group(s) at risk: Warning signs could include (a) pattern of discrimination with the purpose or effect of impairing the enjoyment of certain human rights; (b) exclusionary ideologies that purport to justify discrimination; (c) specific identification of groups and their association with a specific political identity or opinion (including possible compulsory identification or registering of group membership in a way that could potentially lead to the group being targeted in the future); and (d) demonization of groups in political or social discourse.
- Violations of human rights and humanitarian law, which may become massive or serious: Armed conflict in which violations of international humanitarian law disproportionately affect a specific group (e.g. intentional massacre of unarmed civilians, civilian targeting during military campaigns, one-sided physical brutality); (b) violations of

civil and political rights affecting a specific group (e.g. murder—particularly directed against community leaders, torture, mutilation, rape and sexual violence, abduction, population movement/ethnic cleansing, expropriation, destruction of property, looting, lack of freedom of speech/press/assembly/religion; (c) serious or massive violations of economic, social and cultural rights (e.g. destruction of subsistence food supply, denial of water or medical attention, man-made famine, redirection of aid supplies; (d) instances of discrimination (e.g. access to work and resources, political marginalization, restricted movement, education; and (e) a climate of impunity in which these events unfold.

- Additional warning signs: Lack of institutional framework for individuals within the territory and subject to the jurisdiction of a member state to seek justice, redress, and demand accountability; (b) concentration of power (economic/political) in one or few groups to the detriment of others; (c) existence of and support to militias that could carry out attacks against groups by proxy; (d) perceived or real external support to groups that could become targets due to being seen as "collaborators" with external enemies; (e) withdrawal of rights associated with citizenship from specific groups; (f) hate speech, incitement to violence, or humiliation of a group in the media; and (g) forced relocation, segregation, isolation, or concentration of a group.

- A history of genocide or discrimination: A history of violence against a group may presage renewed episodes of repression or counter-movements against prior oppressors. Important elements that may indicate the weight of past experience are (a) a history of vilification or dehumanization of a group; (b) the use of symbols, flags, or markings to conjure previous abuse; (c) denial of past genocides and atrocities; and (d) celebration of instances of perceived or actual abuse of a group.[11]

An interview with the special adviser and his immediate staff conducted in New York on 9 February 2006 indicated that in the year and a half since his appointment, the special adviser had pursued the following approaches to implementing his mandate. First, he had sent ten briefing notes to the Secretary-General, the contents of some of which had been shared with the Security Council. Second, he had looked for ways to engage in advocacy for prevention, which he felt was an important part of his mandate. Third, he had looked for ways to identify populations at risk.

Fourth, wherever possible, the special adviser encouraged dialogue between minorities and their governments to improve understanding and head off problems. Fifth, he looked for opportunities to encourage regional and subregional organizations to engage in preventive activities to protect minorities. Sixth, he had visited Darfur and Côte d'Ivoire and had prepared reports on both.[12] An advisory council of six prominent personalities had been established to support his activities. The special adviser is an ex officio member of this council. The council's mandate is to provide guidance and support to the special adviser and to contribute to the broader efforts of the UN to prevent genocide.

The special adviser on the prevention of genocide is pioneering new approaches to genocide prevention that represent an important part of the intellectual history of preventive diplomacy at the UN. The special adviser started as a part-time official, giving 30 percent of his time to the position, and the groundwork for the office was still being put in place in 2006. That year he had at his disposal the services of a human rights officer, a political officer, and a secretary.[13]

While the foundations of the office of special adviser were being laid, mass killings were being perpetrated in Darfur, and Secretary-General Annan sought to use his influence to ameliorate the situation. One must admit that Darfur has been a massive failure for the international community. How did this happen?

In March 2003, the UN resident coordinator in Khartoum, Sudan, gave an interview to a reporter from the BBC World Service, drawing the world's attention to the ethnic cleansing that was taking place in Darfur. Previously, the resident coordinator had sent reports to UN headquarters about the ethnic cleansing. Immediately after the report was aired, the high commissioner for human rights initiated a fact-finding exercise, asking the governments of Sudan and neighboring Chad for their consent to the dispatch of such a mission. (Thousands of refugees from Darfur had fled to Chad.) This urgent mission first went to Chad, and on its return, the high commissioner received the green light for the team to go to Darfur. Based on the findings from the missions, the high commissioner submitted a major report to the UN Commission on Human Rights and was invited by the Security Council to present the report on 7 May 2004, which was done in the presence of the Secretary-General and the executive director of the World Food Programme, who had just conducted a humanitarian mission to the area.[14] Following the high commissioner's appearance before the Security Council, its president made a public statement underlining the gravity of the situation.[15]

When OCHA head Jan Egeland sought to draw attention to the atrocities in Darfur, his statements drew strong protests from the Sudanese government. After that, Egeland concentrated on providing humanitarian relief on the ground.

As of the time of writing, December 2006, the killings in Darfur continued unabated, notwithstanding the efforts of a contingent of African Union peacekeepers on the ground. The death toll in Darfur had reportedly risen from some 50,000 in 2004 to some 300,000, and the number of refugees and internally displaced persons remained in the millions.[16] Throughout this period, massacres and atrocities continued to be perpetrated against the innocent people of Darfur. The government of Sudan has so far refused to accept a UN peacekeeping force in Darfur.

What did Secretary-General Annan do during this period? How was preventive diplomacy being carried out—if at all? The evidence shows that the Secretary-General did make some efforts. He made a personal visit to Darfur, supported the African Union, had contacts with the government of Sudan and other governments, reported to the Security Council, made public statements, and advocated policy options. Could the Secretary-General have taken other steps? Yes. It seems clear that the Secretary-General should have raised the stakes by formally invoking Article 99.

The situation in Darfur has persisted for different reasons. Geographically, Sudan is the largest country in Africa with oil and other strategic resources. It is not a country that can be threatened with foreign intervention. Darfur is the size of France, and here also external intervention would be no easy matter. Sudan is a strategic ally of the United States in the war against terrorism, and it sells the bulk of its oil to China. Sudan has major economic dealings with other powerful countries of the international community as well. The permanent members of the Security Council all have their own interests to protect.

Furthermore, Sudan has had a long-running war between its north and south in respect of which a peace agreement was concluded just before the onset of the Darfur unrest in 2002. It is a legitimate concern that actions taken to deal with the Darfur crisis should not have put at risk the implementation of the North-South Agreement. Furthermore, Sudan is able to benefit from African cover, namely that the African Union and African countries should be in the lead on peacemaking and peacekeeping in Darfur.

In the face of these complex elements, how can the United Nations and its Secretary-General reconcile realpolitik with principle, namely, the responsibility to protect? There are times when the only way of dealing with great moral challenges is to stand up and be counted in the verdict of history. Darfur was a situation that called for a moral stance in the face of massive, persistent, and continuing atrocities and crimes against humanity. It was one situation in which the Secretary-General should have chosen the high ground over diplomatic expediency. He did not.

The position of special adviser on the prevention of genocide is an important one, and Secretary-General Ban Ki-moon decided to retain and strengthen it. He made the position a full-time one and increased its staff. The first special adviser has charted the way in establishing the office, and the foundations have thus been laid to develop new vistas in the development and practice of preventive diplomacy.

Members of the Advisory Committee of the Secretary-General on the Prevention of Genocide believe that the signs of genocide are visible long before the killings begin, often for a period of years.[17] They feel that the UN needs some mechanism at the heart of the international system that is designed to ring the necessary warning bells. The position of special adviser should therefore act in anticipatory, proactive, and preventive ways as part of the broader Action Plan to Prevent Genocide that Secretary-General Annan advanced.[18] It involves preventing armed conflict, protecting civilians in armed conflict, ending impunity, providing early and clear warning, and taking decisive action.

The advisory committee feels that the real need is to search for measures that prevent extensive human rights abuses or genocide-prone behavior. If the special adviser is to fully exercise what should be a broad anticipatory, proactive, and preventive approach, it is important that he or she not be restricted from addressing situations where violence is not imminent or already happening. The role of the special adviser, committee members feel, is to help provide strong moral authority on the need to act wisely before it is too late and thus avoid immense human suffering.

Members of the advisory committee feel that to effectively discharge the special adviser's mandate, the holder of the position needs to be both a clear voice of moral obligation and a source of good advice about the practical steps needed to discharge that obligation. The special adviser's office needs to be able to engage in effective information collection and analysis ranging worldwide on developments relating to massive or serious violations of human rights and humanitarian law; to select and act quickly on new situations of imminent danger, giving early warning and helping mobilize appropriate responses; to respond not only to new but to ongoing crises that raise issues within his or her brief; and to promote enhanced preventive capacity through other elements in the UN system and by engaging in educational outreach and networking. What the UN needs most from the special adviser is careful analysis of human rights and political developments, committee members argue.

According to advisory committee members, the special adviser should continue to build a network with other key players (international, regional, and subregional organizations, academics, and nongovernmental organizations) to strengthen collective preventive efforts. There is room, in particular, to work with regional organizations, encouraging their activity in this field. Many forms of concerted action are possible among multiple actors. In all of this, nongovernmental organizations can be very helpful. The special adviser should therefore:

- Establish an ongoing process, drawing on readily available information from all sources, to identify targets, scapegoats, and outgroups.
- Monitor trends of hatred and dehumanization toward the groups identified in such a vulnerable position.
- Help build internal capacity of member states for early, ongoing conflict resolution, including essential concepts, such as the development of a national prevention system in every country; techniques (e.g., negotiation and mediation); and institutions (e.g., an independent judiciary).
- Help leaders and the public understand the merits of these enterprises, showing how a country caught in deep antagonisms would find that such measures serve its own interests.
- Identify predisposing factors, for example, economic deterioration, social disorganization, and an alienated population with prospects of war and/or revolution in the background. The earlier such problems are identified and the better they are understood, the greater the opportunity for international organizations to help.
- Enlist the help of key member states that have a strong interest in the problem of genocide and how to overcome it and persuade them to commit intellectual, technical, financial, and moral resources.

Prevention and Protection

The central task of the special adviser must be to help the Secretary-General prevent genocide and protect people from genocide. This will require active behind-the-scenes cooperation with all the entities of the UN system working on prevention, partner organizations, regional preventive mechanisms, and academic and research institutions to help advise the Secretary-General about situations where he or she may need to deploy his preventive efforts. It would be helpful to the special adviser if a partner academic or research organization would maintain a database of potential risk situations, specifically a watch list. This is best done outside the UN, as the existence and maintenance of such a list within the organization would likely engender leaks and diplomatic protests in an environment in which developing countries in particular are already sensitive to intrusions into their internal affairs.

Based on consultations with the partners indicated in the preceding paragraph, the special adviser could personally send a brief to the Secretary-General about situations of high concern at the start of each quarter after discreetly and personally consulting the head of the Department of Political Affairs and the high commissioner for human rights. The special adviser could also suggest behind-the-scenes approaches that the Secretary-General might undertake or that he or she might approve on his or her behalf. Such measures might include discussions with the head of the relevant regional organization or the deployment of a discreet fact-finding mission on behalf of the UN and the regional organization. Great care would need to be exercised to ensure that this does not become a routine interoffice exercise that could leak and spoil the effort. The most careful and sensitive diplomacy would be called for.

In cases of acute concern where the special adviser considers that stronger measures might be needed, he or she would need to assess the options of the Secretary-General in raising the matter with the head of state or government concerned and advising the Security Council discreetly about such a situation. The adviser would also provide the Secretary-General with an analysis of the risks involved in the situation; the contribution that the Security Council, the head of Department of Political Affairs, or the high commissioner might make; and the potential advantages or pitfalls of involvement by the Secretary-General. The responsibility to protect would need to be pursued simultaneously with the practice of preventive diplomacy.

Where the situation seems to call for it and the political context is positive, the deployment of a small corps of UN goodwill ambassadors could be considered for a short period as a calming, preventive, and protective device. In training national peacekeepers for rapid deployment missions as well as in planning for UN peacekeeping, specialized courses could be provided in the role of UN goodwill ambassadors.

In cases of acute concern, the special adviser would need to weigh the options and advise the Secretary-General of the pros and cons of alerting the state parties to the provisions of the Convention on the Prevention and Punishment of Genocide, briefing the Security Council informally or raising the matter under Article 99 of the Charter. In such a situation, the role of the under-secretary-general for political affairs would be central, as the Secretary-General would be embarking on highly sensitive political options that should only be undertaken after careful consideration.

International and Regional Cooperation

The prevention of genocide calls for diplomacy with international and regional partners to sensitize them to the need for preventive measures and to elicit their continuing support in this endeavor. One way of proceeding on this mission would be for the special adviser to engage in continuous contacts with the heads of regional organizations, their conflict prevention mechanisms, and their human rights organizations and leaders to draw insights from one another and move forward cooperatively. After initial contacts with these entities, the special adviser, with the blessings of the Secretary-General, could make policy addresses to each of these entities with a view to laying down lines of cooperation and joint endeavor. Eventually, when the time is ripe, the special adviser could prepare the ground for the Secretary-General to conclude memoranda of understanding with the heads of each regional organization on cooperation in preventing genocide. The purpose would be to help raise awareness, promote policies, and develop practical cooperation to prevent genocide.

High-Level Policy Statements

In close concert with the Secretary-General, the special adviser could aim for the occasional adoption of high-level policy statements expressing a commitment to cooperate to prevent genocide. One could aim, eventually, for such a statement at the assemblies of the principal regional organizations and at the General Assembly. The purpose of such policy statements would be to sensitize members of regional organizations about the issues related to genocide and foster a commitment to practical cooperation.

Cooperation with Human Rights Bodies

Many activities of UN and regional human rights bodies facilitate beneficial cooperation to prevent genocide. Within the framework of the UN Human Rights Council, there are several parallel efforts to implement the Durban Declaration and Programme of Action against Racism, Racial Discrimination, and Xenophobia. Including an item on preventing genocide would seem natural in these efforts. ECOSOC's Permanent Forum on Indigenous

Issues and, if it continues, the former Human Rights Sub-Commission Working Group on Indigenous Populations would be natural partners for attempts to prevent genocide. An independent expert of the Office of the High Commissioner for Human Rights (OHCHR) deals with the protection of minorities, and there is room for cooperation here as well. The field offices and national offices of the OHCHR can be helpful across the board, as indeed can the high commissioner. The OSCE's high commissioner on national and ethnic minorities and the Council of Europe's commissioner for human rights are also natural partners. The regional commissions on human rights and offices such as that of the OSCE on democracy and human rights can make a useful contribution. Careful diplomacy and a certain measure of advocacy might be required when forming these partnerships, keeping in mind that the primary role of the high commissioner for human rights is advocacy.

National Policy Statements and Preventive Measures

It could be a key objective of the special adviser, in cooperation with the UN high commissioner for human rights and other partners, to promote adoption of national policy statements on preventing genocide in multi-ethnic countries. In his final report on prevention, Secretary-General Annan called for the promotion of national prevention systems.[19] National policy statements on the prevention of genocide in multi-ethnic countries would be a good start toward this end. There would naturally be sensitivities in this matter, and the special adviser would need to be prudent in pursuing this course of action. It would require a step-by-step approach, starting with countries that are positively inclined and spreading out to others in time.

Cooperation with Nongovernmental Organizations and Academic and Research Bodies

Nongovernmental organizations and scholars and researchers have already made an important contribution toward developing preventive strategies and institutions, and their continuing efforts will be crucial in supporting efforts of the special adviser and the mission of genocide prevention. One way of drawing on the efforts of this talent and advocacy pool might be to work with them in organizing an annual seminar or conference on the prevention of genocide. Each conference could lead to the publication of a book on the topic that contains the latest research, national, regional, and international policy developments, and generally promotes scholarship and thinking in this field.

Preventing Terrorism

The current times have been deemed the age of terror.[20] It is therefore fitting that this be considered in a study of the intellectual history of preventive diplomacy at the UN. How preventive diplomacy might be relevant to the struggle against terrorism is very important, especially in the context of the danger of nonstate actors who might resort to nuclear terrorism.[21]

In an address to the closing plenary of the International Summit on Democracy, Terrorism, and Security in Madrid on 10 March 2005, Secretary-General Annan highlighted the dangers of nuclear terrorism:

> Perhaps the thing that is most vital is to deny terrorists access to nuclear materials. Nuclear terrorism is still often treated as science fiction. I wish it were. But unfortunately we live in a world of excess hazardous materials and abundant technological know-how, in which terrorists clearly state their intention to inflict catastrophic casualties. Were such an attack to occur, it would not only cause widespread death and destruction, but would stagger the world economy and thrust tens of millions of people into dire poverty. Given what we know of the relationship between poverty and infant mortality, any nuclear terrorist attack would have a second death toll throughout the developing world.
>
> That such an attack has not yet happened is not an excuse for complacency. Rather, it gives us a last chance to take effective preventive action.
>
> That means consolidating, securing, and when possible eliminating potentially hazardous materials, and implementing effective export controls. Both the G8 and the UN Security Council have taken important steps to do this, and to plug gaps in the non-proliferation regime. We need to make sure these measures are fully enforced and that they reinforce each other. I urge the Member States of the United Nations to complete and adopt, without delay, the international convention on nuclear terrorism.[22]

Both the General Assembly and the Security Council have been prominent in the struggle against terrorism. The General Assembly has adopted numerous resolutions setting down policies and strategies, and the Security Council, especially after September 11, 2001, has adopted a series of binding resolutions setting out policies and strategies for countering terrorism.

In resolution 48/122, adopted on 20 December 1993, the General Assembly unequivocally condemned all acts, methods, and practices of terrorism and called on states to take all necessary and effective measures to prevent, combat, and eliminate terrorism, in accordance with international standards of human rights. In resolution 49/60, adopted by consensus on 9 December 1994, the General Assembly declared that criminal acts intended or calculated to provoke a state of terror within the general public, a group of persons, or particular persons for political purposes are unjustifiable, regardless of whether a political, philosophical, ideological, racial, ethnic, religious or any other motive is invoked to justify them.

On 14 September 2005, the UN adopted the International Convention for the Suppression of Acts of Nuclear Terrorism. According to this convention, any person commits an offense if that person unlawfully and intentionally possesses radioactive material or makes or possesses a device with the intent to cause death or serious bodily injury or with the intent to cause substantial damage to property or to the environment. It is also an offense to use radioactive material or a radioactive device in any way or to use or damage a nuclear facility in a way that risks the release of radioactive material:

i. With the intent to cause death or serious bodily injury; or
ii. With the intent to cause substantial damage to property or the environment; or
iii. With the intent to compel a natural or legal person, an international organization, or a State to do or refrain from doing an act.[23]

In 2006, the General Assembly adopted the Global Counter-Terrorism Strategy, in which it resolved to undertake measures to address the conditions conducive to the spread of terrorism and to strengthen and make the best possible use of the UN's capacity in areas such as conflict prevention, negotiation, mediation, conciliation, judicial settlement, rule of law, peacekeeping, and peacebuilding to contribute to the successful prevention and peaceful resolution of prolonged unresolved conflicts. It invited the UN to improve coordination in planning a response to a terrorist attack using nuclear, chemical, biological, or radiological materials.

In resolution 1269 (1999), the Security Council called on all states to cooperate to prevent and suppress terrorist acts and to prevent and suppress in their territories, through all lawful means, the preparation and financing of any acts of terrorism. After the terrorist attacks on September 11, 2001, the Security Council, acting under Chapter VII of the UN Charter, decided that all states should take the necessary steps to prevent the commission of terrorist acts, including providing early warning to other states through the exchange of information. The Security Council also decided that all states should prevent and suppress the financing of terrorist acts.

In the same resolution, the Security Council decided to establish a committee consisting of all of its members to monitor implementation of its resolution with the assistance of appropriate expertise and called on all states to report to the committee periodically on the steps taken to implement the resolution. The Security Council recognized that many states would require assistance in implementing the resolution's requirements and invited states to inform the council's Counter-Terrorism Committee of areas in which they required such support. In that context, the council invited its Counter-Terrorism Committee to explore ways in which states could be assisted and, in particular, to explore with international, regional, and subregional organizations in its resolution 1377 (2001):

- The promotion of best practices in the areas covered by Resolution 1373 (2001), including the preparation of model laws as appropriate
- The availability of existing technical, financial, regulatory, legislative, or other assistance programs that might facilitate the implementation of Resolution 1373 (2001)
- The promotion of possible synergies between these assistance programs[24]

The Security Council continued to press preventive action in its resolution 1624 adopted on 14 September 2005, which called on states to adopt such measures as might be necessary and appropriate and in accordance with international law to prohibit by law incitement to commit a terrorist act or acts and to prevent such conduct. The resolution further called on states to deny safe haven to any persons for which there is credible and relevant information giving serious reasons to consider that they have been guilty of such conduct.

The Security Council also called on states to continue international efforts to enhance dialogue and broaden understanding among civilizations to prevent the indiscriminate targeting of religions and cultures and to take all measures necessary and appropriate and in accordance with their obligations under international law to counter incitement of terrorist acts motivated by extremism and intolerance and to prevent the subversion of educational, cultural, and religious institutions by terrorists and their supporters.[25]

The council called on states to report to the Counter-Terrorism Committee on the steps they have taken to implement the resolution. The council directed the Counter-Terrorism Committee to include states' efforts to implement its resolution in the committee's dialogue with member states.

The council also directed the committee to work with member states to help build capacity, including through spreading best legal practices and promoting exchange of information.

The goal of the committee's dialogue with member states is prevention. This dialogue is being carried out through submission of written reports by member states, the exchange of comments and views between the committee and member states, and visits to member states for discussions on preventive strategies. To date, the Counter-Terrorism Committee has visited Albania, Algeria, the Former Yugoslav Republic of Macedonia, Jordan, Kenya, Malaysia, Morocco, the Philippines, Tanzania, and Thailand. The visits aim, among other things, to assess whether deficiencies are attributable to needs that could be met through technical assistance and to propose solutions to correct them.

The preventive thrust in counterterrorism strategies was particularly highlighted by Secretary-General Annan in his March 2005 address in Madrid, where he laid out a five-pronged preventive strategy: 1) to dissuade disaffected groups from choosing terrorism as a tactic to achieve their goals; 2) to deny terrorists the means to carry out their attacks; 3) to deter states from supporting terrorists; 4) to develop state capacity to prevent terrorism; and 5) to defend human rights in the struggle against terrorism.[26]

In addition to highlighting the dangers of nuclear terrorism, the Secretary-General drew attention to the dangers of biological terrorism:

> Few threats more vividly illustrate the imperative of building state capacity than biological terrorism, which could spread deadly infectious disease across the world in a matter of days. Neither states nor international organizations have yet adapted to a new world of biotechnology, full of promise and peril.[27]

The Secretary-General called for a major initiative to build up local health systems that would be in the front line of such a situation.

Nontraditional Threats to Security

Contemporary security studies warn of new dangers such as global terrorism and the accelerated horizontal and vertical proliferation of weapons of mass destruction. Moreover, in a rapidly globalizing world, the threats have become ever stronger with the emergence and proliferation of technologies that facilitate the spread of weapons of mass destruction to both state and nonstate actors and the dangers of terrorists using weapons of mass destruction. In a globalizing and multidimensional security environment, the meaning of security is no longer confined to state or national security and the preservation of territorial integrity.

At the Second Training Programme on Coping with Non-Traditional Security Threats, which took place in New York on 4–6 December 2006 and was organized by the Geneva Centre for Security Policy and the UN Department of Political Affairs, discussion focused on the point that the sources of insecurity were no longer restricted to threats to national borders and that they were not primarily military in nature.

In addition, participants noted that conflict and security often have regional dynamics and contexts. Consequently, regional analysis and coherent regional strategies are essential. It was particularly stressed that no single country can achieve its security or safety against threats in isolation and that beyond regional analysis and cooperation, there is a need for international and global cooperation. Furthermore, security and development objectives have become increasingly interdependent.[28]

Participants in the training program discussed war economies and resource conflicts because they considered that at least a quarter of today's wars and armed conflicts had resource dimensions, were economically motivated, and had killed over five million people. Some wars sought to assert control over natural resources, such as oil, diamonds, gold, timber, gems, drugs, crops, and water. Migration and population are also seen as closely related to strategic security. At the end of 2005, it was pointed out, there were 20.8 million refugees and internally displaced and stateless persons and hostility toward immigrant communities was accelerating in host countries. Migration, demography, and population movements need to be analyzed and integrated within conflict prevention strategies.

International terrorism and transnational organized crime were also seen as new security issues. According to the U.S. National Counterterrorism Center's report of April 2006, some 11,000 terrorist attacks had occurred in 2005, resulting in close to 15,000 deaths. Nuclear proliferation continues to be a serious concern. The five original nuclear weapons states possess some 27,000 nuclear weapons, and India, Israel, North Korea, and Pakistan have the capacity to produce nuclear weapons now as well. The global stockpile of plutonium and highly enriched uranium that could be used to make nuclear weapons stands at 4,000 tons, which would enable the production of 200,000 crude nuclear weapons. Of this, an estimated 1,850 tons were highly enriched uranium, enough for tens of thousands of nuclear weapons. In addition, there are some 100 civilian-operated nuclear facilities worldwide with varying degrees of security.[29] The 2006 report of the Independent Commission on Weapons of Mass Destruction offered sixty recommendations to rid the world of nuclear, biological, and chemical weapons and to prevent the spread of such weapons and weapon capability to more states and nonstate actors. The IAEA has reported that between 1993 and 2003, some 540 incidents of trafficking in nuclear technology had taken place.[30]

Dealing with these and other danger to international security is "a daunting challenge."[31] How will future UN security policies and preventive diplomacy seek to cope with these evolving threats to national, regional, international, and human security? Other than on the issue of HIV/AIDS, the Security Council does not have a track record of tapping into scholarly thinking on new security threats, and the Secretary-General, other than through the occasional report on conflict prevention, has not sought to provide the Security Council with an annual global analysis of evolving security threats. Pérez de Cuéllar's concept of maintaining a comprehensive global watch over threats to human security had this in mind. It is all the more important that this concept be brought back into UN strategic thinking.

By informal agreement with the Security Council, the Secretary-General could commission an annual scholarly study of evolving global threats to human security and make it available to the council. This would require developing closer working relations with the global community of security scholars, something that could be facilitated by the Department of Political Affairs. The demonstrated interest of the Secretary-General in such a project would add weight to it. The annual study, or a Secretary-General's synthesis of such a study, could be presented to the Security Council, which could hold an annual thematic discussion of new global security threats.

Depending on the content of the yearly analysis and the deliberations of the Security Council, it might be useful for the Secretary-General or the president of the Security Council to engage in preventive diplomacy regarding new threats to human security on a case-by-case basis.

Conclusion

An important initiative has been launched at the UN to draw on diplomacy to prevent genocide. This initiative is still at an early stage and needs broad-based support to succeed. The General Assembly and the Security Council have established an impressive legal framework on preventing nuclear terrorism, and the Counter-Terrorism Committee of the Security Council is endeavoring to promote international cooperation to prevent terrorism through dialogue. The process is at a fairly early stage, and it remains to be seen what results it will yield. The nontraditional threats to security that are on the horizon call for dynamic and innovative responses. As a matter of principle, there must be room to marshal preventive diplomacy.

10

Cooperative Preventive Diplomacy with Regional and Subregional Organizations

- The Contours of Cooperation
- Regional and Subregional Arrangements
- Ideas for Future Cooperation
- Conclusion

The Contours of Cooperation

Cooperation on preventive diplomacy is part of the broader process of UN cooperation with regional and subregional organizations. The Secretary-General is in ongoing contact with the leaders of regional and subregional organizations and has been convening high-level meetings with the leadership of those organizations biennially. Six such meetings have been held so far. At these meetings, broad cooperation efforts are discussed and conflict prevention has been an item of particular focus. The meetings among the Secretary-General and the leaders of regional and subregional organizations provide an opportunity to review areas or issues of concern and discuss how efforts might be coordinated to prevent, mitigate, or resolve conflicts.

The Security Council has held meetings to discuss cooperation with regional organizations for maintaining international peace and security, including preventive measures. At its fourth meeting away from headquarters, held in Nairobi in 2006, the Security Council sought to intensify cooperation with the peace and security institutions of the African Union and discuss cooperation between the union and the UN on the situation in Darfur.

The Secretariat, particularly the Department of Political Affairs, is in regular contact with the conflict prevention arrangements of regional and subregional organizations to exchange views and information with them generally or on particular situations. A practice has developed whereby cooperation meetings are held, for the most part annually, between the UN Secretariat and the secretariats of regional organizations such as the African Union and the OAS. Again, these contacts and meetings provide opportunities to pool efforts using preventive diplomacy regarding particular situations, to the extent that circumstances allow.

At the request of the conflict-prevention arrangements of regional or subregional organizations, the Secretariat has also sought to provide advice or technical assistance to establish or strengthen the regional and subregional mechanisms. One example is when the Organization of African Unity, the predecessor organization to the African Union, was setting up its conflict prevention mechanism, situation room, and secretariat. The Africa I Division of the Department of Political Affairs developed a close relationship with the members of the OAU secretariat who were working with the OAU mechanism, and the two institutions exchanged information about the work of their regional political divisions, their experience in preparing risk assessments, their relations with the Security Council, their efforts to establish databases for early warning and prevention, and the operations of the situation room of the Department of Peacekeeping Operations.

Subsequently, the Department of Political Affairs has sent experts to the African Union to help deepen its early-warning and prevention arrangements. It has provided similar support to ECOWAS. In his 2005 annual report, Secretary-General Annan noted that the UN and the African Union were working together closely through the deployment of a UN assistance cell in Addis Ababa.[1] The UN had conducted staff exchange programs with the African Union and ECOWAS, and discussions were under way for similar arrangements with the Economic Community of Central African States. He further reported that contacts on peace and security in Southeastern Asia had increased between the UN and ASEAN. The UN and the Commonwealth of Independent States had also sought to strengthen cooperation in the area of conflict prevention; a memorandum of understanding had been signed to that effect between the UN's Tajikistan Office of Peacebuilding and the executive secretariat of the Commonwealth.[2]

One cannot underestimate the value of this cooperation between the UN and regional and subregional organizations. Those organizations have been doing a fairly heavy part of the lifting when it comes to global efforts to prevent, mitigate, and resolve conflicts. The more effective these regional and subregional arrangements can become with UN support, the better will be the prospects for preventive diplomacy and action to head off conflicts.

Regional and Subregional Arrangements

Prominent experiments with preventive diplomacy take place at the regional level and can be useful as part of a global effort at mitigating armed conflict. Five such experiments are worth discussing here.

The OAU's Mechanism for Preventing, Managing, and Resolving Conflict

The predecessor of the African Union, the Organization of African Unity, had nearly a decade of experience in conflict prevention before the African Union took over. The mechanism for conflict prevention, management, and resolution was established at the twenty-ninth ordinary session of the OAU Assembly of Heads of State and Government in June 1993. It provided for a conflict prevention secretariat, an urgent response body comprised of African diplomats and political leaders, and a role for the secretary-general of the OAU.

The mechanism was established to operate according to six guiding principles:

- It was based on the OAU charter.
- It was meant to emphasize the sovereign equality of member states.
- It based itself on the imperative of the peaceful settlement of disputes.
- It emphasized the prevention of conflicts over peacekeeping or peace enforcement.
- It revolved around the central organ, the geographically balanced bureau elected annually by the summit of the heads of state and government. Parties to a conflict could bring their case to a meeting of the central organ in camera. Implementation of the central organ's decisions, arrived at through persuasion and mediation, required the parties' consent.
- The mechanism was operational at the level of ambassadors based in Addis Ababa (meeting twice a month), the OAU ministers (meeting at least twice a year), and heads of state and government (meeting once a year).[3]

Salim Ahmed Salim, the OAU's secretary-general, led the way in developing the practice of African preventive diplomacy, which was characterized by the following elements:

- Emphasis on processes of national dialogue to resolve internal disputes

- Strictures against the resort to force in internal or international disputes or conflicts
- The doctrine of democratic legitimacy, namely that military overthrow of democratically elected governments would not be accepted. This doctrine was subsequently further solidified in Decisions AHG/ Dec. 141 (XXXV) and AHG/Dec. 142 (XXXV) on Unconstitutional Changes of Government.
- An emphasis on respect for norms of human rights and humanitarian law—a breakthrough in African regional cooperation[4]

Unfortunately, the mechanism's attempts to intercede or make recommendations were often not heeded. As an official of the OAU put it, the "central organ cannot enforce the decisions without the consent of the parties, much as enforcement may look attractive. It is a matter of persuasion, mediation, and coordination with the parties."[5]

Nevertheless, the OAU's experience with the mechanism provides a solid body of practice for its successor, the continental early warning system of the African Union. When the OAU gave way to the African Union, it passed to the latter's secretariat a situation room staffed by six people; a unit for conflict prevention, management, and reconciliation staffed by eight analysts; and an early warning unit staffed by two experts.

The Continental Early Warning System of the African Union

According to Article 12 of the Protocol Relating to the Establishment of the Peace and Security Council of the African Union, a continental early warning system, to be known as the Early Warning System, will be established to facilitate the anticipation and prevention of conflicts. The system will consist of an observation and monitoring center, to be known as the situation room, located at the Conflict Management Directorate of the union, that will be responsible for data collection and analysis on the basis of an appropriate early warning indicators module; and direct linkage of data collected and processed by the observation and monitoring units of the regional mechanisms to the situation room through appropriate means of communication.

The protocol mandates the African Union's commission to cooperate with the UN, its agencies, other relevant international organizations, research centers, academic institutions, and nongovernmental organizations to facilitate the effective functioning of the Early Warning System. The system is mandated to develop an early warning module based on clearly defined and accepted political, economic, social, military, and humanitarian indicators, which will be used to analyze developments within the continent and recommend the best course of action.

According to the protocol, the chair of the commission will use the information gathered through the Early Warning System "promptly" to advise the African Union's Peace and Security Council on potential conflicts and threats to peace and security in Africa and recommend the best course of action. The chair of the commission shall also use this information to discharge the responsibilities and functions entrusted to him or her.

The member states of the African Union are committed to facilitate early action by the Peace and Security Council and/or the chair of the commission based on early warning information. The chair of the commission is mandated—in consultation with member states and the regional mechanisms, the UN, and other relevant institutions—to work out the practical details to establish the Early Warning System and to "take all the steps required for its effective functioning."[6] As of the time of writing, this process is being set in motion.

It is noteworthy that Article 13 of the protocol, which enables the Peace and Security Council to perform its responsibilities, provides for the establishment of an African standby force to be composed of contingents with varied skills and training, with civilian and military components in their countries of origin and ready for rapid deployment at appropriate notice. The member states are required to take steps to establish standby contingents for participation in peace support missions decided on by the Peace and Security Council or intervention authorized by the assembly. The strength and types of such contingents, their degree of readiness, and the general location shall be determined in accordance with established African Union peace support standard operating procedures and shall be subject to periodic reviews depending on prevailing crisis and conflict situations.

The Early Warning System is a dynamic vision of conflict prevention that is eagerly awaited by Africans and by the wider international community.

The ASEAN Regional Forum

The ASEAN Regional Forum (ARF) is the longest-running regional experiment in preventive diplomacy. It is particularly interesting because it has sought to draw on preventive diplomacy in a part of the world that has been and remains sensitive to intrusions in internal affairs. The ASEAN experience thus has particular significance for the practice of preventive diplomacy elsewhere.

The idea of the ARF emerged as the threat of communism waned after 1989 and as the Vietnamese-Cambodian conflict came to a close by 1991. While the communist threat was diminishing, there nevertheless remained pressing security issues in the entire Asia-Pacific that required urgent attention. Since there had never been an Asia-Pacific-wide security forum of any type, by 1991 ASEAN leaders had put forward their own model of regular diplomatic consultations as the model to be followed for dialogue and cooperation on security issues in the region.[7] The ARF was created in 1992, one year before the conflict prevention mechanism of the OAU, as a means of coping with the multitude of complex post–Cold War conflicts, some of which were inherited from the Cold War era and some of which were new challenges.

The ARF is based on the fundamental principles of ASEAN's Treaty of Amity and Cooperation (TAC), which was concluded in 1976:

- Mutual respect for the independence, sovereignty, equality, territorial integrity, and national identity of all nations
- The right of every state to lead its national existence free from external interference, subversion, or coercion
- Noninterference in the internal affairs of one another
- Settlement of differences or disputes by peaceful means
- Renunciation of the threat or use of force
- Effective cooperation among parties[8]

Thus, the TAC is built on the principle of equality, sovereignty of states, and noninterference in each other's domestic affairs. Noninterference is a sine qua non of ASEAN diplomacy, which was promulgated in the founding Bangkok Declaration (1967) and the Zone of Peace, Freedom, and Neutrality (1971).

Another key principle is that of self-restraint, which ASEAN endorsed in 1992. The declaration on the South China Sea of 22 July 1992 stated that ASEAN foreign ministers would "urge all parties concerned to exercise restraint with a view to creating a positive climate for the eventual resolution of all disputes."[9]

A concept paper for the ARF drafted by Singaporean officials in March 1995 noted that the ARF should progress at a pace comfortable to all participants and should not move too fast for those who want to go slowly.[10]

The ARF follows ASEAN's consultative style of conflict prevention. Through its history, ASEAN has developed a framework for intensive discussion, consultation, and deliberation of matters of mutual interest to foster good neighborliness and cooperation and to avoid exacerbating bilateral disputes. The framework consists of annual and ad hoc meetings among foreign ministers, meetings among other ministers (finance, economic, and environment ministers), and meetings and discussions among officials (the ASEAN standing committee and the meeting of senior officials).

The ARF follows this same consultative and consensual style. Decisions within the ARF are to be made by consensus. At the second ARF meeting in Brunei in August 1995, ministers agreed that ASEAN should be the driving force, that the process should move at a pace comfortable to all participants, and that it should be evolutionary—that is, going through three phases: promotion of confidence-building, development of preventive diplomacy, and elaboration of approaches to conflicts—with conflict management and resolution as the ultimate goal.

The 1995 paper called for various confidence-building measures. Annex A consisted of measures that could be taken immediately, such as developing principles to ensure common understanding, adopting comprehensive approaches to security, creating transparency through voluntary statements of defense policy positions, participating in the UN conventional arms register, enhancing contacts between government and military officials, observers at military exercises, and annual seminars for defense officials and military officers on select international security issues.[11] Annex B contained confidence-building measures to be implemented over the medium and long term, including exploring further a regional arms register, creating a regional security studies center or coordinating existing security activities, creating a maritime information database, using cooperative approaches to sea lanes or communication (exchange of information and training), creating mechanisms to mobilize relief assistance in the event of natural disasters, establishing zones of cooperation in areas such as the South China Sea, implementing systems of prior notification of major military deployments that have regionwide application, and encouraging arms manufacturers and suppliers to disclose the destination of their arms exports.[12]

ASEAN decided on a two-track approach to implement these recommendations. Track I activities are carried out by the ARF governments. Track II is the responsibility of strategic studies institutes and nongovernmental organizations. Institutions such as the ASEAN Institutes of Strategic and International Studies and the Conference on Security and Cooperation in the Asia-Pacific (CSCAP) are Track II conveners. Within CSCAP, each member state may establish a national council. ASEAN-ISIS and CSCAP are responsible for conducting seminars, the results of which are discussed in ARF meetings. CSCAP's functions include activities to foster greater transparency with regard to military activities, the formation of a register of regional arms, enhanced interaction among member states and regular exchanges of defense white papers, exchanges among military personnel, the presence of outside observers at military exercises, and the creation and development of centers dealing with regional peacekeeping. A complete list of Track I and II activities is available on the Internet site of the ASEAN secretariat.[13]

More recently, ASEAN foreign ministers have been organizing retreats that provide informal venues for candid discussions, a feature that was formalized at the July 2001 annual ministerial meeting. According to Dato M. Hassan, director general of the Institutes of Strategic and International Studies in Malaysia, retreats "offer pragmatic opportunities for members to 'interfere' in each other's affairs without the blare and glare of publicity. Their confidence building and conflict prevention relevance in the Southeast Asian context should not be underestimated."[14] ASEAN secretariat official M. C. Abad, Jr., added: "ASEAN itself is a confidence building mechanism. . . . It prevents conflicts by managing interdependence and promoting integration giving its members stakes in each other's peace, stability and prosperity."[15]

Among the accomplishments attributed to the ASEAN ways of working are the reconciliation and conflict prevention between Malaysia and Indonesia during *konfrontasi* (confrontation) in the 1960s and between Malaysia and Singapore following the latter's separation in 1965. Other examples are containment of differences between Thailand and Malaysia over Thai Muslim separatist issues and the Communist Party of Malaya, and reconciliation between Indonesia and Singapore following the Indonesian marines incident of 1968.[16] This is not to say that fundamental differences have been solved. However, as a conflict prevention mechanism, it has worked relatively well.

Intra-ARF communication at the intergovernmental level was agreed on in two forms: 1) an Intersessional Support Group on Confidence Building Measures and 2) intersessional meetings on cooperative activities, including peacekeeping. These were both to be co-chaired by ASEAN and non-ASEAN participants, and the meetings were to be held between ARF summits.

For example, at the second ARF meeting, it was agreed that Indonesia and Japan would co-chair the intersessional meetings on confidence-building measures; Malaysia and Canada would co-chair the intersessional meetings on peacekeeping; and Singapore and the United States would co-chair the intersessional meetings on search and rescue coordination and cooperation. The chair of the ARF is coupled with the ASEAN chair. Thus, the ARF chair rotates each year depending on the host ASEAN country. At the third ARF meeting, it was decided that Track I activities were to be carried out in the first half of the calendar year while Track II activities would take place in the second half.

One may point to the fact that the ARF seems to avoid the language and methods of realistic balance-of-power approaches, identifying threats, and forging corresponding alliances, which may also contribute to avoiding the realist security dilemma of perpetually spiraling insecurity. But it has used confidence-building measures that include security dialogues, exchanges between national defense colleges, disaster relief, voluntary exchanges of information on military exercises, and the circulation of papers to the intersessional group on confidence-building measures. Other confidence-building measures include bilateral exchanges to discuss security perceptions, high-level defense exchanges, military exchanges, training, annual defense policy statements, the publication of white papers, and participation in the UN Conventional Arms Register.[17] One noteworthy development is Beijing's announcement in November 1995 of its first arms control and disarmament white paper.[18]

Some points about ASEAN's preventive diplomacy are:

- It is about diplomacy and relies on diplomatic and peaceful methods such as negotiation, inquiry, mediation, and conciliation.
- It is noncoercive. Military action or the use of force is not part of ASEAN's approach.
- It focuses on timely prevention rather than curative action. Preventive diplomacy methods are most efficiently deployed at an early stage of a dispute or crisis.
- It requires trust and confidence. Preventive diplomacy can be exercised successfully only where there is a strong foundation of trust and confidence among the parties involved and when it is conducted on the basis of neutrality, justice, and impartiality.
- It operates on the basis of consultation and consensus. Any preventive diplomacy effort can be carried out only through consensus after careful and extensive consultation among ARF members, with due consideration for the need of timeliness.
- It is voluntary. Preventive diplomacy practices are to be employed only at the request of all the parties directly involved in the dispute and with their clear consent.
- It applies to conflict between and among states.

- It is conducted in accordance with universally recognized principles of international law and interstate relations embodied, inter alia, in the UN Charter, the five principles of peaceful coexistence, and the TAC.[19]

ARF ministers have been responsive to calls to implement preventive diplomacy measures. At the ninth ARF in Brunei in July 2002, ministers "recognized the importance of making further progress on preventive diplomacy."[20] A paper that was read at that meeting called on the ARF chair to perform a role in good offices and/or a role in coordination between ARF meetings, including:

- Promoting confidence-building among ARF members by facilitating information exchange and dialogue between and among ARF members, such as holding conferences and workshops
- Fostering cooperation between ARF members by facilitating cooperation between ARF members and by facilitating discussion on potential areas of cooperation
- Facilitating discussion on norm-building in the ARF to enhance mutual understanding
- Encouraging exchange of information and highlighting issues that can affect regional security by serving as a conduit for information-sharing between ARF members;
- Serving as a focal point for consultations among ARF members on the basis of consensus of all ARF members. Upon prior consent of directly involved states and the consensus of all ARF members, the ARF chair may convene an ad hoc meeting of all ARF members at an appropriate level.
- Liaising with external parties, such as heads of international organizations and Track II organizations on an informal basis and with prior consultation with all ARF members and their consent[21]

The Conflict Early Warning and Response Mechanism of the Intergovernmental Authority on Development

In 1995–1996, the secretariat of the Intergovernmental Authority on Development (IGAD) was mandated to produce a framework and provisions for its new responsibilities in conflict prevention, management, and resolution. A cooperative project between the IGAD governments, IGAD's secretariat, and international and national nongovernmental organizations started soon. Its founding principles were first adopted in the Khartoum

Declaration of November 2000 and then specified in a protocol that was approved by all member states in January 2002.[22]

For the functioning of the system, each IGAD member state is required to establish a conflict early warning and response mechanism (CEWARN) unit, composed of the government, the military, members of civil society, and research institutions. Their key functions are to verify, analyze, and comment on information coming from independent field monitors (part-time project-funded monitors have started their work in IGAD countries). A central unit located in Addis Ababa acts as a clearinghouse and manages a database and Internet communication center. At the highest political level, the system is coordinated by the steering committee of permanent secretaries of IGAD member states and a technical committee comprised of the heads of units in each member state and the coordinator of the technical unit in Addis Ababa. An important feature of CEWARN is its immediate linkage to high-level decision makers in IGAD countries and IGAD's executive secretary.

The Organization of American States

The inter-American system includes the Inter-American Treaty of Reciprocal Assistance (Rio Treaty, 1947), the charter of the OAS (1948), and the American Treaty on Pacific Settlement (Pact of Bogotá, 1948). The treaties of Tlatelolco and Ayacucho concerning control of nuclear weapons and arms limitation are also relevant. The Pact of Bogotá provides for good offices and mediation by a government or private citizen as agreed to by the parties. It also provides for investigation and conciliation under the authority of a five-member commission established by the OAS council. Resort to arbitration and judicial settlement is also provided for.

Preventive diplomacy in the OAS is exercised through the good offices of the secretary-general as well of member states individually and in groups. Friendly intercessions in emerging disputes are a long-standing part of the inter-American tradition. Two cases of preemptive mediation involving the OAS are the territorial disputes between Ecuador and Peru (1981) and between Guatemala and Belize (1972).[23]

The OSCE High Commissioner on National Minorities

In 1990, the Conference on Security and Co-operation in Europe (which later became the Organization for Security and Co-operation in Europe, OSCE) established the position of high commissioner on national minorities to provide early warning and, as appropriate, action at the earliest possible stage in the case of tensions involving national minority issues that have not yet developed beyond an early warning stage. In the judgment of the high commissioner, these situations could develop into a conflict within the OSCE area, affecting peace, stability, or relations between participating states, requiring the attention of and action by the council. Within this mandate, based on OSCE principles and commitments, the high commissioner is required to work in confidence and to act independently of all parties directly involved in the tensions.

The high commissioner should be an eminent international personality with long-standing relevant experience from whom an impartial performance of the function may be expected. By way of early warning, the high commissioner was mandated to:

- Collect and receive information regarding national minority issues from sources specified in the mandate
- Assess at the earliest practicable stage the role of the parties directly concerned, the nature of the tensions and recent developments therein and, where possible, the potential consequences for peace and stability within the Conference on Security and Co-operation in Europe area

To this end, the high commissioner is able to pay a visit to any participating state and communicate in person with the parties directly concerned to obtain first-hand information about the situation of national minorities. Some procedural requirements have been established for the exercise of parts of these functions. During a visit to a participating state, the high commissioner may discuss the questions with the parties while obtaining first-hand information from all parties directly involved and where appropriate promote dialogue, confidence, and cooperation between them.

If, on the basis of exchanges of communications and contacts with relevant parties, the high commissioner concludes that there is a prima facie risk of potential conflict, he or she may issue an early warning, which will be communicated promptly by the chair to the Committee of Senior Officials. The high commissioner may recommend that he or she be authorized to enter into further contact and closer consultations with the parties concerned with a view to possible solutions, according to a mandate to be decided by the Committee of Senior Officials.

Ideas for Future Cooperation

Strengthened UN cooperation with these regional and subregional arrangements can be of great advantage in early warning and preventive diplomacy.

How, then, can preventive diplomacy cooperation be strengthened between the UN and the regional and subregional arrangements?

This topic has come up for consideration at the biennial meetings of the Secretary-General and the leaders of the regional and subregional organizations. At the third high-level meeting between the UN and regional organizations, held in 2001, the participants agreed on a framework for cooperation in peacebuilding that listed strengthening "existing national and regional mechanisms for prevention, conflict resolution and peace-building" as an item of cooperation.[24] At the fifth high-level meeting between the UN and regional organizations, participants noted that cooperation in preventing armed conflict was a fundamental element of countering challenges to international peace and security and that "current cooperation at the working level should be pursued with renewed vigor."[25]

The participants agreed on a framework for cooperation in confronting new challenges to international peace and security, including international terrorism. This framework envisaged further working-level consultations on issues discussed at the meeting, including the establishment of a coordination center or advisory council at a high working level between the UN and regional organizations "to confront new challenges to international peace and security." Subsequent to the meeting, technical workshops were held between member states and regional organizations to discuss capacity-building and cooperating on early warning and preventive diplomacy.[26]

In January 1993, the Security Council invited regional organizations to improve coordination with the UN and has since been mindful of the declaration adopted by the General Assembly in December 1994 on enhancing cooperation between the UN and regional organizations. At an open meeting on 11 April 2003, the Security Council discussed "The Security Council and Regional Organizations: Facing New Challenges to International Peace and Security." It held another open meeting on 20 July 2004 to discuss cooperation between the UN and regional organizations in stabilization processes. Representatives of the African Union, the European Union, the Arab League, ASEAN, the North Atlantic Treaty Organization, the Commonwealth of Independent States, the OSCE, the Organization of the Islamic Conference, and ECOWAS took part in the meeting.

A presidential statement adopted after the meeting emphasized that the Security Council has primary responsibility for maintaining international peace and security and that effectively addressing the numerous conflict situations confronting the international community would require an increased level of cooperation with regional organizations, where appropriate. Member states and heads of regional organizations participating in the meeting stressed their interest in enhancing cooperation between the UN and regional organizations in maintaining international peace and security. They also considered that regular dialogue on specific issues between the council and regional organizations would bring significant added value in this regard.[27] The Security Council welcomed ongoing high-level meetings of the Secretary-General and regional organizations and the consensus reached over modalities of cooperation in conflict and principles of cooperation in peacebuilding.

From time to time, the Security Council has been briefed by the heads of some regional organizations. At an open meeting on 7 May 2004, for example, the minister for foreign affairs of Bulgaria, as the OSCE's chair, briefed the Security Council on the organization's activities on various issues of peace and security in Europe.[28] The OSCE chair has addressed the council on other occasions. The heads of other regional organizations have also addressed the Security Council.

The formal cooperative activities described above are undoubtedly of value but still leave open the question of how practical cooperation between the Security Council and regional organizations in support of preventive diplomacy might be further developed. Several considerations come to mind. In the first place, a regional organization might decide to act within its own procedures and wish to keep the matter there. That is the essence of preventive diplomacy, and in such a case there might not be any need to keep the Security Council advised of the matter. In the second place, the head of the regional organization might be in discreet contact with the Secretary-General, which might be adequate to the particular situation. In the third place, the secretariat of the regional organization and the United Nations might share information and maintain contacts.

Notwithstanding all of the above, something fundamental is still lacking. The international community is entitled to expect that the Security Council and the regional organizations will contribute to maintaining a true global watch over threats to international peace and security and that the watch will be systematic. At the present time, as illustrated in the chapter on the Security Council, whether the Security Council is briefed about potential trouble spots depends on whether the Secretariat chooses to brief it about a situation or whether a member state chooses to raise it. This is a weakness in the organization of preventive diplomacy globally.

A system of internal regional rapporteurs inside the Security Council would address this weakness. If the Security Council established such a system, a regional rapporteur could be regularly briefed by regional or subregional organizations in his or her area of responsibility. This would deepen cooperation between the UN and regional organizations for preventive diplomacy. The rapporteur might even lead a visiting mission to the regional organization from time to time. In the absence of such a system, biennial briefings by each regional organization in informal consultations of the Security Council is a possible solution. Such briefings would give the regional organization an opportunity to share—confidentially—its assessment with the Security Council.

Currently, too much is left to chance cooperation between the secretariats of the UN and regional organizations. Cooperation regarding preventive diplomacy must also move more in the direction of cooperation with the Security Council itself as part of the process of developing a genuine global watch over threats to international peace and security.

Conclusion

It is fitting to conclude this chapter with a plea for more direct cooperation between regional organizations and the Security Council on preventive diplomacy. A solid foundation of cooperation between the UN and regional organizations has been laid between their secretariats. Some formal activity has also been taking place inside the Security Council itself, such as general or specific cooperative meetings with regional organizations. The next step must involve conscious efforts by the Security Council, with the cooperation of the regional organizations, to set in place a genuine cooperative global watch with preventive diplomacy at its center.

Conclusion: Some Thoughts for the Future

At the end of this journey of the idea of preventive diplomacy at the UN, one crucial conclusion stands out—namely, that preventive diplomacy is and will remain one of the great ideas at the UN for as long as the organization lasts. Whenever there is a possibility that diplomacy might help head off conflict or emergencies, the effort should be considered by the Secretary-General, the president and members of the Security Council, and, possibly, by the president of the General Assembly.

There will be cases where there are reasonable prospects of success, and that is a matter of judgment. In such cases, there must be a moral duty to try preventive diplomacy. There will be cases where preventive diplomacy is not likely to be effective. One must accept this and not engage in a futile effort that is doomed to failure. Again, this is a question of judgment. Preventive diplomacy is more art than science.

Preventive diplomacy may be marshaled not only in respect of disputes or crises but also in respect of the great threats that face humankind. Again, this is a matter of judgment, particularly for the Secretary-General. What is at issue is careful diplomacy, not moral posturing. Through information-gathering and analysis, discreet contacts, and consultations, the Secretary-General might be able to help move the agenda along on an issue that is vital for the future of human security and welfare. The prevention of genocide is one such example. Another example is the danger of terrorism combined with weapons of mass destruction. Again, it will be up to the judgment of the Secretary-General whether and how he or she gets involved.

The proliferation of small arms could be a topic where the Secretary-General might be able to work with key partners discreetly behind the scenes. There are strong economic interests involved in this issue, and the last thing a Secretary-General should do is point the finger of accusation. But contacts and consultations with governments and corporations might yield results over time.

The Secretary-General will need to be careful to avoid becoming caught in the cross-fire of national interests or politics. Global warming is undoubtedly an example of such an issue, where the threat to human security is high but the positions of governments are quite divided. The Secretary-General would need to be prudent about getting involved in such an issue and should seek to exercise influence cautiously. Secretary-General Ban Ki-moon has already made a good beginning in sounding the alert on this issue.

A Secretary-General has many responsibilities and needs to balance them. The constituency of the UN—"We the Peoples"—looks to the Secretary-General for moral and political leadership. This is indeed important. But leadership must be combined with moral authority and wise judgment. The articulation of issues will require careful diplomacy. A Secretary-General who is constantly lecturing or hectoring governments will soon lose effectiveness. A Secretary-General who is mainly a preacher probably will not have too many opportunities to engage in preventive diplomacy. Tact, judgment, discretion, and prudence must all influence the exercise of leadership and the pursuit of advocacy.

Because of the potential usefulness of preventive diplomacy and the need to cultivate the art, it would be wise to retain its distinctiveness as an idea, even while recognizing the value of broader preventive strategies. The practitioner of preventive diplomacy swims in the stream of broader preventive strategies. But the practitioner of preventive diplomacy must develop and sharpen specialized skills. Analyses of ideas and policies must retain the distinctiveness of the idea of preventive diplomacy, keeping a particular focus on the Secretary-General.

This requires that the UN Secretariat, particularly the Department of Political Affairs and the Executive Office of the Secretary-General, be optimally equipped to support the role of the Secretary-General in exercising preventive diplomacy. The political department is central when it comes to crisis situations, and the executive office is central when it comes to global threats as well as crisis situations. The recent High-level Panel on Threats, Challenges and Change devoted a large part of its report to the need to strengthen the Secretariat's capacity in supporting the preventive diplomacy role of the Secretary-General. But in Secretary-General Annan's subsequent report, the panel's ideas were not given practical followup.

The resources of the political department that supports the preventive diplomacy role of the Secretary-General and the Security Council must be strengthened as a matter of urgency. The department's focus on preventive diplomacy must be sharpened, whatever else is done on broader preventive strategies. Subsuming preventive diplomacy under preventive actions generally does not fit the bill.

At different times and by different persons, the idea has been floated that there should be a special representative of the Secretary-General on preventive diplomacy who would work within the Department of Political Affairs and under the leadership of the under-secretary-general for political affairs. The arguments advanced in favor of this idea have been that the head of the political department, while being the principal political adviser of the Secretary-General, is also weighed down by the demands of running a large and complex department and of advising the Secretary-General on political situations and issues across the globe. Under the guidance of the head of the political department, someone focusing on preventive diplomacy would be able to sharpen the concentration on this vital function. This is an attractive idea worth pursuing.

This book has illustrated that regional and other representatives of the Secretary-General are often able to engage in valuable preventive diplomacy on the ground. The Secretary-General's special representative for West Africa is a case in point. The United Nations Institute for Training and Research runs a program of seminars and consultations to help sharpen the skills of special representatives and similar officials. The practice of preventive diplomacy could usefully be highlighted in this already valuable program.

In 1987, Secretary-General Pérez de Cuéllar advanced the idea that the UN system should maintain a comprehensive global watch over threats to human security. This idea retains its value and could profit from discussions within the interagency consultation processes in the UN system. The establishment of a war risk reduction center is a related idea that has been put forward in the academic literature. This idea could also benefit from further exploration, probably within the academic and research community, as a start.

An issue that should be highlighted, however, is the following: The Security Council and the Secretary-General are mandated to watch over the maintenance of international peace and security, mindful of threats or breaches, potential or actual. So far, the Security Council, a highly political body, has had mainly a case-by-case focus, although on issues such as HIV/AIDS, it has pursued a thematic focus on threats to international security. If the Security Council is to be able to enhance its potential to exercise preventive diplomacy in the future, should it, or the UN Secretariat, be responsible for maintaining a global security watch? And should consideration also be extended to new and nontraditional threats to security?

One could think of quite a few issues on which the evidence clearly shows that the Security Council is ill prepared. What, for example, are the security implications of rising oceans or of global migratory movements, as just two examples? This is not to suggest that the Security Council engage in unending deliberations on such topics. But the Security Council is entitled to receive factual briefings and analyses on matters such as these. Without a doubt, much information and analyses are already available in the research and scholarly community. It is necessary to organize a global security watch in such a manner that the information and analysis are made available to the Security Council—as the leading security organ of the international community—in an organized and digestible manner. There is a possibility, here also, for the president and members of the Security Council or the Secretary-General to marshal preventive diplomacy when it seems appropriate.

The Secretary-General, who spearheads the preventive diplomacy of the United Nations, could take the lead in developing a global watch over issues affecting the future and welfare of the planet. This means that the Secretary-General should use suitable occasions to alert the world to pressing dangers in a manner calculated to win respect and gain confidence. The issues may concern the environment, international or human security, the protection of groups at risk, the prevention of terrorism, or the control of weapons of mass destruction. People look to the Secretary-General to help define and alert the world to the pressing issues requiring attention.

Second, the Secretary-General should encourage the preventive diplomacy role of sister institutions. This means continued and energized support for international, regional, and subregional arrangements to prevent conflicts and atrocities. It also means the exercise of the competence entrusted to the Secretary-General to bring matters that he or she thinks might affect the maintenance of international peace and security to the Security Council's attention. The Secretary-General should pay particular attention to the prevention of genocide and the prevention of terrorists' access to weapons of mass destruction.

As part of the exercise of preventive diplomacy, the Secretary-General of the future would do well to use her or his authority to help promote and build up prevention systems nationally, subregionally, and internationally. The development of institutions of prevention is crucial, and it is an area where preventive diplomacy can yield rich dividends in the future.

Third, the Secretary-General should take the lead in implementing a diplomacy of democracy and human rights at the country level. The key strategic idea here should be to help countries develop or enhance their national protection systems. Constitutions and laws should be reflective of international human rights norms. National courts should be able to draw on international human rights norms and jurisprudence. Human rights should be taught in schools and institutions of higher learning. There should be institutions such as a national commission on human rights as well as arrangements for early warning and urgent response to head off grievances before they deteriorate. Strengthening national protection systems should be a flagship idea for the Secretary-General.

Arguments have also been put forward for a return to the ideas first advanced by President George H. W. Bush to establish a coordinator of electoral assistance supported by an electoral commission at the United Nations. The promotion of democracy as a strategy of conflict prevention requires renewed dynamism.

Fourth, the alleviation of extreme poverty should be a priority objective of the Secretary-General. This would require the UN system to bring the concept of preventable poverty into focus and to highlight situations where, having regard for the resources available within a country, there is a consistent pattern of gross violations of economic and social rights. The implementation of the Millennium Development Goals would provide the broader framework for such strategies.

Fifth, the empowerment of women must be a leading priority for the Secretary-General. This is an issue of strategy as well as of justice. Gender inequality is so pervasive as to make our world far removed from the vision of the Universal Declaration of Human Rights. Women as leaders, mothers, monitors, and participants can help us deal with the problems of the environment, conflicts, and poverty. Empowering women is enabling humanity.

Sixth, the Secretary-General must engage in a diplomacy of protection, particularly with respect to groups at risk. Coming after Rwanda and Srebrenica, Darfur is a deep stain on the United Nations. The diplomacy of protection has not been up to the mark to date. Unless the UN is able to protect people, the peoples of the UN will have little respect for it. Aerial protection might have helped the people of Darfur.

Seventh, the Secretary-General should take the lead in striving for an ethical world order—a world of conscience and of values. The Secretary-General must be the personal embodiment of such ethics. The Secretary-General is looked on as a moral leader of the world and must be above reproach on issues of personal or professional ethics.

The use of preventive diplomacy should not be left to the Secretary-General alone. The UN Charter provides room to exercise preventive diplomacy by the Secretary-General as well as by the Security Council or the General Assembly. The funds and specialized agencies of the United Nations system as well as committed nongovernmental organizations, such as the International Committee of the Red Cross and the International Crisis Group, and individuals have a role to play.

From the point of view of maintaining a global watch over threats to international peace and security, the current arrangements inside the Security Council still have one fundamental deficiency that can be easily corrected: The council is too dependent on the Secretariat or a member state to bring potential threats to international peace and security to its attention. The council has not organized itself to help it take a systematic periodic look at the global scene and to benefit from briefings or advice that could be available to it. The council owes it to the international community to systematize its efforts in this respect.

From the perspective of guarding the world against threats to international peace and security, existing arrangements within the Security Council have a considerable shortfall—the body is too dependent on the Secretariat and member states to bring to its attention potential challenges to international stability. The council should develop mechanisms and procedures that would allow it to better take advantage of advice and information that could be available to it and undertake systemic reviews. As the preeminent body charged with maintaining world order, the Security Council has an obligation to remedy such deficiencies. This book has also argued for a system of internal regional rapporteurs inside the Security Council.

It is imperative that the Security Council make its global watch more systematic over potential threats that could endanger the maintenance of international peace and security. Ways must be found to help the council keep track of nontraditional threats to security.

The "Peoples of the United Nations," particularly the scholarly and research community, can play a useful role in helping take forward the idea of a global security watch and in furthering understanding of the salience of the idea of preventive diplomacy and how it might be enhanced in the future. By focusing on the intellectual journey of the idea of preventive diplomacy at the UN, the United Nations Intellectual History Project has begun tapping into the veins of the available diplomatic and scholarly materials. The project is thus an important undertaking, drawing a bridge between academia and the policy world in order to shed light on the UN's ideational history and the political context in which it is embedded.

This endeavor has attempted to open these exploratory shafts. Others will follow, and more veins will be pursued as further materials are unearthed. One thing is clear: the idea of preventive diplomacy is one of the great UN ideas that will be around for as long as the world organization exists, for behind it is a simple faith that whatever might be done to head off crises or conflicts should be considered. Preventive diplomacy will not always be viable or successful, as illustrated by Secretary-General Lie's involvement in the Korean situation and more recently the failure of the world body to take effective action to protect the vulnerable people of Darfur from egregious human rights abuses. But it might be decisive in averting war, as exemplified by the role of Secretay-General U Thant during the Cuban missile crisis and the UN's deployment of troops to the Former Yugoslav Republic of Macedonia. The viability of preventive diplomacy will only be clear on a case-by-case basis. One should therefore always be prepared to consider it, using judgment, tact, and discretion.

Notes

Series Editors' Foreword

1. Craig N. Murphy, *The UN Development Programme: A Better Way?* (Oxford: Oxford University Press, 2006).

2. D. John Shaw, *UN World Food Programme and the Development of Food Aid* (New York: Palgrave, 2001).

3. Maggie Black, *The Children and the Nations* (New York: UNICEF, 1986); and Maggie Black, *Children First: The Story of UNICEF* (Oxford: Oxford University Press, 1996).

4. Thomas G. Weiss and Sam Daws, eds., *The Oxford Handbook on the United Nations* (Oxford: Oxford University Press, 2007).

5. Louis Emmerij, Richard Jolly, and Thomas G. Weiss, *The Power of UN Ideas: Lessons from the First 60 Years* (New York: UNIHP, 2005), 7. For a review of the initial volumes, see Robert J. Berg, "The UN Intellectual History Project: Review of a Literature," *Global Governance* 12, no. 3 (2006): 325–341.

6. See S. Neil MacFarlane and Yuen Foong-Khong, *Human Security and the UN: A Critical History* (Bloomington: Indiana University Press, 2006).

7. Roger Normand and Sarah Zaidi, *Human Rights at the UN: The Political History of Universal Justice* (Bloomington: Indiana University Press, 2008).

8. Boutros Boutros-Ghali, *An Agenda for Peace 1995* (New York: UN, 1995) (contains the original 1992 document and the 1995 supplement); Boutros Boutros-Ghali, *An Agenda for Development 1995* (New York: UN, 1995); and Boutros Boutros-Ghali, *An Agenda for Democratization* (New York: UN, 1996).

9. *Programme Planning: Preparation of the Next Medium-Term Plan: Note by the Secretary-General: Enclosure: Some Perspectives on the Work of the United Nations in the 1990s*, A/42/512, 2 September 1987.

10. Kofi A. Annan, *Prevention of Armed Conflict* (New York: UN, 2001).

11. Louis Emmerij, Richard Jolly, and Thomas G. Weiss, *Ahead of the Curve? UN Ideas and Global Challenges* (Bloomington: Indiana University Press, 2001), xi.

Preface and Acknowledgments

1. Carnegie Commission on Preventing Deadly Conflict, *Preventing Deadly Conflict: Final Report* (Washington, D.C.: Carnegie Commission on Preventing Deadly Conflict, 1997). See also David A. Hamburg, *No More Killing Fields: Preventing Deadly Conflict* (New York: Rowman and Littlefield, 2002).

Secretaries-General on Preventive Diplomacy

1. Andrew W. Cordier and Wilder Foote, *Public Papers of the Secretaries-General of the United Nations*, vol. 1, *Trygvie Lie, 1946–1953* (New York: Columbia University Press, 1969), 134.

2. General Assembly, "Introduction to the Report of the Secretary General on the Work of the Organization, 16 June 1959–15 June 1960," *General Assembly Official Records*, 1960, 15th Session, Supplement No. 1A (A4390/Add.1), 5–7.

3. U Thant, *View from the UN: The Memoirs of U Thant* (Garden City, N.Y.: Doubleday, 1978), 31–32.

4. Kurt Waldheim, *The Challenge of Peace* (New York: Rawson Wade Publishers Inc., 1980), 5–6.

5. *Programme Planning: Preparation of the Next Medium-Term Plan: Note by the Secretary-General: Enclosure: Some Perspectives on the Work of the United Nations in the 1990s*, A/42/512, 2 September 1987, 3.

6. Boutros Boutros-Ghali, *An Agenda for Development 1995* (New York: United Nations, 1995).

7. Kofi Annan, *In Larger Freedom: Towards Development, Security and Human Rights for All* (New York: UN, 2005).

8. Ban Ki-moon, "Address to the United Nations International School-United Nations Conference on 'Global Warming: Confronting the Crisis,'" UN press release SG/SM10893, 1 March 2007.

Introduction

1. Joel Larus, ed., *From Collective Security to Preventive Diplomacy* (New York: John Wiley & Sons, 1965).

2. Richard I. Miller, *Dag Hammarskjöld and Crisis Diplomacy* (New York: Oceana, 1961).

3. Brian Urquhart, *Hammarskjöld* (New York: Alfred K. Knopf, 1972).

4. Boutros Boutros-Ghali, *An Agenda for Peace: Preventive Diplomacy, Peacemaking and Peace-Keeping* (New York: United Nations, 1992).

5. Kofi Annan, *Prevention of Armed Conflict: Report of the Secretary-General* (General Assembly document A/55/985), 7 June 2001; Kofi Annan, *Interim Report of the Secretary-General on the Prevention of Armed Conflict* (General Assembly document A/58/365), 12 September 2003; Kofi Annan, *Progress Report on the Prevention of Armed Conflict: Report of the Secretary-General* (General Assembly document A/60/891), 18 July 2006.

6. General Assembly resolution 377 (V), 3 November 1950.

7. As H. G. Nicholas cautioned, " If the action of one or more of the members violates the Charter, the Secretary-General's duty is clear, but when the time comes, as it must, for healing the breach . . . the Secretary-General's partiality, though it be the partiality of righteousness, is likely to be an offence in the nostrils of the returned prodigal." H. G. Nicholas, *The United Nations as a Political Institution*, 4th ed. (Oxford: Oxford University Press, 1971), 172.

8. Prior to the U.S. invasion of Grenada, the Grenadian Permanent Mission to the United Nations wrote a detailed letter to Secretary-General Waldheim on 19 August 1981, setting out the circumstances that led them to believe that Grenada was about to be invaded by the United States and asking the Secretary-General to use his good of-

fices to prevent this. Alas, there was nothing the Secretary-General could do to prevent the American juggernaut. A copy of the letter, provided to him when he was special assistant to the head of the UN human rights program, is in the possession of the author.

9. See Brian Urquhart, *Hammarskjöld,* 262–292 and 293–314. Hammarskjöld considered the Lebanon operation "a classical case of preventive diplomacy," the main object of which was to keep the Cold War out of the Middle East (256).

10. Victor-Yves Ghebali brings this point out well: "Semantically speaking, the phrase 'preventive diplomacy' emerged within the United Nations during the Cold War period. In the late 1950's-early 60's, Secretary-General Dag Hammarskjöld coined it just to describe the residual function which, according to him, the UN could hope to play in a bipolar international system. In this perspective, 'preventive diplomacy' was not considered as an approach for the prevention of potential conflicts, but rather for the preservation of nascent conflicts from the magnetic attraction of the East-West confrontation. Over time, the meaning of the phrase evolved to mean the management of potential conflicts, as demonstrated, for example, by the 1988 General Assembly Special Declaration on Conflict Prevention and Elimination [A/43/51 of 5 December 1988]. With the collapse of communism, preventive diplomacy found a new lease on life: Secretary-General Boutros Boutros-Ghali included it in his *Agenda for Peace* (1992) on an equal footing with such concepts as peacekeeping, peacemaking, peace enforcement, and peacebuilding. Since then the United Nations has turned it into a major political priority." See Victor-Yves Ghebali, "Preventive Diplomacy as Visited from the OSCE," in *The OSCE and Preventive Diplomacy,* ed. Victor-Yves Ghebali and Daniel Warner, PSIO Occasional Paper No. 1/99 (Geneva: Program for the Study of International Organizations, Geneva Graduate Institute of International Studies, 1999), 7, available online at hei.unige.ch/psio/fichiers/OSCE%201.99.pdf (accessed 27 September 2007).

11. Ghebali correctly notes that "a full-fledged preventive diplomacy process normally includes three stages: early warning, early action and peace-building measures. Although distinct in abstract terms, they actually form a continuum." Ibid., 15.

12. Mohammed Bedjaoui, "Preventive Diplomacy: Development, Education and Human Rights," in *Preventive Diplomacy,* ed. Kevin Cahill (New York: Basic Books, 1996), 37.

1. Preventive Diplomacy in the Concert of Europe, the Hague Peace Conferences, the League of Nations, and the UN Charter

1. "Secretary-General, Addressing Student Conference, Compares Challenge of Climate Change to Cold War–Era Nuclear Threat," UN press release SG/SM 10893, 1 March 2007.

2. Kalevi J. Holsti, *Peace and War: Armed Conflicts and International Order 1648–1989* (Cambridge: Cambridge University Press, 1991).

3. F. H. Hinsley, *Power and the Pursuit of Peace* (Cambridge: Cambridge University Press, 1967), 1.

4. Ibid., 63.

5. Ibid., 79.

6. *The Cambridge Modern History* (New York, 1907–1925), 10:3, cited in René Albrecht-Carrié, *The Concert of Europe 1815–1914* (New York: Harper and Row, 1968), 15.

7. See John Lowe, *The Concert of Europe: International Relations 1814–1870* (London: Hodder and Stoughton, 1994).

8. Ibid., 39.

9. Ibid., 225.

10. Ibid., 233.

11. Hinsley, *Power and the Pursuit of Peace*, 233.

12. Ibid.

13. See James Brown Scott, *The Hague Peace Conferences of 1899 and 1907: A Series of Lectures Delivered before the Johns Hopkins University in the Year 1908* (Boston: Johns Hopkins University Press, 1908).

14. See David W. Wainhouse, *International Peace Observation* (Baltimore, Md.: Johns Hopkins University Press, 1966), 8.

15. Arthur W. Rovine, *The First Fifty Years: The Secretary-General in World Politics 1920–1970* (Leiden, Netherlands: Sijthoff, 1970), 59.

16. Ibid., 65.

17. See Wainhouse, *International Peace Observation*, 48.

18. Ibid., 72.

19. Leland Goodrich and Anne Simons, *Charter of the United Nations: Commentary and Documents*, 3rd ed. (New York: Columbia University Press, 1969), 589.

20. Ibid., 589; *Final Report of the Preparatory Commission* (Preparatory Commission document PC/20), 23 December 1945, 87.

21. Stephen Schwebel, *The Secretary-General of the United Nations: His Political Powers and Practice* (Cambridge, Mass.: Harvard University Press, 1952), 23–26.

22. Boutros Boutros-Ghali, *Building Peace and Development 1994, Annual Report on the Work of the Organization* (New York: United Nations, 1994).

23. The proposal to establish a UN Staff College, which had been around since 1969, was implemented in 1995, and the college began operations in 1996. In July 2001, the General Assembly approved the Statute of the United Nations System Staff College. On 1 January 2002, the college began its operations as a distinct institution within the UN system.

24. This section, like the preceding one, is based on the experience of the author. For a recent account on the proceedings of the Security Council, see Chinmaya R. Gharekhan, *The Horseshoe Table: An Inside View of the UN Security Council* (Delhi: Pearson/Longman, 2006).

25. See "Blair Gives Backing for Darfur No-Fly Zone: Washington Develops Air Strike Plan for Sudan," *Financial Times*, 13 December 2006.

26. See Kurt Bassuener, "A No-Flight Zone Is Key," *International Herald Tribune*, 1 February 2006, 6. See also Bertrand G. Ramcharan, "Contemporary Challenges of Human Rights Protection: A Call for Preventive Strategies," *Rutgers Law Journal* 37, no. 2 (2006): 495–516. This article states that "from the outset of the Darfur crisis it has been evident that aerial policing of the situation would be the only means of exercising protection over the civilian population being preyed upon by pro-government forces" (515).

27. *Security Council Official Records,* 1st Year, 70th Meeting, 20 September 1946, 404. See also Goodrich and Simons, *Charter of the United Nations,* 591.

28. See Goodrich and Simons, *Charter of the United Nations,* 592.

29. See *Letter Dated 25 June 1950 from the Representative of the United States of America to the Secretary General Transmitting a Communication to the President of the Security Council Concerning an Act of Aggression upon the Republic of Korea* (Security Council document S/1495), 25 June 1950; and "Cablegram Dated 25 June 1950 from the United Nations Commission on Korea to the Secretary General Concerning Aggression upon the Republic of Korea," S/1496, 25 June 1950.

30. *Security Council Official Records,* 5th Year, 473rd Meeting, 25 June 1950, 3.

31. *Security Council Official Records,* 11th Year, 748th Meeting, 30 October 1956.

32. Ibid., 591–592.

33. *Security Council Official Records,* 16th Year, 964th Meeting, 28 July 1961, para. 86.

34. *Security Council Official Records,* 14th Year, 847th Meeting, 7 September 1959, 2–3.

35. S/4381, 13 July 1960. See also *Security Council Official Records,* 15th Year, 873rd Meeting, 13 July 1960, 1–2.

36. *Security Council Official Records,* 16th Year, 962nd Meeting, 22 July 1961, paras. 2–3. See Goodrich and Simons, *Charter of the United Nations,* 590.

37. See Goodrich and Simons, *Charter of the United Nations,* 592–593.

38. In 1972, on the initiative of Waldheim, the General Assembly put the problem of international terrorism on its agenda. Kurt Waldheim, *The Challenge of Peace* (New York: Rawson, Wade Publishers, 1977), 4.

2. UN Policies and Doctrines of Preventive Diplomacy

1. See M. J. Peterson, *The UN General Assembly* (London: Routledge, 2006).

2. See UNITAR, *Presidents of the General Assembly Speak Out* (New York: United Nations Institute for Training and Research, 1986), 20.

3. See International Conciliation no. 444, October, in James Hyde, *1948: Peaceful Settlement. A Survey of Studies in the Interim Committee of the United Nations General Assembly* (New York: Carnegie Endowment for International Peace, 1948).

4. See also "Prevention of Armed Conflict," General Assembly resolution A/Res/57/337, 3 July 2003; and Security Council resolution 1366 (2001), 30 August 2001, both on Kofi Annan's *Prevention of Armed Conflict.*

5. See also Edward C. Luck, *UN Security Council: Practice and Promise* (London: Routledge, 2006).

6. *United Nations Programme of Action to Prevent, Combat and Eradicate the Illicit Trade in Small Arms and Light Weapons in All Its Aspects,* General Assembly document A/CONF.192/115, 20 July 2001.

7. "United Nations Declaration and Programme of Action for a Culture of Peace," General Assembly document A/Res/53/243, 1999.

8. See Leon Gordenker, *The UN Secretary-General and Secretariat* (London: Routledge, 2005).

9. Arthur W. Rovine, *The First Fifty Years: The Secretary-General in World Politics 1920–1970* (Leyden, Netherlands: Sijthoff, 1970), 249–250.

10. This point was made by James S. Sutterlin in his comments on an earlier draft of this book.

11. Rovine, *The First Fifty Years,* 225.

12. *General Assembly Official Records,* Third Session, Supp. no. 1, 5 July 1948.

13. Andrew W. Cordier and Wilde Foote, *Public Papers of the Secretaries-General of the United Nations,* vol. 1, *Trygve Lie, 1946–1953* (New York: Columbia University Press, 1969), 156.

14. Ibid., 167.

15. Ibid.

16. Cordier and Foote, *Public Papers,* 1:171.

17. Ibid., 187–188.

18. Brian Urquhart cites Ralph Bunche's description of this concept: "The important aim of the UN 'presence' is the establishment of some sort of UN arrangement on the spot with a purpose of watching local developments, holding a finger on the pulse and keeping UN Headquarters fully informed about developments in that area. For the most part those who constitute and lead the 'presence' operation, whatever its form, are expected to play their role pretty much by ear, to give well considered advice where needed and requested, to intervene as necessary but always delicately and diplomatically, and to keep constantly in consultation with the Secretary-General for advice and guidance." Brian Urquhart, *Hammarksjöld* (New York: Alfred A. Knopf, 1972), 294–295.

19. Ibid., 57.

20. Ibid., 338. See "Statement by Secretary General on Principles Regarding Political Fact-Finding or 'Good Offices' Missions," UN press release SG/849, 27 August 1959.

21. See Richard I. Miller, *Dag Hammarskjöld and Crisis Diplomacy* (New York: Oceana, 1961).

22. Brian Urquhart, *Hammarskjöld* (New York: Alfred A. Knopf, 1972), 47.

23. Ibid., 47.

24. Ibid., 235.

25. Ibid., 308–309.

26. Ibid., 255.

27. Ibid., 256.

28. Kai Falkman, *To Speak for the World: Speeches and Statements by Dag Hammarskjöld* (Stockholm: Atlantis, 2005), 137–138.

29. "Introduction to the Annual Report," *General Assembly Official Records,* 15th Session, Supp. no. 1A, 31 August 1960, 4.

30. U Thant, *View from the UN: The Memoirs of U Thant* (Garden City, N.Y.: Doubleday, 1967), 27.

31. Ibid., 31.

32. Ibid., 33.

33. Kurt Waldheim, *The Challenge of Peace* (New York: Rawson, Wade Publishers, 1980), 5–6.

34. Ibid., 2.

35. Ibid., 1.

36. Ibid., 12.

37. Ibid., 4.

38. Ibid., 80.

39. Ibid., 8.

40. Ibid., 48.

41. Ibid., 40–41.

42. Ibid., 82–84.

43. Kurt Waldheim, *In The Eye of the Storm: The Memoirs of Kurt Waldheim, Secretary-General of the United Nations 1972–1982* (London: Weidenfeld and Nicolson, 1985), 1–11, 156–169.

44. Ibid., 177–186.

45. Ibid., 182.

46. Javier Pérez de Cuéllar, "The Role of the UN Secretary-General," Cyril Foster Lecture, Oxford University, 1986, 4. Published as UN press release SG/SM/3870, 13 May 1986.

47. "The Office for Research and the Collection of Information," UN document ST/SGB/SB/223, 1 March 1987.

48. Stephen Schwebel, *The Secretary General of the United Nations: His Political Powers and Practice* (Cambridge: Harvard University Press, 1952), 23–26.

49. *Programme Planning. Preparation of the Next Medium Term Plan. Note by the Secretary General. Enclosure: Some Perspectives on the Work of the United Nations in the 1990s,* UN document A/42/512, 2 September 1987, 2. (Hereafter *Perspectives for the 1990s.*)

50. Ibid., 2.

51. Ibid., 3.

52. Ibid., 8.

53. Ibid., 3.

54. Ibid.

55. *Perspectives for the 1990s,* 4.

56. Ibid.

57. *Perspectives for the 1990s,* 6.

58. Ibid., 7.

59. Boutros Boutros-Ghali, "Challenges of Preventive Diplomacy: The Role of the United Nations and Its Secretary-General," in *Preventive Diplomacy: Stopping Wars before They Start,* ed. Kevin M. Cahill (New York: Basic Books, 1996), 16–34.

60. *Report of the Panel on United Nations Peace Operations* (General Assembly document A/55/305-S/2000/809), 21 August 2000, section G.

61. *Supplement to An Agenda for Peace: Position Paper of the Secretary General on the Occasion of the Fiftieth Anniversary of the United Nations* (General Assembly document A/50/60, S/1995/1), 3 January 1995, 2–3.

62. "Note by the President of the Security Council," (Security Council document S/23500) 31 January 1992, 3, available online at http://www.stimson.org/cnp/pdf/S23500_UNSC.pdf (accessed 16 September 2007).

63. Boutros Boutros-Ghali, *An Agenda for Peace: Preventive Diplomacy, Peacemaking and Peace-keeping* (New York: United Nations, 1992), 11, 7–8.

64. Ibid., 8.

65. Ibid., 13.

66. Ibid.

67. Boutros-Ghali, *An Agenda for Peace.*

68. "An Agenda for Peace: Preventative Diplomacy and Related Matters," General Assembly resolution 47/120A, 18 December 1992, Part VII: Role of the General Assembly in Preventive Diplomacy.

69. Ibid.

70. Ibid.

71. Chinmaya R. Gharekhan and Boutros Boutros-Ghali, *The Horseshoe Table: An Inside View of the UN Security Council* (Delhi: Longman, 2006).

72. Department of Political Affairs, "A Report on Preventive Diplomacy," March–December 1992. In an interview with the author in Geneva on 2 August 2006, Mr. Petrovsky provided the author with a copy of the confidential report he had submitted to Secretary General Boutros-Ghali. This report was never published.

73. Ibid., 1.

74. Boutros Boutros-Ghali, *Building Peace and Development: Report on the Work of the Organization from the Forty-Eighth to the Forty-Ninth Session of the General Assembly* (New York: United Nations, 1994), paras. 790–791.

75. "An Agenda for Development: Report of the Secretary-General" (General Assembly document A/48/935), 6 May 1994, para. 44. Published as Boutros Boutros-Ghali, *An Agenda for Development 1995* (New York: United Nations, 1995).

76. *An Agenda for Development,* para. 3.

77. Ibid., para. 16.

78. Ibid., para. 18.

79. Ibid., para. 21.

80. Ibid., para. 20.

81. Ibid., para. 22.

82. Ibid., para. 23.

83. Boutros Boutros-Ghali, *An Agenda for Democratization* (New York: United Nations, 1996).

84. Ibid., 9–10.

85. Ibid., 53.

86. Ibid., 54.

87. Ibid., 55.

88. *Prevention of Armed Conflict: Report of the Secretary-General* (Security Council document S/2001/574), 7 June 2001.

89. Danilo Türk, assistant secretary-general for Political Affairs, UN Department of Political Affairs, Keynote Speech at Seminar on Conflict Prevention and Peace-Building in Southeast Asia, Manila, Philippines, 19–21 February 2002.

90. This account of the Kofi Annan period is based on Tapio Kaanninen and C. Kumar, "The Evolution of the Doctrine and Practice of Early Warning and Conflict Prevention in

the UN System," in *Conflict Prevention in Practice: Essays in Honour of Jim Sutterlin,* ed. Bertrand G. Ramcharan (Leiden, Netherlands: Martinus Nijhoff, 2005), 45–60.

91. *Progress Report on the Prevention of Armed Conflict: Report of the Secretary-General* (General Assembly document A/60/891), 18 July 2006.

92. Ibid.

93. Ibid., 12.

94. Ibid., 30.

95. Ban Ki-moon, "Acceptance Speech," New York, 3 October 2006, available online at http://www.un.org/News/dh/infocus/sg_elect/ban_speech.htm (accessed 3 October 2007); "Chad: Ban Ki-moon Proposes Peacekeeping Force with Some 11,000 Personnel," UN News Centre, 23 February 2007, available online at http://www0.un.org/apps/news/ story.asp?NewsID=21661&Cr=chad&Cr1 (accessed 3 October 2007); Ban Ki-moon, "Address to the United Nations International School-United Nations Conference on 'Global Warming: Confronting the Crisis,'" UN News Centre, 1 March 2007, available online at http://www.un.org/apps/news/infocus/sgspeeches/search_full.asp?statID=70 (accessed 3 October 2007).

96. General Assembly, "Introduction to the Report of the Secretary General on the Work of the Organization, 16 June 1959–15 June 1960," *General Assembly Official Records*, 1960, 15th Session, Supplement No. 1A (A4390/Add.1), 5–7.

3. The Practice of Preventive Diplomacy by the Security Council

1. See the International Peace Academy, "From Promise to Practice: Strengthening UN Capacities for the Prevention of Violent Conflict," report on Security Council Workshop, 9–10 February 2001, West Point, New York, 1.

2. See, for example, Elizabeth Cousens, "Conflict Prevention," in *The UN Security Council: From the Cold War to the 21st Century,* ed. David. M. Malone (Boulder, Colo.: Lynne Rienner, 2004), 101–116; and Thomas G. Weiss, "The UN's Prevention Pipe-Dream," *Berkeley Journal of International Law* 14, no. 2 (1997): 501–515.

3. See Bertrand G. Ramcharan, *The Security Council and Human Rights* (The Hague: Martinus Nijhoff, 2002).

4. "On the Role of the Security Council in the Prevention of Armed Conflict," Security Council resolution 1366 (2001), 30 August 2001, 3.

5. Cousens, "Conflict Prevention," 114.

6. Ibid., 114–115.

7. "Report of the Security Council 1 August 2004–July 2005," *General Assembly Official Records,* 60th Session, Supplement No. 2 (A/60/2), 21 September 2005.

8. "Report of the Security Council 16 June–31 July 2002," 27 September 2002, *General Assembly Official Records,* 57th Session, Supplement No.2 (A/57/2), 3.

9. Ibid.

10. "Report of the Security Council 1 August 2003–31 July 2004," 29 September 2004, *General Assembly Official Records,* 59th Session, Supplement No. 2 (A/59/2), 4–5.

11. "Report of the Security Council 1 August 2002–31 July 2003," 23 September 2003, *General Assembly Official Records,* 58th Session, Supplement No. 2 (A/58/2), 4.

12. "Report of the Security Council 1 August 2003–31 July 2004, 29 September 2004," 7.

13. "Groups of friends" is a term used at the UN to refer to a group of countries that take a particular interest in a country on a situation and concert their efforts to help promote solutions to problems affecting that country or situation.

14. "Report of the Security Council 1 16 June–31 July 2002," 27 September 2002, 4–5.

15. "Report of the Security Council 1 August 2002–31 July 2003," 23 September 2003, 5.

16. Ibid., 2 and 167.

17. Ibid., 2.

18. "Report of the Security Council 1 August 2003–31 July 2004," 29 September 2004, 8.

19. "Report of the Security Council 1 August 2004–July 2005," 21 September 2005, 11.

20. B. G. Ramcharan, "Preventing War between Eritrea and Yemen over the Hanish Islands," in *Conflict Prevention in Practice: Essays in Honour of Jim Sutterlin*, ed. B. G. Ramcharan (Leiden, Netherlands: Martinus Nijhoff Publishers, 2005), 166–167.

21. "Report of the Security Council 16 June 2000–15 June 2001," 30 June 2001.

22. Ibid., 479.

23. Ibid., 568–569.

24. See Peter Van Walsum, "Conflict Containment: The Security Council Mission to East Timor," in *Conflict Prevention in Practice*, ed. Bertrand G. Ramcharan, 191–198 (Leiden, Netherlands: Martinus Nijhoff, 2005).

25. Marrack Goulding, "Observation, Triage, and Initial Therapy. Fact-Finding Missions and Other Techniques," in *Preventive Diplomacy*, ed. Kevin M. Cahill (New York: Basic Books, 1996), 144–153.

26. Ibid.

27. "Declaration on Fact Finding by the United Nations in the Field of the maintenance of International Peace and Security," General Assembly resolution 46/59, 9 December 1991. See also Axel Berg, "The 1991 Declaration on Fact-Finding by the United Nations," *European Journal of International Law* 4, no. 1 (1992): 107–114.

28. "Report of the Security Council 1 August 2002–31 July 2003," 23 September 2003, 2.

29. "Report of the Security Council 1 August 2004–31 July 2005," 21 September 2005, 12.

30. *Report of the Security Council Mission to Central Africa, 21 to 25 November 2004* (Security Council document S/2004/934), 30 November 2004; "Report of the Security Council 1 August 2004–31 July 2005," 21 September 2005, 7.

31. UN News Centre, "Security Council Mission Recommends Dozens of Peacebuilding Actions for Central Africa," 23 November 2005, available at http://www.monuc.org/news.aspx?newsID=9100.

32. Ibid.

33. See Michael Doyle and Nicholas Sambanis, *Making War and Building Peace: United Nations Peace Operations* (Princeton, N.J.: Princeton University Press, 2006).

34. Collier, *Development and Conflict*, 7–8.

35. Kofi Annan, *In Larger Freedom: Towards Development, Security and Human Rights for All* (New York: United Nations, 2005).

36. For its agenda, see "Provisional Agenda," PBC/OC/1/1, 21 June 2006.

37. Paraphrased from "Post-Conflict Peacebuilding," Security Council resolution 1645 (2005), 20 December 2005, 2.

38. *Letter dated 21 June 2006 from the President of the Security Council Addressed to the Secretary-General* (Peacebuilding Commission document PBC/OC/1/2), 21 June 2006.

39. *Progress Report on the Prevention of Armed Conflict: Report of the Secretary-General* (General Assembly document A/60/981), 18 July 2006, para. 109.

40. *Letter Dated 3 August 2006 from the Permanent Representative of Ghana to the United Nations Addressed to the Secretary-General* (Security Council document S/2006/610), 3 August 2006.

41. *Report of the 5509th Meeting of the Security Council* (Security Council document S/PV.5509), 9 August 2006, 3.

42. Ibid., 8.

4. The Practice of Preventive Diplomacy by the Secretaries-General

1. UNITAR, *The Quiet Approach: A Study of the Good Offices Exercised by the United Nations Secretary-General in the Cause of Peace* (New York: UNITAR, 1972).

2. Ibid., 15–17.

3. Bertrand G. Ramcharan, *Humanitarian Good Offices: The Good Offices of the Secretary-General in the Field of Human Rights* (The Hague: Martinus Nijhoff, 1983).

4. Trygve Lie, *In the Cause of Peace: Seven Years with the United Nations* (New York: Macmillan, 1954), 215.

5. Ibid.

6. Arthur W. Rovine, *The First Fifty Years: The Secretary-General in World Politics, 1920–1970* (Leiden, Netherlands: Sijthoff, 1970), 229.

7. "Complaint of Detention and Imprisonment of United Nations Military Personnel in Violation of the Korean Armistice Agreement," General Assembly resolution 906 (IX), 10 December 1954.

8. Rovine, *The First Fifty Years*, 282.

9. *Security Council Official Records*, 11th Year, 751st Meeting, 31 October 1956, 2.

10. *Second and Final Report of the Secretary-General on the Plan for an Emergency International United Nations Force* (General Assembly document A/3302), 6 November 1956.

11. Rovine, *The First Fifty Years*, 295.

12. Arthur M. Schlesinger, Jr., "Foreword," in Robert Kennedy, *Thirteen Days: A Memoir of the Cuban Missile Crisis* (New York: W.W. Norton, 1999), 7.

13. Kennedy, *Thirteen Days*, 169.

14. Rovine, *The First Fifty Years*, 379.

15. Ibid., 380–381.

16. See Brian Urquhart, *Ralph Bunche: An American Odyssey* (New York: W.W. Norton, 1993), 426–429.

17. Ibid., 428.

18. Ibid., 429.

19. Ibid.

20. Ibid.

21. According to a UN publication on peacekeeping, "It was probably the most dangerous situation confronting the world since the Cuban Missile Crisis of October, 1962." See *The Blue Helmets: A Review of United Nations Peacekeeping* (New York: United Nations, Department of Public Information, 1985), 78.

22. See Kurt Waldheim, *In the Eye of the Storm: The Memoirs of Kurt Waldheim, Secretary-General of the United Nations 1972–1982* (London: Weidenfeld and Nicolson, 1985), 60–61.

23. "The Six-Point Agreement," 11 November 1973, available online at http://www .mfa.gov.il/MFA/Foreign+Relations/Israels+Foreign+Relations+since+1947/1947-1974/ 17+The+Six-Point+Agreement-+11+November+1973.htm.

24. For more about the Kilometer 101 Agreement and UNDOF, see James O. C. Jonah, *What Price Survival of the United Nations? Memoirs of a Veteran International Civil Servant* (Ibadan: Evans Brothers, 2006).

25. Henry Kissinger, *Crisis: The Anatomy of Two Major Foreign Policy Crises* (New York: Simon and Schuster, 2003), 175–176.

26. Ibid., 358–359.

27. See *Letter of 25 October 1973 from Secretary-General to President of Security Council* (Security Council document S/11049), 25 October 1973.

28. *Report of the Secretary General to the Security Council Pursuant to Resolution 340 (1973)* (Security Council document S/11052/Rev.1), 27 October 1973.

29. For an account of the work of the commission, see Ramcharan, *Humanitarian Good Offices*, 129–138.

30. Marrack Goulding, *Peacemonger* (Baltimore, Md.: Johns Hopkins University Press, 2003).

31. Javier Pérez de Cuéllar, *Pilgrimage for Peace: A Secretary General's Memoir* (New York: St. Martin's Press, 1997), 392–393.

32. Secretary-General Pérez de Cuéllar's letters to the parties have never been published. The letters are in the possession of the author, who was a member of the discreet fact-finding mission to Bulgaria and Turkey.

33. This is taken from the mission's confidential report to the Secretary-General, a copy of which is in the possession of the author but which has never been published.

34. This summary is based on Ramcharan, "Preventing War Between Eritrea and Yemen over the Hanish Islands," in *Conflict Prevention in Practice: Essays in Honour of Jim Sutterlin,* ed. B. G. Ramcharan, 157–168 (Leiden, Netherlands: Martinus Nijhoff Publishers, 2005).

35. Interview with Secretary-General Boutros Boutros-Ghali, 23 July 2004, Geneva, Switzerland.

36. *Letter dated 18 June 1996 from the Secretary-General to the President of the Security Council* (Security Council document S/1996/447), 19 June 1996.

37. Ibid., 1.

38. Ibid., 2. See also B. G. Ramcharan, "Preventing War between Eritrea and Yemen over the Hanish Islands," in *Conflict Prevention in Practice: Essays in Honour of Jim Sutterlin,* ed. B. G. Ramcharan (Leiden, Netherlands: Martinus Nijhoff Publishers, 2005), 164.

39. "Secretary-General Appeals for Maximum Restraint in Letters to Presidents of Eritrea and of Yemen," UN press release SG/SM/6033, 15 August 1996, available online at http://www.un.org/news/Press/docs/1996/19960815.sgsm6033.html (accessed 27 September 2007).

40. Text taken from the notes on the informal meeting of the council; in author's possession.

41. UN press briefing, 19 August 1996, available online at http://www.un.org/News/briefings/docs/1996/19960819.dbaug19.html (accessed 9 September 2007).

42. This account is based on Jack Christofides, "How Good Offices Changed the Nature of the Border Dispute Between Nigeria and Cameroon," in *Conflict Prevention in Practice: Essays in Honour of James Sutterlin,* ed. B. G. Ramcharan (Leiden, Netherlands: Martinus Nijhoff, 2006), 211–218.

43. *Land and Maritime Boundary between Cameroon and Nigeria (Cameroon v. Nigeria: Equatorial Guinea intervening),* International Court of Justice no. 94 (10 October 2002).

44. "At Secretary-General's Invitation, Presidents of Cameroon, Nigeria, Meet in Paris to Discuss Bakassi Peninsula, Other Issues," UN press release SG/SM/8368, AFR/476, 6 September 2002.

45. A summary of the judgment is contained in "Land and Maritime Boundary between Cameroon and Nigeria (Cameroon v. Nigeria: Equatorial Guinea intervening)," ICJ press release 2002/26, 10 October 2002.

46. "Secretary-General Calls on Cameroon, Nigeria to Respect International Court of Justice's Judgment on Border Dispute," UN press release SG/SM/8429, 11 October 2002, available online at http://www.unis.unvienna.org/unis/pressrels/2002/sgsm8429.html (accessed 14 September 2007).

47. "Statement by Secretary-General Kofi Annan Following His Geneva Meeting with Presidents of Cameroon, Nigeria," UN press release SG/SM/8495, 18 November 2002, available online at http://www.unis.unvienna.org/unis/pressrels/2002/sgsm8495.html (accessed 14 September 2007)

48. *Letter Dated 17 March 2004 from the Secretary-General to the President of the Security Council (Cameroon-Nigeria Mixed Commission)* (Security Council document S/2004/298), 16 April 2004.

49. See United Nations Office for West Africa, Dakar, Mixed Commission on Cameroon-Nigeria, Final Communiqué of the First Meeting, Yaoundé, 1–2 December 2002.

50. United Nations Office for West Africa, Dakar, Mixed Commission on Cameroon-Nigeria, Final Communiqué of the Third Special Meeting, Abuja, 12 July 2003.

51. United Nations Office for West Africa, Dakar, Mixed Commission on Cameroon-Nigeria, Final Communiqué, Eleventh Meeting, Yaoundé, 18–19 August 2004.

52. Ibid.

53. "Transcript of Press Conference with UN Secretary-General and Presidents of Cameroon, Nigeria, Held at Palais Des Nations, Geneva, 31 January," UN press release SG/SM/9143/Rev. 1, 5 February 2004.

54. Andrew Cordier and Wilder Foote, eds., *Public Papers of the Secretaries-General of the United Nations,* vol. 5, *Dag Hammarskjöld, 1960–1961* (New York: Columbia University Press), 461.

55. Ibid.

56. Ibid.

57. Ibid.

58. The reports of the Independent Inquiry Committee into the United Nations Oil-for-Food Programme can be found online at http://www.iic-offp.org/documents.htm (accessed 9 September 2007). See also Jeffrey A. Meyer and Mark G. Califano, *Good Intentions Corrupted: The Oil-for-Food Scandal and the Threat to the U.N.* (New York: Public Affairs, 2006).

59. United Nations Staff Union, "Resolution Adopted by the Emergency General Meeting of New York Staff," *Bulletin of the United Nations Staff Union,* 13 March 2006, available online at http://www.unstaff.org

60. See, for example, "In a Shift, Annan to Fill Out a U.N. Form Disclosing His Finances," *New York Times,* 16 September 2006. The Secretary-General ended his term amid such issues, which did not promote public trust.

61. Iain Guest, a seasoned observer of the commission, found this "bizarre" for a Secretary-General. Iain Guest, "Take a Seat and Take Your Lumps, America: Human Rights Council I," *International Herald Tribune,* 23 March 2006, 4.

5. Preventive Diplomacy during the Cuban Missile Crisis

1. Schlesinger has written that even as President Kennedy pursued bilateral negotiations, "he prepared to enlist the United Nations in fallback plans in case bilateral negotiations faltered." Arthur Schlesinger, Jr., "Foreword," in Robert Kennedy, *Thirteen Days: A Memoir of the Cuban Missile Crisis* (New York: W.W. Norton and Company, 1999) 12. Richard Neustadt and Graham Allison have noted that the issue in the missile crisis was one of diplomacy as well of defense. Richard E. Neustadt and Graham T. Allison, "Afterword," in Robert Kennedy, *Thirteen Days,* 135.

2. Robert Kennedy, *Thirteen Days: A Memoir of the Cuban Missile Crisis* (New York: W.W. Norton, 1999), 54.

3. U Thant, *View from the UN: Memoirs of U Thant* (Garden City, N.Y.: Doubleday, 1978), 31.

4. Kennedy, *Thirteen Days,* 169.

5. "Resolution of Council of Organization of American States, Meeting as the Provisional Organ of Consultation on October 23, 1962," *U.S. Department of State Bulletin* 722 (1962): 47, available online at http://home.att.net/~slomansonb/CubanMissile.html (accessed 9 September 2007).

6. The OAS resolution was transmitted to the Security Council and published in *Letter from the Secretary General of the OAS to the President of the Security Council* (Security Council document S/5193), 25 October 1962.

7. See Ramses Nassif, *U Thant in New York, 1961–1971: A Portrait of the Third UN Secretary-General* (New York: St. Martin's Press, 1988), 37.

8. Ibid., 33.

9. Dino Brugioni, *Eyeball to Eyeball: The Inside Story of the Cuban Missile Crisis* (New York: Random House, 1990), 502.

10. Kennedy, *Thirteen Days*, 153.

11. U Thant, *View from the UN*, 161–162.

12. "Procès Verbaux," UN Security Council document S/PV.1025, 25 October 1962, para. 92.

13. "Procès Verbaux," Security Council document S/PV.1024, 24 October 1962, para. 111.

14. Ibid., para. 112.

15. Ibid., para. 115.

16. Ibid., para. 126.

17. Thant, *View from the UN*, 163 and part III, appendices A–E.

18. John Bartlow Martin, *Adlai Stevenson and the World* (Garden City, N.Y.: Anchor Press/Doubleday, 1978), 730.

19. Ibid.

20. Ibid.

21. Thant, *View from the UN*, 166.

22. Ibid.

23. Martin, *Adlai Stevenson and the World*, 730.

24. Thant, *View from the UN*, 167.

25. Ibid.

26. Barbara Leaming, *Jack Kennedy: The Education of a Statesman* (New York: W.W. Norton, 2006), 409. Of the Cuban missile crisis meetings, the author states, "my accounts of the meetings and quotations from participants during the Cuban crisis between August 1962 and November 1962 are based on the taped transcripts printed in *The Presidential Recordings John F. Kennedy: The Great Crises*, vol. 1, Timothy Naftali, ed., vol. 2, Timothy Naftali and Philip Zelikow, eds., and vol. 3, Philip Zelikow and Ernest May, eds. (New York: Norton & Company, 2001), plus the accounts by notetakers present at the meetings contained in the documents in FRUS 10 and 11" (484). For the quotes involving Ball, the author cites transcripts of telephone calls between JFK and Ball, 24 October 1962, *FRUS*, 11. In his memoirs, Andrei Gromyko discusses the Cuban missile crisis briefly and declares the outcome a victory for the Soviet Union. He does not refer to the role of U Thant. See Andrei Gromyko, *Memoirs* (New York: Doubleday, 1989), 179–180. V. Zubok and C. Pleshakov, who are conversant with the archives of the Soviet Union, also do not discuss U Thant's role in their book, *Inside the Kremlin's Cold War* (Cambridge, Mass.: Harvard University Press, 1996).

27. Martin, *Adlai Stevenson and the World*, 731.

28. Adlai Stevenson, note to U Thant, 25 October 1962, Box S-0872, Papers of UN Secretary-General U Thant (1961–1971), United Nations Archives and Records Centre, New York. Theodore Sorensen, apparently referring to this intervention of Stevenson, wrote: "A second U Thant proposal, negotiated through Stevenson urging both sides to avoid unnecessary contact during the next few days, was more acceptable . . . [to President Kennedy]." See Theodore C. Sorensen, *Kennedy* (New York: Harper and Row, 1965), 710.

29. See Department of State to the Mission of the United States, telegram 1105, 26 October 1962, available online at http://www.yale.edu/lawweb/avalon/diplomacy/forrel/ cuba/cuba083.htm (accessed 4 October 2007). This and subsequent citations to tele-

grams in this chapter are part of "Cuban Missile Crisis: 1961 [sic; 1962]," a component of the Yale Law School's Avalon Project of document collections in U.S. diplomatic history.

30. Mission to the United Nations to the U.S. Department of State, telegram 1484, 26 October 1962, available online at http://www.yale.edu/lawweb/avalon/diplomacy/forrel/cuba/cuba086.htm.

31. The mission to the United Nations had earlier reported on the previous conversation at 11:30 AM in telegram 1479 from New York, transmitted at 4 PM. Since Stevenson was still in Washington, Yost and Plimpton had represented the U.S. side. At the earlier meeting, the U.S. side had made the same points as at the second meeting. See the Avalon Project's annotation 1 of Mission to the United Nations to the U.S. Department of State, telegram 1484, 26 October 1962, at http://www.yale.edu/lawweb/avalon/diplomacy/forrel/cuba/cuba086.htm.

32. Mission of the United States to the United Nations to U.S. Department of State, telegram 1494, 27 October 1962, available online at http://www.yale.edu/lawweb/avalon/diplomacy/forrel/cuba/cuba093.htm (accessed 4 October 2007).

33. Adlai Stevenson to U Thant, 27 October 1962, Box S-0872, Papers of UN Secretary-General U Thant (1961–1971), United Nations Archives and Records Centre, New York.

34. See Laurence Chang and Peter Kornbluh, eds., *The Cuban Missile Crisis, 1962: A National Security Archive Documents Reader* (New York: The New Press, 1992, 1998), 93–94.

35. Thant, *View from the UN*, 169. In contrast, British prime minister Harold Macmillan's initial reaction to U Thant's intercession was bluntly negative. He told President Kennedy after U Thant's first appeal, "I think that's rather tiresome of him because it looks sensible and yet its very bad!" This remark was made in a telephone conversation between Kennedy and Macmillan on 24 October 1962 at 5:00 PM. See Ernest May and Philip Zelikow, eds., *The Kennedy Tapes: Inside the White House During the Cuban Missile Crisis* (Cambridge, Mass.: The Belknap Press of Harvard University Press, 1997), 387. U Thant had been provided with a transcript of the relevant parts of this conversation, including the above remark of Macmillan. A carbon copy of parts of the minutes of the conversation are among U Thant's papers at the United Nations Archives and Records Centre. Arthur Schlesinger wrote of U Thant's first appeal: "U Thant made an unexpected intervention . . . but from our point of view it equated aggression and response, said nothing about the missiles already in Cuba, permitted work to go forward on the sites and contained no provisions for verification." See Arthur Schlesinger, Jr., *A Thousand Days: John F. Kennedy in the White House* (Boston: Houghton Mifflin, 2002), 820.

36. On the visit to Cuba, see Thant, *View from the UN*; and Ramses Nassif, *U Thant in New York: Portrait of the Third UN Secretary-General, 1961–71* (New York: St. Martin's Press, 1988). In Nassif's assessment, "U Thant's greatest achievement in his ten-year tenure was his intervention in the Cuban missile crisis of October 1962, when the world came close to a nuclear holocaust" (25).

37. "Procès Verbaux," Security Council document S/PV.1025, paras. 91–94.

38. Thant, *View from the UN*, 194.

39. Ibid.

6. The Practice of Preventive Diplomacy by Representatives of the Secretary-General and UN Subregional Offices

1. See Connie Peck, "Special Representatives of the Secretary-General," in *The UN Security Council,* ed. David Malone (Boulder, Colo.: Lynne Rienner, 2004), 322–339.

2. See Richard Miller, *Dag Hammarskjöld and Crisis Diplomacy* (New York: Oceana Publications, 1961), 326–327.

3. Vratislav Pechota, *The Quiet Approach: A Study of the Good Offices Exercised by United Nations Secretary-General in the Cause of Peace* (Geneva: UNITAR, 1972), 12.

4. Ibid., 11–12.

5. Ahmedou Ould-Abdallah, *Burundi on the Brink 1993–1995: A UN Special Envoy Reflects on Preventive Diplomacy* (Washington, D.C.: United States Institute for Peace Press, 2000).

6. Ibid., 56–58.

7. Ibid.

8. *Report of the Secretary General Pursuant to Security Council Resolution 721(1991)* (Security Council document S/2380), 11 December 1991, Annex III: "Concept for a United Nations Peace-keeping Operation in Yugoslavia, as discussed with Yugoslav leaders by the Honourable Cyrus R. Vance, Personal Envoy of the Secretary General and Marrack Goulding, Under-Secretary-General for Special Political Affairs, November/December 1991."

9. *Algeria: Report of Eminent Panel, July–August 1998,* 10 September 1998, available online at http://www.un.org/NewLinks/dpi2007/ (accessed 9 September 2007).

10. Ibid., 26–27.

11. Kieran Prendergast, who was under-secretary-general for political affairs, considered this discreet good offices exercise a good example of preventive diplomacy that was under way during the terms of office of Secretaries-General Pérez de Cuéllar, Boutros-Ghali, and Annan. Conversation with the author, UN headquarters, New York, 16 November 1994.

12. "Enhancing the United Nations Effectiveness in Peace and Security: A Report Submitted to the Secretary-General of the United Nations by Under-Secretary-General Marrack Goulding," New York, 30 June 1997, paras. 5.12–5.15. The author was provided a copy of the report in his capacity as a political director in the Department of Political Affairs, where he served under Goulding and his successor, Kieran Prendergast.

13. Marrack Goulding, "Practical Measures to Enhance the United Nations' Effectiveness in the Field of Peace and Security: Report Submitted to the Secretary-General of the United Nations," New York, 30 June 1997, 26–27.

14. Report of the High-level Panel on Threats, Challenges and Change, *A More Secure World: Our Shared Responsibility* (New York: United Nations, 2004).

15. Kofi Annan, *In Larger Freedom: Towards Development, Security and Human Rights for All* (New York: UN, 2005).

16. The French text of the statement is taken from UNOWA's Web site, www.un.org/unowa. The short English translations are by the author. The *Security Council Official Records* ([UN document PV 5509], 9 August 2006), carries a more detailed version of the

presentation and mentioned other threats, such as the development of piracy on the high seas.

17. *Letter Dated 26 November 2001 from the Secretary-General Addressed to the President of the Security Council* (Security Council document S/2001/1128), 29 November 2001; *Letter Dated 11 December 2004 from the Secretary-General Addressed to the President of the Security Council* (Security Council document S/2005/16), 11 January 2005.

18. *Letter Dated 11 December 2004 from the Secretary-General Addressed to the President of the Security Council.*

19. Paul Collier, "Development and Conflict," Centre for the Study of African Economics, Department of Economics, Oxford University, 1 October 2004, 1, available at http://www.un.org/esa/documents/Development.and.Conflict2.pdf.

20. Ibid., 2.

21. Ibid., 3.

22. "The UN Office for West Africa," 1, available online at www.un.org/unowa/unowa/bckgrdnew.pdf (accessed 9 September 2007).

23. Ibid.

24. *Letter Dated 3 August 2006 from the Permanent Representative of Ghana to the United Nations Addressed to the Secretary General* (Security Council document S/2006/610), 3 August 2006, 4–5.

25. *Security Council Official Records,* 61st Year, 5509th Meeting, 9 August 2006, 7.

26. "ECOWAS-EU-UNOWA Framework of Action for Peace and Security," 3, available online at http://www.un.org/unowa/unowa/studies/eu-ecowas-unowa.pdf (accessed 27 September 2007).

27. Special Representative Ahmedou Ould-Abdallah, interview with author, New York, 20 September 2006.

28. *Youth Unemployment and Regional Insecurity in West Africa,* UNOWA issue papers, second edition, August 2006, available at http://www.un.org/unowa/unowa/studies/yunemp-v2-en.pdf.

29. *Life after State House: Addressing Unconstitutional Changes in West Africa,* UNOWA issue papers, March 2006, available at http://www.un.org/unowa/unowa/studies/lash-en.pdf.

30. Ibid., 12.

31. *Security Council Official Records,* 61st Year, 5509th Meeting, 9 August 2006 (Resumption 1), 24.

32. He had also negotiated an agreement that they defray significant parts of the cost of the boundary-delimitation exercise.

33. Plenary Debate, *General Assembly Official Records,* 8th Plenary Meeting, 16 September 2005, A/60/PV.8, 18.

34. *Report of the Secretary-General on the Work of the Organization* (General Assembly document A/61/1), 16 August 2006, para. 59.

35. *Statement by the President of the Security Council* (Security Council document S/PRST/2006/38), 9 August 2006.

7. The Preventive Role of UN Peacekeepers and Observers

1. See chapter 2 above.

2. Lester Pearson, *Peace in the Family of Man* (Toronto: Oxford, 1957).

3. Oliver Ramsbotham, Tom Woodhouse, Hugh Miall, and Gareth Schott, *Contemporary Conflict Resolution,* 2nd ed. (Cambridge: Polity Press, 2005), 331.

4. "The Four Faces of Peace," The Honourable Lester Bowles Pearson's Acceptance Speech upon Presentation of the Nobel Peace Prize in 1957, available online at http://www.unac.org/en/link_learn/canada/pearson/speechnobel.asp (accessed 9 September 2007).

5. General Assembly, "Introduction to the Report of the Secretary General on the Work of the Organization, 16 June 1959–15 June 1960," *General Assembly Official Records,* 1960, 15th Session, Supplement No. 1A (A4390/Add.1), 5–7.

6. Ibid., 143–144.

7. Paul Collier, "Development and Conflict," Centre for the Study of African Economics, Department of Economics, Oxford University, 1 October 2004, 7–10.

8. *Report of the Secretary-General on the Former Yugoslav Republic of Macedonia* (Security Council document S/24923), 9 December 1992.

9. Ibid.

10. Ibid. Security Council resolution 795, 11 December 1992, established the preventive deployment in the Former Yugoslav Republic of Macedonia.

11. *Report of the Secretary-General Pursuant to Security Council resolution 795 (1992)* (Security Council document S/26099), 13 July 1993.

12. Text taken from the original cable of UNPROFOR, in the files of the author.

13. Background paper submitted by the FYROM Command to Brainstorming Exercise on the Future of UNPROFOR, Zagreb-Mokrice, 15–17 February 1994. Paper in the possession of the author, who participated in the exercise.

14. Henryk Sokalski, *An Ounce of Prevention: Macedonia and the UN Experience in Preventive Diplomacy* (Washington, D.C.: United States Institute for Peace, 2003), 108. See also Abiodun Williams, *Preventing War: The UN and Macedonia* (Lanham, Md.: Rowman & Littlefield, 2000).

15. Ibid.

16. On the occasion of the United Nation's fiftieth anniversary in 1995, the foreign ministers of Canada and the Netherlands organized a ministerial meeting to generate political support for enhancing UN rapid deployment capabilities. Canada and the Netherlands announced the creation of an informal group of countries called the Friends of Rapid Deployment. The group is composed of about fifty states with an equivalent number participating as observers.

17. Government of The Netherlands, "A UN Rapid Deployment Brigade: A Preliminary Study," revised version, April 1995.

18. See Howard Peter Langille, "Conflict Prevention: Options for Rapid Deployment and UN Standing Forces," in *Peacekeeping and Conflict Resolution,* ed. Tom Woodhouse and Oliver Ramsbotham, 219–253 (London: Frank Cass, 2000).

19. Government of Canada, *Towards a Rapid Reaction Capability for the United Nations* (Ottawa: Department of Foreign Affairs and International Trade and Department of National Defence, 1995).

20. Langille, "Conflict Prevention: Options for Rapid Deployment and UN Standing Forces," 157–158.

21. Report of the High-level Panel on Threats, Challenges and Change, *A More Secure World: Our Shared Responsibility: Report of the Secretary-General's High-level Panel on Threats, Challenges and Change* (New York: United Nations, 2004), 59; see also 86.

22. This account is based on Angela King, "Internal Conflict Prevention: The UN Observer Mission to South Africa (UNOMSA) 1992," in *Conflict Prevention in Practice*, ed. Bertrand G. Ramcharan (Leiden, Netherlands: Martinus Nijhoff, 2005), 151–156.

23. Ibid.

24. Ibid.

8. Preventive Diplomacy in the Economic, Social, Human Rights, and Humanitarian Fields

1. See Frances Stewart, *The Root Causes of Conflict: Some Conclusions,* Working Paper no. 18, Queen Elizabeth House Working Paper Series, Oxford University, June 1998.

2. "Ad Hoc Group to Study Problems of East-West Trade in Implementation of Commission Resolution 9(XVI)," E/ECE resolution 4 (XVIII), 4 May 1963.

3. "Further Work of the Ad Hoc Group to Study Problems of East-West Trade in Implementation of Commission Resolution 9 (XVI)," E/ECE/553/Add.3, 23 March 1965.

4. "Work of the Committee on the Development of Trade," E/ECE/ resolution 2 (XXII), 28 April 1967, 1.

5. I have reviewed the historic contribution of the ECE as a forum of East-West confidence-building measures on economic and social issues in Bertrand G. Ramcharan, "Equality and Discrimination in International Economic Law (VIII): The United Nations Regional Economic Commissions," *The Yearbook of World Affairs 1978* (Boulder, Colo.: Westview Press, 1978), 268–285.

6. See Yves Berthelot and Paul Rayment, "The ECE: A Bridge between East and West," in *Unity and Diversity in Development Ideas: Perspectives from the UN Regional Commissions,* ed. Yves Berthelot (Bloomington: Indiana University Press, 2004), 64.

7. See Bertrand G. Ramcharan, *The International Law and Practice of Early Warning and Preventive Diplomacy: The Emerging Global Watch* (Dordrecht, Netherlands: Martinus Nijhoff, 1991), 143–144.

8. See ibid., 144–146.

9. "International Decade for Natural Disaster Reduction," General Assembly resolution 44/236, 22 December 1989, available online at http://www.un.org/documents/ga/res/44/a44r236.htm (accessed 16 September 2007).

10. Ibid., 146–148.

11. Ibid., 148–154.

12. See Department of International Economic and Social Affairs, *World Economic Survey 1989: Current Trends and Policies in the World Economy* (New York: United Na-

tions, 1989), available at http://www.un.org/esa/policy/wess/WESS%20since%201948/world%20economic%20survey%201989.pdf.

13. "Proposals to Improve the Work of the United Nations in the Early Identification, Analysis and Forecasting of World Economic Developments," ECOSOC document E/1990/80, 6 June 1990.

14. Ibid.

15. "United Nations Millennium Declaration," General Assembly resolution 55/2, 8 September 2000.

16. Ibid.

17. Ibid.

18. "Proposals to Improve the Work of the United Nations in the Early Identification, Analysis and Forecasting of World Economic Developments," para. 31.

19. *Substantive Issues Arising in the Implementation of the International Covenant on Economic, Social and Cultural Rights: Poverty and the International Covenant on Economic, Social and Cultural Rights. Statement Adopted by the Committee on Economic, Social and Cultural Rights on 4 May 2001* (ECOSOC document E/C.12/2001/10), 10 May 2001, para. 11.

20. See Bertrand G. Ramcharan, *Humanitarian Good Offices in International Law* (The Hague: Martinus Nijhoff, 1983).

21. See Luise Druke, *Preventive Action for Refugee Producing Situations* (Frankfurt: Peter Lang, 1989).

22. See Bertrand G. Ramcharan, "Early Warning at the United Nations: The First Experiment," *International Journal of Refugee Law* 1, no. 3 (1989): 379–386.

23. See Thomas G. Weiss and David A. Korn, *Internal Displacement: Conceptualization and Its Consequences* (London: Routledge, 2006).

24. See David Forsythe, *Humanitarian Politics: The International Committee of the Red Cross* (Baltimore, Md.: Johns Hopkins University Press, 1977).

25. "Study and Investigation of Situations which Reveal a Consistent Pattern of Violations of Human Rights," Commission on Human Rights resolution 8 (XXIII), 16 March 1967. See generally B. G. Ramcharan, *The Concept and Present Status of the International Protection of Human Rights: Forty Years after the Universal Declaration* (Dordrecht: Martinus Nijhoff Publishers, 1989).

26. See Bertrand G. Ramcharan, *A United Nations High Commissioner in Defence of Human Rights* (The Hague: Martinus Nijhoff, 2004).

27. The Human Rights Committee, the Committee on Economic, Social and Cultural Rights, and the Committee on the Rights of the Child.

28. *Report of the Committee on the Elimination of Racial Discrimination* (General Assembly document A/48/18), 15 September 1993, annex I, available online at http://www.unhchr.ch/tbs/DOC.NSF/8e9c603f486cdf83802566f8003870e7/9d43bba5cf6507718025655d003f980e?OpenDocument#A%2F48%2F18E (accessed 14 September 2007).

29. *Report of the Committee on the Elimination of Racial Discrimination,* annex III, Prevention of Racial Discrimination, including Early Warning and Urgent Procedures: Working Paper adopted by the Committee on the Elimination of Racial Discrimination, 126–130, quote on 127.

30. Ibid., 127–128.

31. Ibid., 128–129.

32. Ibid., 127.

33. Ibid., 129.

34. *Report of the United Nations High Commissioner for Human Rights and Follow-up to the World Conference on Human Rights* (ECOSOC document E/CN.4/12), 28 December 1999.

35. *Report of the United Nations High Commissioner for Human Rights* (General Assembly document A/61/36), 2006, para. 3.

36. Ibid., paras. 3–4.

37. The UPR refers to a new process, the universal periodic review, to be operated by the Human Rights Council. Under this process, every UN member will be scrutinized for its human rights record.

38. *Report of the United Nations High Commissioner for Human Rights* (General Assembly document A/61/36), 2006, para. 75.

39. Felix Schnyder, "Les Aspects juridiques actuels du Problème des réfugiés," *Recueil des Cours de l'Académie de la Haye* 114 (1965-I): 335–450.

40. Ibid.

41. Saddrudin Aga Khan, "Legal Problems Relating to Refugees and Displaced Persons," *Recueil des Cours de l'Académie de la Haye* 149 (1976-I): 347.

42. Ibid., 349.

43. "UN Asks Hong Kong to Delay Deportations," *New York Times,* 17 December 1989.

44. Interview with François Fouinat, former chef de cabinet to High Commissioner Sadako Ogata, Geneva, 6 December 2006.

45. The information related here was provided in an interview with Ambassador Teferra Shiawl-Kidanekal in New York on 20 September 2006.

46. See Weiss and Korn, *Internal Displacement: Conceptualization and its Consequences.*

47. For more about the Handyside and Klaas cases, see Clare Ovey, Robin C. A. White, and Francis Geoffrey Jacobs, *Jacobs and White: The European Convention on Human Rights*, 4th ed. (Oxford: Oxford University Press, 2006).

48. See Martin Scheinin et al., "The Case Law of the Human Rights Committee," Turku/Abo, Institute for Human Rights, Abo Akademi University, 2003, 400.

49. Louis Henkin, "Democracy and Liberty as Human Rights," in *Towards Implementing Universal Human Rights: Festschrift for the Twenty-Fifth Anniversary of the Human Rights Committee,* ed. Nisuke Ando (Leiden: Martinus Nijhoff, 2004), 173–180.

50. Louis Henkin, "Democracy and Liberty as Human Rights," in *Commemorative Volume on the Occasion of the Twenty-Fifth Anniversary of the Human Rights Committee,* ed. Nisuko Ando (Leiden: Martinus Nijhoff), 173–180, quote on 176. Professor Larry Diamond has also asserted the universal right to democratic governance in Larry Diamond, *Promoting Democracy in the 1990s: Actors and Instruments, Issues and Imperatives: A Report to the Carnegie Commission on Preventing Deadly Conflict* (New York: The Commission, 1995), 60–68.

51. Boutros Boutros-Ghali, *An Agenda for Democratization* (New York: United Nations, 1996).

52. "The Situation in Bosnia and Herzegovina," Security Council resolution 1423 (2002), 12 July 2002.

53. Gregory H. Fox, "Democratization," in *The UN Security Council: From the Cold War to the 21st Century*, ed. David Malone (Boulder: Lynne Rienner Publishers, 2004), 69–84, esp. 69.

54. Kevin Cahill, ed., *Preventive Diplomacy* (New York: Basic Books, 1996), vii.

55. *An Agenda for Peace: Preventive Diplomacy, Peacemaking, and Peace-Keeping: Report of the Secretary-General* (Security Council document S/24111-A/47/277), 17 June 1992, para. 19.

56. *Progress Report on the Prevention of Armed Conflict: Report of the Secretary-General* (General Assembly document A/60/891), 18 July 2006, paras. 46–47.

57. "The Manila Declaration of 1988, Issued on 6 June 1988 at the Conclusion of the International Conference of Newly Restored Democracies, Held at Manila, from 3 to 6 June 1988," General Assembly document A/43/538, 16 August 1988, Annex, 3–4, available online at http://www.icnrd6.com/previous.php (accessed 14 September 2007); "Doha Declaration: Building Capacity for Democracy, Peace and Social Progress," 31 October 2006, available online at http://www.icnrd6.com/outcome.php (accessed 14 September 2007).

58. Korea, Haiti, Costa Rica, and Cambodia.

59. George H. W. Bush, "Address to the United Nations," 1 October 1990, available online at http://www.millercenter.virginia.edu/scripps/digitalarchive/speeches/spe _1990_1001_bush (accessed 14 September 2007).

60. See the Web site of the United Nations Electoral Assistance Division, available at http://www.un.org/Depts/dpa/ead/overview.html (accessed 28 September 2007).

61. The author was then special assistant to the head of the Human Rights Centre, and many of the demarches of UNHCR were made to him.

62. Suddrudin Aga Khan, *Study on Human Rights and Mass Exoduses*, ECOSOC document E/CN.4/1503, 11 March 1981.

63. See ibid. See also *Refugees. Dynamics of Displacement. A Report for the Independent Commission on International Humanitarian Issues* (London, Zed Books, 1986), 137.

64. See Ramcharan, "Early Warning at the United Nations," 379–386.

65. See International Commission on Intervention and State Sovereignty, *The Responsibility to Protect* (Ottawa: The International Development Research Center, 2001).

66. See Bertrand G. Ramcharan, ed., *The Protection Role of National Human Rights Institutions* (Leiden, Netherlands: Martinus Nijhoff, 2005).

9. Preventive Diplomacy in an Age of Genocide, Terrorism, and Nontraditional Threats to Security

1. General Assembly resolution 60/1, 24 October 2005.

2. General Assembly resolution 96 (1), 11 December 1946.

3. See Samantha Power, *Problem from Hell: America and the Age of Genocide* (New York: Perennial, 2002). See also David Hamburg, *No More Killing Fields: Preventing*

Deadly Conflict (New York: Rowman & Littlefield, 2002); and David and Beatrix Hamburg, *Learning to Live Together: Preventing Hatred and Violence in Child and Adolescent Development* (Oxford: Oxford University Press, 2004).

4. See the study on the question of genocide by Mr. Nicodeme Ruhashyankiko, special rapporteur of the Sub-Commission on Prevention of Discrimination and the Protection of Minorities, *Study on the Question of the Prevention and Punishment of the Crime of Genocide* (ECOSOC document E/CN.4/Sub.2/416), 4 July 1978; see also Mr. B. Whitaker, special rapporteur, *Study on the Question of the Prevention and Punishment of the Crime of Genocide* (ECOSOC document E/CN.4/Sub.2/1985/6), 16 July 1985.

5. See Bertrand G. Ramcharan, *Humanitarian Good Offices in International Law* (The Hague: Martinus Nijhoff, 1983).

6. "Genocide Is a Threat to Peace Requiring Strong, United Action, Secretary-General Tells Stockholm International Forum," UN press release SG/SM/9126, 26 January 2004, available online at http://www.un.org/News/Press/docs/2004/SGsm9126.doc.htm (accessed 28 September 2007).

7. "UN Secretary-General Kofi Annan's Plan to Prevent Genocide," UN press release SG/SM/9197, 7 April 2004, available online at http://www.preventgenocide.org/prevent/UNdocs/KofiAnnansActionPlantoPreventGenocide7Apr2004.htm (accessed 14 September 2007).

8. *Letter dated 12 July 2004 from the Secretary-General addressed to the President of the Security Council* (Security Council document S/2004/567), 13 July 2004, available online at http://www.un.org/Depts/dpa/prev_genocide/appointment.pdf.

9. "On the Role of the Security Council in the Prevention of Armed Conflicts," Security Council resolution 1366 (2001), 30 August 2001.

10. See *Letter Dated 12 July 2004 from the Secretary-General Addressed to the President of the Security Council* (Security Council document S/2004/567), 13 July 2004.

11. *Report of the Secretary-General on the Implementation of the Five Point Action Plan and the Activities of the Special Adviser on the Prevention of Genocide* (ECOSOC document E/CN.4/2006/84), 9 March 2006.

12. The special adviser briefed the Security Council for the first time on 14 November 2006.

13. In 2007 Secretary-General Ban Ki-moon made the position full time and appointed Francis Deng as special adviser.

14. *Report of the UN High Commissioner for Human Rights and Follow-Up to the World Conference on Human Rights. Situation of Human Rights in the Darfur Region of the Sudan* (ECOSOC document E/CN.4/2005/3), 7 May 2004.

15. *Statement by the President of the Security Council* (Security Council document S/PRST/2004/18), 26 May 2004.

16. "U.S. Official: Sudan Darfur Deaths May Reach 300,000," Associated Press, 4 October 2004; "Darfur Death Toll May be 300,000, Say UK lawmakers," Reuters, 30 March 2005, available online at http://www.alertnet.org/thenews/newsdesk/L30582172.htm (accessed 14 September 2007).

17. Interview of members of the Advisory Committee of the Secretary-General on the Prevention of Genocide by the author, 2 February 2007, New York.

18. "UN Secretary-General Kofi Annan's Plan to Prevent Genocide."

19. Kofi Annan, *Progress Report on the Prevention of Armed Conflict: Report of the Secretary-General* (General Assembly document A/60/891), 18 July 2006.

20. Strobe Talbott and Nayan Chanda, eds., *The Age of Terror: America and the World after September 11* (New York: Basic Books, 2001).

21. See Allison, *Nuclear Terrorism.* See also Mohamed Elbaradei and Jonas Gahr Store, "How the World Can Combat Nuclear Terrorism," *Financial Times*, 15 April 2006, 13.

22. Kofi Annan, "A Global Strategy for Fighting Terrorism," Keynote Address to the Closing Plenary of the International Summit on Democracy, Terrorism and Security, 10 March 2005, available online at http://summit.clubmadrid.org/keynotes/a-global-strategy-for-fighting-terrorism.html#transcripcion (accessed 14 September 2007).

23. "International Convention for the Suppression of Acts of Nuclear Terrorism," 14 September 2005, 4, available at http://untreaty.un.org/English/Terrorism/English_18 _15.pdf.

24. "Threats to International Peace and Security Caused by Terrorist Acts," Security Council resolution 1377 (2001), 12 November 2001, 3.

25. "Threats to International Peace and Security (Security Council Summit 2005)," Security Council resolution 1624, 14 September 2005.

26. Annan, "A Global Strategy for Fighting Terrorism."

27. Ibid.

28. "Coping with Non-Traditional Security Threats," Concept Paper, Geneva Centre for Security Policy, December 2006.

29. Ibid.

30. Vladimir A. Orlav, "Illicit Nuclear Trafficking & the New Agenda," *IAEA Bulletin* 46, no. 1 (June 2004): 55.

31. Ibid.

10. Cooperative Preventive Diplomacy with Regional and Subregional Organizations

1. *Report of the Secretary-General on the Work of the Organization* (General Assembly document A/60/1), 8 August 2005, 13, available online at http://www.un.org/documents/secretariat.htm (accessed 14 September 2007).

2. Ibid., 12–13.

3. See International Peace Academy and the Organization of African Unity, *Report of the Cairo Consultation: The OAU Mechanism for Conflict Prevention, Management and Resolution* (New York: IPA, 1994), 19.

4. Salim A. Salim, "The Priorities and Challenges of the OAU on the Eve of the New Millenium: Resolving Conflicts," *OAU Conflict Management Bulletin* 1, no. 5 (August–September 1996): 4–5.

5. International Peace Academy and the Organization of African Unity, *Report of the Cairo Consultation.*

6. Protocol Relating to the Establishment of the Peace and Security Council of the African Union, adopted by the 1st Ordinary Session of the Assembly of the African

Union, Durban, 9 July 2002, 18, available online at www.africa-union.org/root/au/organs/ psc/Protocol_peace%20and%20security.pdf (accessed 14 September 2007).

7. On ASEAN as a security community, see Amitav Acharya, *Constructing a Security Community in Southeast Asia: ASEAN and the Problem of Regional Order* (London: Routledge, 2001); and Ralf Emmers, *Cooperative Security and the Balance of Power in ASEAN and the ARF* (London: Routledge, 2003).

8. "Treaty of Amity and Cooperation in Southeast Asia," 24 February 1976, available at http://www.aseansec.org/1217.htm.

9. ASEAN Declaration on the South China Sea (1992), Manila, Philippines, 22 July 1992, available online at http://www.aseansec.org/5233.htm (accessed 14 September 2007).

10. ASEAN Regional Forum, "Concept and Principles of Preventive Diplomacy," available online at http://www.aseanregionalforum.org/PublicLibrary/TermsofReferences andConceptPapers/tabid/89/Default.aspx (accessed 2 October 2007).

11. Ibid., 7–9.

12. Ibid., 8–9.

13. A list of ARF Track I and Track II activities are available online at http://www .aseanregionalforum.org/PublicLibrary/ARFActivities/tabid/92/Default.aspx.

14. Dato M. Hassan, director general, Institute of Strategic and International Studies (ISIS), Malaysia, "Regional Mechanisms for Conflict Prevention," presentation at the Seminar on Conflict Prevention, Manila, 20–21 February 2002.

15. Medardo C. Abad, Jr., "Enhancing ASEAN-UN Cooperation in Conflict Prevention and Peacebuilding in the 21st Century," presentation at the Seminar on Conflict Prevention, Manila, 20–21 February 2002.

16. See Robin Ramcharan, *Southeast Asian Security: Pitfalls of the Regional Approach*, PSIS Occasional Paper no. 1, Geneva, Programme for Strategic and International Studies, 1998.

17. John Garofano, "Power, Institutions, and the ASEAN Regional Forum: A Security Community for Asia?" *Asian Survey* 42, no. 3 (2002): 517.

18. State Council of the People's Republic of China, *White Paper: Arms Control and Disarmament,* November 1995. See also R. Manning, R. Montaperto, and B. Roberts, *China, Nuclear Weapons and Arms Control: A Preliminary Assessment* (New York: Council on Foreign Relations, 2000).

19. "Concept and Principles of Preventive Diplomacy," reproduced in Institute of Defence and Strategic Studies, *A New Agenda for the ASEAN Regional Forum,* Monograph no. 4 (Singapore: Institute of Defence and Strategic Studies, 2002), 88–93. The five principles of cooperation, also known as the Panchsheel, are mutual respect for each other's territorial integrity and sovereignty, mutual nonaggression, mutual noninterference in each other's internal affairs, equality and mutual benefit, and peaceful coexistence. The Panchsheel was put forward by Premier Zhou Enlai in talks with the Indian government in Beijing from December 1953 to April 1954 concerning Tibet. In June 1954, the Five Principles were included in the joint communiqué issued by Premier Zhou Enlai and Prime Minister Jawaharlal Nehru. Since then the Panchsheel's principles have been adopted in other international documents as norms for relations between countries. See

generally the Wikipedia entry on "Principles of Peaceful Coexistence," available online at http://en.wikipedia.org/wiki/Five_Principles_of_Peaceful_Coexistence.

20. Bandar Seri Begawan, "Chair's Statement," Ninth Meeting of the ASEAN Regional Forum, 31 July 2002. Available at www.aseansec.org/12003.htm.

21. "Enhanced Role of the ARF Chair," reproduced in Institute of Defence and Strategic Studies, *A New Agenda for the ASEAN Regional Forum,* 94–97.

22. The Intergovernmental Authority on Development is committed to assisting its member states (Djibouti, Eritrea, Ethiopia, Kenya, Somalia, Sudan, and Uganda). The IGAD mission is to assist and complement the efforts of member states to achieve, through increased cooperation, food security and environmental protection; promotion and maintenance of peace, security, and humanitarian affairs; and economic cooperation and integration. For more information, see http://www.igad.org/about/mission.html.

23. L. Ronald Scheman and John W. Ford, "The Organization of American States as Mediator," in *International Mediation in Theory and Practice,* ed. Saadia Touval and I. William Zartman (Boulder, Colo.: Westview, 1985), 197–232.

24. See *Letter Dated 12 February 2001 from the Secretary-General to the President of the Security Council* (Security Council document S/2001/138), 14 February 2001, annex I.

25. See "Fifth High-level Meeting between UN and Regional Organizations Concludes Following Two-Day Discussion of Main Challenges to International Peace and Security," the statement issued by Secretary-General Kofi Annan at the conclusion of the meeting, UN press release SG/2084, 30 July 2003, available online at http://www.un.org/News/Press/docs/2003/sg2084.doc.htm (accessed 14 September 2007).

26. Ibid.

27. See *Statement by the President of the Security Council* (Security Council document S/PRST/2004/27), 20 July 2004.

28. *General Assembly Official Records,* 59th Session, Supplement No. 2, General Assembly document A/59/2, 20 August 2004, 17.

Index

About the Author

Bertrand G. Ramcharan is Professor of International Human Rights Law at the Geneva Graduate Institute of International Studies, Chancellor of the University of Guyana, and Senior Fellow at the Ralph Bunche Institute for International Studies at The CUNY Graduate Center. He has a doctorate in international law from the London School of Economics and Political Science and is a Barrister at Law of Lincoln's Inn. He was a member of the UN Secretariat for thirty-two years. He served in the position of Deputy and then UN High Commissioner for Human Rights ad interim (2003–2004) at the level of Under-Secretary-General. Previously he had been director and political/legal advisor with the international peacemakers and peacekeepers in the Former Yugoslavia, Director of the Africa Division of the Department of Political Affairs, and head of the speech-writing service of the Secretary-General. He has taught as an Adjunct Professor at Columbia University, as a law professor at the University of Ottawa, and as Visiting Professor of International Law at Lund University, Sweden. He is the author or editor of over twenty-five books on international law, human rights, and the United Nations. He is a Commissioner of the International Commission of Jurists and Member of the Permanent Court of Arbitration.

About the United Nations Intellectual History Project

Ideas and concepts are a main driving force in human progress, and they are arguably the most important contribution of the United Nations. Yet there has been little historical study of the origins and evolution of the history of economic and social ideas cultivated within the world organization and of their impact on wider thinking and international action. The United Nations Intellectual History Project (UNIHP) is filling this knowledge gap about the UN by tracing the origin and analyzing the evolution of key ideas and concepts about international economic and social development born or nurtured under UN auspices. The UNIHP began operations in mid-1999 when the secretariat, the hub of a worldwide network of specialists on the UN, was established at the Ralph Bunche Institute for International Studies of The CUNY Graduate Center.

The UNIHP has two main components, oral history interviews and a series of books on specific topics. The seventy-nine in-depth oral history interviews with leading contributors to crucial ideas and concepts within the UN system provide the raw material for this and other volumes in the series. In addition, complete and indexed transcripts are available to researchers and the general public in an electronic book format on a CD-ROM distributed by the secretariat.

The project has commissioned fifteen studies about the major economic and social ideas or concepts that are central to UN activity, which are being published by Indiana University Press.

- *Ahead of the Curve? UN Ideas and Global Challenges,* by Louis Emmerij, Richard Jolly, and Thomas G. Weiss (2001)
- *Unity and Diversity in Development Ideas: Perspectives from the UN Regional Commissions,* edited by Yves Berthelot with contributions from Adebayo Adedeji, Yves Berthelot, Leelananda de Silva, Paul Rayment, Gert Rosenthal, and Blandine Destremeau (2003)
- *Quantifying the World: UN Ideas and Statistics,* by Michael Ward (2004)
- *UN Contributions to Development Thinking and Practice,* by Richard Jolly, Louis Emmerij, Dharam Ghai, and Frédéric Lapeyre (2004)
- *The UN and Global Political Economy: Trade, Finance, and Development,* by John Toye and Richard Toye (2004)

- *UN Voices: The Struggle for Development and Social Justice,* by Thomas G. Weiss, Tatiana Carayannis, Louis Emmerij, and Richard Jolly (2005)
- *Women, Development and the UN: A Sixty-Year Quest for Equality and Justice,* by Devaki Jain (2005)
- *Human Security and the UN: A Critical History,* by S. Neil MacFarlane and Yuen Foong Khong (2006)
- *Human Rights at the UN: The Political History of Universal Justice,* Roger Normand and Sarah Zaidi (2008)
- *Preventive Diplomacy at the UN,* by Bertrand G. Ramcharan (2008)

Forthcoming Titles:

- *The UN and Transnational Corporations: From Code of Conduct to Global Compact,* by Tagi Sagafi-nejad in collaboration with John Dunning
- *The UN and Development Cooperation,* by Olav Stokke
- *The UN and the Global Commons: Development without Destruction,* by Nico Schrijver
- *The UN and Global Governance: An Idea and Its Prospects,* by Ramesh Thakur and Thomas G. Weiss
- *The United Nations: A History of Ideas and Their Future,* by Richard Jolly, Louis Emmerij, and Thomas G. Weiss

The project also collaborated on *The Oxford Handbook on the UN,* edited by Thomas G. Weiss and Sam Daws, published by Oxford University Press in 2007.

For further information, the interested reader should contact:

UN Intellectual History Project
The CUNY Graduate Center
365 Fifth Avenue, Suite 5203
New York, New York 10016–4309
212–817–1920 Tel
212–817–1565 Fax
UNHistory@gc.cuny.edu
www.unhistory.org